THE FRANCIS LEE AUTOBIOGRAPHY

THE FRANCIS LEE AUTOBIOGRAPHY

TRIUMPHS, TREACHERY AND TOILET ROLLS

WITH

BILL BRADSHAW

pitch

First published by Pitch Publishing, 2024

Pitch Publishing
9 Donnington Park,
85 Birdham Road,
Chichester,
West Sussex,
PO20 7AJ
www.pitchpublishing.co.uk
info@pitchpublishing.co.uk

A CIP catalogue record is available for this book from the British Library.

ISBN 978 1 80150 921 3

MIX
Paper | Supporting responsible forestry
FSC® C013056

Printed and bound in the UK on FSC® certified paper in line with our continuing commitment to ethical business practices, sustainability and the environment.

Typesetting and origination by Pitch Publishing

Printed and bound in Great Britain by TJ Books, Padstow

Contents

This book is dedicated to the memory of Francis Henry Lee and the joy he brought to all those who had the pleasure of watching him play – or who were lucky enough to spend any time at all in his company.

Acknowledgements

I WOULD like to thank the Lee family, especially Francis's widow Gill, sons Jonny and Nik, and his daughter Charlotte for their time and support in helping me to complete this project. Thanks go also, of course, to Francis himself for giving up his time so generously to talk me through the various facets of his remarkable life, both in and out of football. He was always a joy to deal with and he was not only generous with his time … the glass was always topped up and I never left his company without a cigar thrust into my top pocket!

The genesis of the book was an enjoyable lunch at Soho's Little Italy restaurant, in Frith Street, back in 2012. I joined my old pal Keith Bishop, a legendary PR guru, and Chris Ronnie, a colourful North West businessman, who had many sports contacts in the Manchester area – including Francis Lee. 'Franny is looking for someone to tell his story, someone to write his book with him,' said Chris. Was I interested? Was I ever! So, thanks to 'Bish' and Chris for a fine lunch – and the nudge for me to call Franny. All journalists love a good story, and Franny's life was not just a good story, it was a great story. He lived at least four lives, not just one: a brilliant, top-class footballer; an entrepreneurial, visionary businessman; a successful racehorse trainer and then football club chairman at his beloved Manchester City. To be taken by Franny inside his extraordinary existence was my privilege.

Thanks to my literary agent Rick Mayston for his patience as we sought to get Franny's story told. I must also thank the gatekeepers of the various Manchester City-dedicated websites for our historical cribs – notably Gary James – for their assiduous attention to detail. And the work of former athlete and journalist Peter Keeling, who chronicled much of Francis's early career in his 1970 book *Soccer Round the World*, was an invaluable touchstone.

Finally, thanks to my wife, Jill, for her immense help and encouragement as I sought to complete the book, and to my son, Kit, and daughter, Holly, for their constant support.

Foreword by Mike Summerbee

FRIENDSHIP IS a priceless gift. It's a gift I was proud to share with Francis Lee, and after our first meeting, when he joined Manchester City in 1967, we were friends for life.

I'd bumped into him occasionally before then, playing against him when he was at Bolton, and I was at Swindon or City. I remember playing at Bolton and being careful to try to stay on the pitch because it seemed like there was a five-foot drop at one point if you strayed off it! But we first really met the day he became a City player.

Francis changed Manchester City's direction when he joined the club from Bolton Wanderers just after the start of the 1967/68 season. We already had a very good team, but he gave us an edge we hadn't had before – a killer instinct that turned a good team into a great team. He was integral to everything we achieved during that glorious era, and without him I doubt we'd have won the trophies we did.

He brought a lot of confidence to the club and the side at that time. Although he was pretty young, Francis already had top-flight experience at Bolton – not many of the City lads had that before our promotion from the Second Division in 1966, just a year before Francis signed. Yet Francis exuded confidence and he spread it through the team, it was infectious.

Joe Mercer, City's great boss of the team in that era, famously said signing Francis was the final piece of the jigsaw, and that's exactly what he was. Once he came in, the team was complete, and our great trophy-winning run was underway.

The thing about Francis that I admired the most was that not only was he at the top of his game continually for City, and for England, he was also running a very successful toilet roll manufacturing business under the name F.H. Lee at the same time. More often than not, he would come to training in a suit, ready to go off to Scandinavia or other parts of Europe to strike deals for his business. He was not just a top footballer, he was a top businessman and he worked as hard off the pitch as he did when he was on it.

On it, he was a joy to play with. That air of confidence was wonderful – but he was never arrogant. He could play at centre-forward or off the right wing, rather like myself. It worked so well. The City forward line was packed with talent, and we were interchangeable at times in that fantastic three-year period when we won the league title, FA Cup,

Football League Cup and European Cup Winners' Cup between 1967/68 and 1969/70.

We had Francis, myself, Neil Young, Tony Coleman and Colin Bell – among others – all able to drive forward and attack. Opponents were often overwhelmed, and it also demonstrated what a fine coach we had in Malcolm Allison.

Incredibly, when Francis first arrived at City in his early 20s, his business was already established and on the up. When training was over, the typical player's life of a round of golf or a session in the pub was not for him – he was off working on his second career. To be a top businessman, you have to be able to be a tough negotiator and do things that aren't always easy, but Francis managed to do that with the same focus and determination he displayed when he was playing football. I often wondered: how can you win titles, play for England at the World Cup and still run a very successful business? It was incredible, but not a surprise to me because I saw how hard he worked to achieve the things he wanted. Francis was an exceptional person.

This included playing for Sir Alf Ramsey's England, which shows just how much on top of his game he was, regardless of his business career. I was lucky enough to win caps and to be around the England squad with him at this time, but I didn't make it to the 1970 Mexico World Cup. Francis did, and he was a key member of Sir Alf's team.

I can't tell you how much it meant to players to pull on that England shirt back then – I'm sure it still does – but this was the era of England as world champions. There was no mass influx of foreign superstars then, so City and all England's top sides were stuffed with homegrown talent ... it was harder to break into the England side, there was so much competition. Francis did that, and he did it with style.

Whatever he did or wherever he went, he brought success with him, and when he left City as a player and went to Derby County, he helped them win the top flight's holy grail, the 1974/75 First Division title. What an inspired signing he was for Derby County, winning the title in his first season. It was also the perfect riposte from Francis to Mr Peter Swales and City for showing him the door! This, and all the rest of his successes, were down to hard work.

Francis left City too soon, not that he wanted to. I don't think Peter Swales liked the strength of characters in the dressing room then and, of course, Francis was one of them. I think there was also a little envy, shall we say, from Swales because of Francis's success in the paper business. Swales was a good businessman, but Francis was in a different league.

I was in the same boat at City. Franny left at the start of the 1974/75 season, and I followed him out of the door at the end of that same season. We both could have offered more to City for a couple of years, for sure.

Of course, after he called time on playing, he built his business further and he then enjoyed a successful spell as a racehorse trainer at his Little Stanneylands home in Cheshire. I fondly remember days out at York races and elsewhere with him. He brought the same enthusiasm and confidence to that venture as he did with football and business.

Later, Francis ended up buying Manchester City from Peter Swales in 1994, and we all know results on the pitch were not great – but he changed things around quite radically. This paved the way for many of the good things that everyone associated with City sees today, including the transformative move from Maine Road to the City of Manchester Stadium, now the Etihad. He deserves a great share of the credit for that, far more credit than he received in the immediate aftermath of his departure as chairman in 1998.

Despite all his achievements – including being appointed a CBE for his services to football and charity in 2016 – Francis never forgot his roots. He did a lot for the community of Westhoughton, his home patch near Bolton, especially the boys' clubs. He would, for example, organise or take part in charity runs down the years. He might have been involved in games on a Saturday, but he'd be there at 9am on a Sunday for a five-mile run.

Francis was like that, a generous man with his time and in many other ways, too. Some years back, I was moving from my home in Romiley, near Stockport, to another house across the road. It got to the point where I needed the funds for a deposit, but the monies from my sale hadn't yet come through. I mentioned it to Francis, and he immediately stepped in and gave me £250,000. What a gesture! I paid him back within three or four weeks, but this underlines the man's generosity.

His contribution to Manchester City will never be forgotten and, through it all, Francis was Francis, true to himself. The last time I saw him was in hospital and, as I walked in, he said, 'What are you doing here?' I was speechless from the start!

We had so many laughs and great times over the years, and he'll be sadly missed by Gill and his wonderful family; by his many friends especially my wife, Tina, myself and our family and everyone who knew him. He'll leave a big gap in my life, but every time I think about him, I'll smile because I know I was fortunate to call him one of my closest friends.

His is a great legacy with many happy memories. Francis Lee was one of a kind.

Chapter One

Early Days

MILLIONAIRE FOOTBALLERS are commonplace in England these days. The unbelievable riches on offer in the Premier League guarantee that any decent journeyman player who plies his trade in the top league in the world will be guaranteed to become a millionaire, even if he stays fit for just a modest number of seasons in the game.

Those at the next level, who are *outstanding* players in the modern game, regularly starring for top-six clubs and perhaps involving themselves in one or two high-level transfers, will be massively wealthy. Such young men would be agog if they read the story of the guy who was probably – almost certainly – England's first millionaire footballer.

That guy isn't George Best, Kevin Keegan, Kenny Dalglish or Alan Shearer. That guy is me: Francis Henry Lee.

Having said that, my millions – earned while I was playing the game in the 1960s and 70s – came from dogged work in my business life rather than my exploits on the pitch. I had a dual way of life … ambitious professional footballer and, at the same time, aspiring businessman.

Yet to say my origins were humble would be an understatement. That's why the likes of Harry Kane, Raheem Sterling and Jack Grealish would be stunned by my story; the story set out in the pages that follow.

Because I was never meant to amount to anything, or so I was told. If I'd taken at face value, the 'advice' offered by those in the business of doling out such pearls of wisdom – my schoolteachers or my first manager at Bolton Wanderers – I'd have given up on making any real mark. I was constantly reminded that my future was strictly limited. I felt like Marlon Brando's character, Terry, in *On the Waterfront*, when he famously said, 'I'm a bum – I gotta one-way ticket to Palookaville.' Except I never did say it, and I never did take any notice of those dishing out career advice. I had my own ideas and my own ambitions. I wasn't listening to that stuff.

I could, I suppose, understand some of their limited thinking. I came from a humble background, from a very, very working-class family in a poor Lancashire town. Not the typical material from which millionaires are cut.

I was a war baby, born on 29 April 1944. As a young kid, I lived in a typical mill-town terraced house – 5 Gladstone Street, Westhoughton – four miles from Bolton, with the city of Manchester 13 miles distant. The folk of Westhoughton worked in the cotton mills or down the colliery. Before moving a little later to a more modern post-war council house, our old home was so cold that we'd go 30 yards up the road to where there was a baker's shop. Not for a warm treat; no, we'd stand with our hands pressed against the outside bakery wall where the ovens were pumping out heat inside, just to get warm before we went to school.

No central heating for us. No washing machine. My mother, Millie, had a big boiler in the scullery, and she'd light a fire beneath it to heat the water, and there would be the rubbing boards for washing the clothes on. It was basic all right, but it was home.

All those terraced houses had fireplaces in the bedrooms upstairs. That's when you knew someone was poorly … when they lit a fire in the bedroom upstairs to keep the patient warm. Whoever was in that room must have been ill! And if they actually brought the bed downstairs, they were bloody ill. It made it easier to carry them out when they died.

I remember walking with my mother past the old churchyard and all the railings had been cut down. I asked her why they'd been cut. 'Oh, they had to be cut down for the war effort,' she said. They'd been removed to recycle for making tanks and planes and ammunition. So, people were poor where I came from. As I grew up in Westhoughton, they had nothing, not even railings.

My father, Colin, worked in the cotton mill, Taylor and Hartley Textile Holdings, on Bolton Road. My mother worked in the same mill till she had the children – me, my brother Arthur and sister Irene. My father became weaving shed foreman and he actually died on the premises many years later. We'd been to Leicester when Manchester City played there in an FA Cup replay. We got beaten that night – Dad saw me score first with a penalty in a ding-dong game that we lost 4-3, and it was foggy on the way back. He didn't get back home until half four in the morning. He then got changed and went straight to work and he died at half seven. He smoked 40 or 50 fags a day, was overweight and he liked a pint or two.

Dad was six feet tall and 17 stone – and he was the smallest in the family! His brothers were enormous. Uncle Harold and Uncle Fred were both six-four; Uncle Arthur was six-three. Dad's father was a horrible little bastard, an ex-miner who wouldn't let any of his lads go down the pit. He really was *horrible* – but, I suppose, he was good in that way. Uncle Harold was killed in the war, fighting in the Far East, while Dad got drafted into the fire brigade in Liverpool.

After the war they'd work all week in the mill but then, come Saturday and the weekend, that was reserved for something special. That's when they'd treat themselves to something a bit different – like picnics at the cricket in summer or football matches in winter. They followed the local cricket team, Westhoughton, and you'd go down to their ground, the Tyldesleys, named after the famous local cricketing family, and there would be 3,000 watching the cricket there. That's why so many good overseas pros used to come to the leagues, and they could then move from there to the county, Lancashire.

Sunday, we had to go to school – Sunday school – in the morning and afternoon. It was at Central Hall Mission Church. I know exactly why we *had* to do that. Yes, we were god-fearing citizens, but also it was the only chance my mum and dad had to get their leg over!

When I got to about seven or eight, as we entered the early 50s, we moved into that new council house on the estate. It would have been 1951 and these were really nice council houses compared with our old terraced home. The new place was in Hazel Avenue, and it had an inside bathroom and toilet, plus an outside toilet as well. This was great as, not long after moving, my younger brother Trevor had arrived, too. The new houses were only 27s 6d. rent or £1.37 a week in today's decimal cash. You can understand the delight when I signed for Bolton as a ground-staff boy in the late 1950s on £5 a week; half my wages paid for the council house rent … it had gone up by a few bob by then!

Life started to improve for working people who had voted out Winston Churchill and the Tories in 1945. But, by 1951, he was back in office and a later Tory prime minister, Harold Macmillan, told the country in 1957 that we'd 'never had it so good'. That was probably true, with rationing finally ended and the economy starting to improve. But I bet he'd never had it as bad as we had in Westhoughton! Macmillan was a very well-to-do chap, educated at Eton and Oxford and he wanted for nothing, certainly not a warm home! He was at the head of a publishing empire and perfectly represented the establishment.

Whereas my family perfectly represented hard work. They weren't particularly sporting. Everybody in the family circle, both mother's side – the Tonge family – and father's side, were either miners or worked in a cotton mill. My father's side were such big fellows, although not particularly athletic; but my mother, Millie's side, certainly were. Her father, Henry, and his brother Frank were both champion wrestlers when it was a real sport, not this modern WWF rubbish. I get my athleticism and smaller stature from mother's side of the family, the Tonges.

I can remember coming out of the house to go to the primary school where 200 kids would go. We used to play football at school during all the breaks and, when it was summer, we'd switch to cricket. I was a good footballer, but I was a bloody good cricketer, too. We played both the main sports all the time. Every minute of the day – there was nothing else to do!

In my early days at school I showed a streak of entrepreneurship that was to flourish as I grew towards adulthood. I started my own mini business selling snacks to my classmates. If we'd never had it so good, what was wrong in trying to make it a little better? I quickly realised that if you could do a good deal, then do it. That was to stand me in good stead as I got older.

And what proved key to me becoming a footballer was the vital schooldays switch I had to make when I got to the age of 11. I was decent at schoolwork and the 11-plus was looming. The 11-plus was the academic test in those pre-comprehensive schooldays that decided a kid's future; whether he or she would go on to an academic education at a grammar school or, for those who failed the test, a secondary modern school, with a curriculum suited to more basic trades and manual work.

There were A and B forms at school, and I was in the A stream. They gave us all a letter to give to our parents with the option of taking the 11-plus – passing that entrance exam meant the prize of going to a grammar school. There would have been a choice of three for me: Bolton Grammar School, Rivington and Blackrod Grammar or Hindley and Abram Grammar. I'd have certainly got into one of them … had I *taken* the exam!

But I decided I wasn't going to even sit the exam. So, I didn't tell my parents about the letter, because I knew going to a grammar would have meant my football options would be limited. I simply wouldn't have made it as a player in a school where football was played occasionally and where rugby union was the main winter sport on the agenda.

For me to progress as a footballer, I had to get into the town schoolboys' team – Horwich and Westhoughton Boys. Just as you had to get into the Bolton Boys, Manchester Boys or Liverpool Boys teams if you were in those school areas.

I'd have played some football at a grammar school, but other sports as well. It wouldn't have been so intense as at a secondary modern, where football was king. If you did well and played for the town team, all the scouts would be there and, if you were decent, there would be the chance to progress to the Lancashire County Schools' side. If you did *that*, you could be picked up by a professional club as one of the 11 to 15 elite schoolboys in the county.

So, when I got my letter about the 11-plus, I looked at the envelope and decided *not* to hand it over to my parents. Days later, my teacher got hold of me and asked why the school had heard nothing from my folks about the exam. I said that my folks didn't want me to take it because they fancied I'd do well in the engineering line and wanted me to go to the secondary modern school until I was 12, and then go to Horwich Technical School, where you could become a draughtsman, engineer or an electrician.

Somehow, my dad found out about my little scheme. You didn't argue with my dad – he'd give you a good hiding if you did, especially for telling lies – and he said to me, 'What's all this about?' I told him that I wanted to be a footballer, but that I couldn't do that if I went to one of the grammars. I told him I wanted to go to Horwich Tech and take my chance at getting into the town team. To my eternal relief and gratitude, my dad said he understood where I wanted to be and why I wanted to go. 'I hope you're making the right decision,' he told me. 'I only hope you're going to be all right with your football.' He knew, though, that Horwich was a good college and they fed kids into the local locomotive works and the aircraft builders, de Havilland – the makers of the famous Comet jet airliner – which became part of Hawker Siddeley.

As it happened, when I went to the secondary modern, I got picked early for the town team even before I moved on to Horwich Tech. My gamble was paying off! I was the smallest boy on the team and my shirt used to come out of the bottom of my shorts! At first people criticised me for not being that good, and for being too weak, but they persevered with me.

I was in the Horwich Secondary Modern school team, too, that was the under-15s and I was three years behind them, no wonder I looked small! I was like a waif, about 4ft 11in and six stone six. And I was picked to play on the wing because I was regarded as a good footballer.

How did I manage that? Well, I was self-taught; I'd play, kicking a ball against the wall on my own or practising dribbling with a bunch of mates. Then there were house matches at school between the four houses. Playing the house matches got me into the secondary modern school team and, from there, into the town team, where I knew there would be scouts.

As far as I was concerned, everything at home revolved around sport. Depending on the time of year, there was a weekly football or cricket match – which I also loved – with our neighbours when we visited my grandma for Sunday tea.

Everything was going according to plan, except it was difficult in that I was playing against much bigger lads. At 13 I went on to Horwich Tech, as planned, after passing my exam. At that time a guy called John Winrow, in Westhoughton, formed his own boys team to play in the Bolton Boys Federation – the side was called Winrows because he had two sons who were footballers. A few of us joined Winrows, and in our first season we won the under-14s championship. Then, the season after that, we won the under-15s, with most of us younger than that. I was by now also playing for Horwich Tech School team and the town team ... and I then got picked for Lancashire Boys when

I was 14. I played twice a day, for the school or the town team in the morning and in the afternoon for Winrows. When you played twice a day, in that type of football, the scouts started asking questions, especially when they were told that I was younger than the age group I was playing in.

When I'd progressed into the Horwich and Westhoughton Boys' team, Dad had stopped watching football and was watching Leigh's rugby league side instead. That puzzled me. Looking back, I think he was worried that I might not turn out to be as good as he'd thought I would be. But that changed after Vic Wilcox, the father of one of my team-mates, urged him to come and watch me. After that, he didn't miss a single game.

And after moving up to Horwich Tech there was an amazing transformation, too, because I started to grow! I shot up from 4ft 11in and six stone six to 5ft 7in and about ten stone. Everybody thought, 'Christ, he's going to be as big as his dad!' But after 15, I stopped growing and I'm only 5ft 7½in now!

Through playing in the Boys Federation, the town team and Lancashire Boys, all the scouts were interested, and I had about six offers from clubs. But they didn't realise I was so young; I was only 13 or 14 then. The town team won the Talbot Cup, a tournament for all town sides in Lancashire, and then the interest really intensified. All the scouts flocked around Lancashire Boys. I went for a trial for the county at Southport, when I was about 15, and I got picked – played well for them – and then got a trial for England Boys. I was playing a *lot* of football.

Alec Rudd, who looked after the Horwich Tech team, had his concerns and he warned me: 'You're playing well, but I'm worried that you're doing too much. You could burn yourself out.' I said, 'No, I'm enjoying it!' and carried on. And then Lancashire Boys put me in for that England Schoolboys' trial and I had to go to Darlington.

Alec Rudd and Joe Wallwork, one of my teachers at Horwich Tech, had driven me up to County Durham in a little Morris Minor. The trial was England North vs England South and I was picked for the North. At half-time we were winning 3-0 and I'd scored two and made one. Job done? Maybe – I was taken off at the interval.

On the way back, we were chugging along in the little Morris and Alec and Joe were puffing away on their fags (with me nearly heaving in the smoke swirling around the back seat). 'Well, Lee,' they said, 'it's a special day for Horwich and Westhoughton Boys because you will be our first schoolboy international.' I didn't feel much like a schoolboy international in the back of that little motor – I felt like asking them to wind down the window because I thought I was about to throw up!

Alec announced at the Monday assembly – when they made the usual sporting announcements – that F.H. Lee would be picked for England Boys. It was a proud day and then we waited for the official call-up. And waited … and I never heard another bloody thing!

I don't know if it was *that* disappointment that made me say to myself, 'I'll bloody show them.' By now the scouts were coming to my house to see my dad: Burnley, Bolton, Wolverhampton to name just a few. The Manchester clubs didn't come knocking because they had a really large influx of Manchester boys – they all seemed to be really big lads, and size, apparently, mattered when it came to picking the England Boys' team. Maybe that's why I wasn't selected.

What happened after that shows they got it wrong because only 18 months after that England trial I'd joined Bolton Wanderers. Not only had I joined them, but I was also playing for them in the First Division, then England's top-flight elite league.

I'd said to my dad, 'I really do think I could be a professional footballer.' He said, 'Look, I've worked 42 years in the mill, and it's been something I've hated every single morning. It's like being in prison. You're the first in the family who can choose what he's going to do.'

Dad often reminded me that he'd been a good player, and he'd always encouraged me with my football. He must have seen something because, from about the age of four, all my Christmas presents were connected to the game – and we'd play almost every day in the house. That was great fun, but it could create the odd problem. One night, I knocked the mantelpiece clock off its perch and it went flying. My mum was in another room, and it was a couple of weeks before she noticed the clock had no glass on it!

When we played together, Dad used to give me the odd dig and knock me around a little. I realised he was trying to toughen me up and I think it really worked. I could more than hold my own with older lads when I was picked to play in older-age-group teams.

What he was saying about me giving football a go and avoiding a life sentence in the mill sounded encouraging, but he added a warning: 'If I allow you to join a club at 15, you must prepare for what you'll have to do if you don't make the grade at 18 and, secondly, prepare yourself for life after the game, because it doesn't last forever.' Those words resonated and stayed with me. It was my creed for life.

The important thing was that my dad, mum and I agreed that I'd give football a go. I had their full support. I then had to go to see the principal of Horwich Tech, a Mr L.G. King, who sat there in his cap and gown, and I gave him a letter from my father. 'What's all this about?' he asked. I told him I thought I had a good chance of making it as a professional player but that if, at 17 or 18, it looked like I wasn't going to make it, I could always go to evening classes and take draughtsmanship qualifications. 'I think you're a complete fool,' he told me. 'You've been badly advised by your parents, and I shall write them a letter accordingly.' Thanks for that, Mr King.

There I was, a fool. I wasn't going to make it. My parents were badly advising me. I wouldn't amount to anything going down that route. I begged to disagree, although I kept that to myself. It wouldn't be the only time someone in authority tried to put me in my place, but I was determined to follow my dream.

So it was that I signed for Bolton Wanderers. Why Bolton? Because my mother didn't want me moving away from home. When I was just 15½, I was playing in their reserve side and the following season it was the first team. I was on my way.

Chapter Two

Shooting Star at Bolton Wanderers

I WAS delighted to be at Bolton Wanderers, signing aged 15, in 1959. They were my local team and a major name in English football at the time … remember, they had won the FA Cup just the year before. That's when they famously ruined the Manchester United fairy tale by beating Matt Busby's cobbled-together team of Munich survivors and willing stand-ins. It came just weeks after the awful air disaster, and Bolton's greatest player, Nat Lofthouse, scored both Wanderers goals.

I'd barely got settled into my life as a ground-staff boy – it was 1960 – and I was thrown in to make my debut alongside the great Nat, aged 35 by now, in the Bolton attack. I'd joined as a starry-eyed kid with my headmaster's warning ringing in my ears. I certainly didn't expect to progress as rapidly as I did. No way did I anticipate being leading scorer for Bolton in the First Division when I was 17, but I'm getting ahead of myself. First, my debut, aged just

16 … it came on Guy Fawkes's Day, Saturday, 5 November 1960, and, pardon the pun, for me, it was a cracker!

The side had one or two injuries, so they turned to me, and I only went and scored on my debut! It was against Manchester City, of all teams, and I grabbed my goal, heading it past the legendary City keeper Bert Trautmann, the one-time German prisoner of war! Quite what Bert must have thought of me, all of 5ft 7½in, putting a header past him, I can only imagine. Nat also scored that day and I managed to get myself booked in a 3-1 win.

I remember looking up at the clock on top of the stand when my header hit the back of the net. It was quarter past three. My time had come!

Talking of time, when I prepared for my very first day as a Bolton player the year before, time conspired against me. My mother had got me up at home in good time for me to report to Burnden Park. After a good breakfast, I walked briskly to the ground, and I was there early for my report time of 9am. I didn't want to be first inside the ground, so I hung around outside, biding my time. I made my way in at about 8.50am and immediately got a dressing-down because I'd got my report time wrong … I should have been there at 8.30am!

But I soon settled in with the rest of the ground-staff lads. In fact, I was their self-appointed gaffer, the foreman of the ground-staff gang. We did a lot of menial tasks around the place; sweeping the terraces, painting whenever and wherever it was required, cleaning the senior players' boots, tidying the changing rooms and baths.

There was, of course, time for teenage pranks. Like when my mate, Carl Davenport, drenched me with a hose. I immediately planned my revenge when I reckoned he'd shot into the toilet. The toilet block was adjacent to the dressing rooms and wasn't covered at the top. I aimed the hose and turned it on, full pressure, over the top of the door. Unluckily for me – and my target – the figure I'd seen steal into the loo was, in fact, a senior member of the office staff! He emerged, pants around his ankles, looking like a drowned rat. I'd certainly got off on the wrong foot!

The Bolton team manager, an old-school chap called Bill Ridding, didn't take to me. We never seemed to hit it off despite my progress on the pitch. But after my great scoring start for the first team against City, I played another six games, and my first away appearance was at Arsenal's famous Highbury Stadium. It was amazing because there I was, in the Arsenal programme at outside-right: 'Mr F.H. Lee' … I had to be called *mister* because I was still an amateur! I didn't get paid for my football, I got just £5 a week gross for all my work as a 16-year-old ground-staff boy, working on the terraces and doing the menial cleaning and suchlike. No reward at all for my football, just for my labouring about the place. Little did they realise, that big

Arsenal crowd, that I was listed as an amateur because I simply wasn't old enough to be a pro! There was a lesson or two for me that day on the pitch, as we lost 5-1.

Just before that game we played Newcastle United at home. They had seasoned professionals in defence, such as Alf McMichael, Dick Keith and Bob Stokoe, who was at centre-half. The fine Welsh player, Ivor Allchurch, was in their forward line, a really talented player. We won it 2-1.

In the same month, Nat bowed out and retired after one injury too many, against Birmingham. Then I got left out and I reverted to the reserves. The season after, I signed professional in May 1961, but I didn't have a good season, playing five senior games. Yet, the following year, when Bolton's ageing side were struggling to avoid relegation again, I was the leading goalscorer. The team grew older together and they sold Dougie Holden, the left-winger, to Preston. He was a good player. Dennis Stevens went, too, moving to Everton, when I was about 18.

But when I was 17, and on my way to being Wanderers' top scorer, there was an incident when we got a penalty. The week before we'd got one and Dennis Stevens had missed it. In all, they'd missed about three in the weeks just beforehand. Then came this one at Burnden Park's Great Lever End and no one wanted to take it! The crowd realised and started booing, and I said to Bryan Edwards, the captain, 'Slim, I'll take it!' He looked at me and said,

'You're not fucking taking it. Stevie, you take it!' So, Stevens took it, and he missed it. At that time I wasn't the most confident about myself. If anyone said anything to me in the dressing room, I'd blush. The manager then had a bit of a go at full time – and he rarely got involved in football affairs – telling us it was all a disgrace. He said it must not happen again and that we should practise penalties. I again said that I'd take them in future and he said to me, 'You might not be in the fucking team!' To which I replied, 'Okay, if I'm in the team, I'll take them.'

Sure enough, we got another one in a game soon after that. I put it on the spot and knocked it in, and that made all the difference to how I felt about myself. All of a sudden I changed. I could walk through that dressing room without blushing or feeling embarrassed about what the senior players were saying to me, because I'd done something that *none* of them wanted to do. It's amazing what little things like that can do for your confidence. It made a difference to me and gave me that personal boost as I moved forward.

But something else happened at this time that told me my card had been marked at Bolton. It signalled I was never going to be flavour of the month with the manager. It began during the close season when I went to pick up my dad from playing panel (crown green) bowling. As I waited for him, I had a half pint of shandy at the bar. Just 20 minutes later, I left the place with my dad. It transpired that the chap sat next to me at the bar used to play alongside the legendary former Bolton forward Joe Smith, a big star either side of the First World War. When I reported at the club next day, Bill Ridding had me in his office. He said I'd been seen drinking the previous day, according to information passed to a director. From this seed grew numerous subsequent tales about me and my so-called drinking.

I'm quite sure that these stories were used by the club as one method to ward off interest in me from other clubs as my form improved on the pitch. Certainly, I heard from connections at three other big clubs that, when they made initial enquiries, they were warned off by Bolton; they were told I was 'a bad lad' who liked a drink. This was all symptomatic of a malaise at Burnden Park that meant they were never likely to make the sort of progress I was keen to enjoy.

When Jimmy Hill led the Professional Footballers' Association (PFA) out of the outdated shackles of the maximum wage – which had limited all players to earn only £20 a week at the turn of the 1960s – it meant that professional football clubs in England had to get to grips with the new deal, and learn fast how to make it work. Bolton, in the 1960s, never did. Now players, more than ever before, needed to be treated like adults, not naughty kids. When the English game became more professional, Bolton could not or would not keep up with the pace of change. It's worth noting that Wanderers' 1958 cup-winning side didn't contain a single player that cost a transfer fee. It was generally accepted that their fine side cost nothing apart from £110 in signing-on fees! The club didn't like spending money.

And, though Nat Lofthouse is rightly a Bolton legend, his attitude in the 1950s to players' terms and conditions jarred with the mood of the times as players steadily moved towards militancy and Jimmy Hill's threatened PFA strike in 1961. That threatened action brought the maximum wage era to an end. Yet Nat wrote in his book, *Goals Galore*, in 1954:

> For me football is pleasure with pay and I can think of no other profession which offers so much to a youngster if he possesses fitness, a quick-thinking brain and a pair of nimble feet.
>
> I know we often hear talk about soccer slaves – but strangely enough, it's not the professional footballer who does the complaining. More often than not it is someone who is in no way associated with the game …
>
> Just think for a moment what a top-class man receives every week. During the season his wages are £15 a week. In the summer they come down to £12 a week. For a win he receives a bonus of

> £2. A draw means a bonus of £1. In addition to this, although the contracts say he 'may' receive a benefit at the end of five years' service, most players are duly rewarded. The maximum benefit is £750, which works out at another £3 a week. Footballers' benefits, unlike those of cricketers, are taxable. Out of my last £750 cheque, I had to pay £280, but that is beside the point.
>
> In addition to our wages and benefits, the Football League hands over to every footballer, on reaching the age of thirty-five, a sum amounting to nine per cent of his wages during his career in League football. This is tax free. A footballer does not have to contribute anything towards the Provident Fund from which this money is drawn. It is all paid from the four per cent levy which clubs hand over to the League out of their gate receipts.
>
> It is important that the people who follow football should know these facts, and it also applies to those who still look upon professional footballers as down-trodden individuals leading a hand-to-mouth existence.

Wow! But that was Bolton in those far-off days. I'd probably have stayed at Bolton far longer than I did had they treated me well; Wyn Davies, who came in from Wrexham as Nat's long-term replacement in 1962, would have stayed longer had they shown more enterprise and ambition. Instead, he left for Newcastle United. We could have built a very useful side at Bolton. Instead, it was a gradual decline and relegation hit the club hard in 1963/64.

I'd top-scored again for Bolton in 1964/65 with 23 in the league, my best return for them. This was the season we just missed out on an immediate promotion back to the top flight after our relegation. Wyn was a great partner in attack, but the way I was treated, as the local lad and ex-amateur, certainly grated. I was leading scorer for five seasons on the trot and they never paid me the top first-team rate. They bought Wyn for £25,000 in 1962 and he was put on top wages, so I asked the manager: 'Why can't I be on top wages – I've scored more goals than him?' They told me it was because I was too young. There was always something.

Wyn and I were good pals, but I noticed the difference in attitude, even to timekeeping. I kept good time, but I noticed Wyn could roll in any time he liked, and he'd be indulged. For me, or the other local lads, it was a different story! There were lots of problems at Bolton but the major one, in my opinion, was the relationship, or lack of one, between the players and management. They just didn't seem to grasp how to engage and get on the right side of players. In broad terms, players tend to be easy-going, and it will work wonders if a club is straight with them and develops them, both as individuals and a team.

Bolton had also failed to keep pace with training or tactics. Ridding was an old-fashioned secretary-manager, a role so far away from the modern-day manager or, more likely, chief coach, as to be laughable.

Around 1958, the same time Bolton had their famous FA Cup triumph, Brazil won the World Cup in Sweden with a kid called Pelé in attack. It ushered in the 4-4-2 formation, which was widely adopted: four at the back, four midfielders and two attackers up front. Yet Bolton carried on regardless with the age-old WM formation with two full-backs, three half-backs and five forwards.

I'd made a firm friend of Freddie Hill, the Bolton forward who had joined them a year or two before me, and he brought back some interesting new ideas and tactics from his time with England Under-23s. They were dismissed out of hand. Ridding's coach, George Taylor, had a simple philosophy: stop your opponents and you'll win. Bottle them up, first and foremost.

Yet the club had fine senior players when I first walked – admittedly, a little late – into Burnden Park. Full-back Roy Hartle was a man of steel down Bolton's right. Wingers feared him, and yet, off the park, he was reserved, with the air of an academic. He became a Tory councillor for the Halliwell ward in the town. Incredibly, he was never booked or sent off in a long career. He liked to tell referees, 'But I played the ball …' And so he did, albeit the man went with it sometimes! Towards the end of his career, Roy faced Manchester City and the winger who became my great pal, Mike Summerbee. Mike was told by coach Malcolm Allison to push it past Hartle and run. Mike obliged and, as he raced past him, Roy scythed him down like a sheaf of corn. Roy would always get up and dust down his stricken opponent before walking away without another word.

On the other flank, Tommy Banks was a similarly imposing full-back and, between them, centre-half and skipper Bryan 'Slim' Edwards was a cultured, gentlemanly centre-half, a one-club man who had 18 years at Burnden, clocking close to 500 games. As the 50s ended, though, this side was ageing, and the wheels were coming off – or being sold off. Nat's injuries forced him to retire just after I first got into the side; I've mentioned the departures of Dennis Stevens and winger Dougie Holden, and they followed midfielder-winger Ray Parry, switching to Blackpool in 1960, and wing-half Derek Hennin moving to Chester in 1961.

This was a club behind the times and haemorrhaging experience and quality. One of the biggest mistakes was in dispensing with Tommy Banks when they did. He was allowed to leave in 1961 for Altrincham, a decision I regarded as a bit of a tragedy and a waste of talent – because

I reckon Tommy had two or three years of top football left in him. He played on for another six years at Altrincham and Bangor City, but he was good enough to have a done a good job at Burnden. True, he had hamstring problems, but he had made his England debut as recently as 1958 and played in all four of his country's 1958 World Cup finals games.

What was going on? Well, it was all part of Bolton's ham-fisted plan to overcome the new financial challenges of football life after the maximum wage was abolished. The plan was simple: rid the club of experienced players expecting to be paid the new, higher wages, and replace them with youngsters who wouldn't expect such terms. What they didn't factor in is that such planning could only result in unbalanced, inconsistent performances from inexperienced players. Bolton never grasped the fact that footballers were worth the rate for the job in just the same way as a time-served craftsman or an in-demand entertainer.

On the playing side, Bolton's training methods had me at a loss at times. Before an important game against Manchester United, Bill Ridding gave his team talk around the boardroom table. He'd chalked a series of lines, and it looked like a map of Crewe station. These lines, we were told, were the paths of Bobby Charlton's runs when he got on the ball.

'Charlton comes along these paths and zooms for goal,' Ridding explained. 'All you have to do is stop him. Easy!'

Fine Bill, that's all right then. Ahead of a cup tie with West Brom, the manager was into another team talk. He turned to speak to our centre-forward, who was hunched in the corner. 'What do you think, Wyn?' he asked. Welsh-speaker Wyn never did say much, but this time he was completely silent. Bill's talk had sent him to sleep!

But I gave my best to Bolton for as long as I could. I knew we could have been doing far better and I was *certain* that I was capable of so much more myself. A return of 92 goals in 139 first-team appearances is a little more than a goal every 1.5 games. Not bad for a young player in a fading team.

So, was it that bad at Bolton? Well, I've no interest in old feuds and I'm hardly likely to indulge in 'what might have beens' on a personal level. I went on to enjoy the kind of success with my subsequent clubs that I could only dream of at Bolton. I also went on to build a good international career, so I'm far from bitter. I'm in a prime position to simply be honest, and I won't pull punches, either. When I decided my time at Bolton was up, in 1967, I got a lot of criticism from the club and from supporters. So they deserve to hear my side of the story.

In my earliest days in the first team, when I was still an amateur, Bolton were clearly getting me on the cheap – very cheap. I was due to sign professional the following year and Bolton always said that if you played for the first team, you got first-team wages. In those days the maximum wage was £20 a week, but they didn't pay me that. Not only that – because I was initially playing as an amateur, I got no bonuses either.

I was probably one of the cheapest players ever to play in the top flight, the old Football League First Division, because my initial take-home pay was £4 12s 6d. or £4.63. I played about six games on that money. It was made up of the £5 a week I got for being a ground-staff boy but then, once my National Insurance stamp of 7s 6d. was deducted, I got £4 12s 6d.

As I've admitted, the season following my debut wasn't a great one for me. I went back into the reserves when I was due to sign professional. Be that as it may, Wanderers always treated their local lads poorly. Bolton would try to knock the stuffing out of you if you were a bit cocky or confident. And they tried it with me after one game when I was 17 … they told me I was dropped to the 'A' team. I refused, and they warned me that I'd be in breach of my contract if I didn't play. I didn't mind playing for the reserves, but the 'A' team? Anyway, as it happened, I did play for the 'A' team … one of the last matches of the season. Who should it be against? Manchester City, at an old training ground called Urmston. Neil Young was one of those playing for City, and we'd be team-mates years later, but I was completely pissed off that day.

Next season, I started like a house on fire and I was knocking the goals in early on, and they gave me a new contract. But they never, ever paid me their top wages. When you went into wage negotiations with the manager, Ridding – who could be a complete so and so – you'd be lined up outside his door and you could hear the 'conversations' from outside. I recall Eric Redrobe, a big centre-forward, complaining that his terms weren't good enough, that he'd scored a lot of goals for the reserves and, instead of £16 a week, he thought he should be on at least £18. Ridding said to him, 'Redrobe, when you came here, you were fucking rubbish. Now I've taught you everything I know, and you're still fucking rubbish!' All the lads could hear this going on.

Another time he dropped Freddie Hill, when we thought he was undroppable, and Ridding was smartly out of the door, going for his lunch. Freddie chased after him and told Ridding he wanted a word. 'What have you left me out of the team for?' asked Freddie. Ridding replied, 'This is an important match tomorrow – I'm trying to win this one!'

Bolton didn't always treat Freddie well and he also had the huge disappointment of a failed transfer to Liverpool in 1964, scuppered by a medical that apparently showed up high blood pressure and blood sugar. It didn't stop him playing at Bolton for 12 years – and he carried on elsewhere for years after that!

As I'd made my way into the Bolton first team, Freddie came into his own at Wanderers and won both Under-23 and full caps for England. Unfortunately, he arrived in the England senior side just as Alf Ramsey took over as manager. Alf, famously, had no real interest in wingers and that closed the door on Freddie after just two full caps. But what a wonderful player Freddie Hill was, so very, very skilful. I never forgot him and much later in my career I made it my business to link up with him on the pitch once again.

Not long after I first made the first team, there was a guy called Bill Pickard, who was a Burnley director, and he sold agricultural machinery. He asked my father if Bolton had signed me as a pro. My dad told him that they hadn't because I'd not been offered a decent pro contract. Bill said they'd always liked me and were still interested in signing me. Then, just before the maximum wage ended, Bolton offered me a new deal at £12 a week. They said I wasn't old enough to be on the same as the seniors, so I put in a transfer request. I always had a dispute with them after that. Bolton repeatedly denied there was any interest in me … even when I knew there certainly was!

Was it me? Was I a difficult bastard, as Bolton would have others believe? No, I don't think so. I was ambitious, yes, and I was opinionated – I always have been – and I'd back myself. But I wasn't difficult, and I think the fact I simply stood my ground made it easy for Bolton to brand me a troublemaker.

Burnley were always after me. Northampton were then on the rise through the leagues – just like Watford under Graham Taylor, 25 years later. Their Welsh manager, Dave Bowen, wanted me. I wouldn't have gone there, as I thought they were a team of cloggers, to be honest. I got injured against them on a frosty pitch – it was my own fault, and I didn't do it again. But Spurs, who were a huge club at this time, having so brilliantly won the league and FA Cup double in 1960/61, also wanted me. I knew that their manager, Bill Nicholson, was an admirer of mine.

I was top scorer for those five seasons on the trot at Bolton, from 62/63 through to 66/67, and it's amazing how many clubs I later learned wanted to sign me during those days. It was all a bit of a struggle, even so. Despite Bolton's Lofthouse-inspired cup win in 1958 and decent seasons in the league – finishing fourth in the top flight in 1959 and sixth in 1960 – Nat's retirement and the club's failure to adapt to the new economics of the game heralded the end of Bolton's time as one of England's bigger teams.

Even in our relegation season, in 1963/64, I was the club's top scorer. It didn't stop us dropping into the Second Division for the first time in 29 years. On the other hand, it hadn't stopped my form up front attracting interest from many of the top-flight clubs. So many seemed to be given the familiar club line that I wasn't for sale, or that I was supposedly trouble. I remember we played and beat Bill Shankly's Liverpool in the League Cup, after a replay. We were drawn away at Anfield and I scored a real cracker from an oblique angle just four or five yards from the byline … in it went into the top corner. We drew that game 1-1 and got them back to Burnden Park, where we beat them 3-2, with Freddie Hill scoring one of our goals. I took a free kick about 30 yards out and it swerved, with the keeper only knocking it down, and Freddie was there to score. A great win bearing in mind we were in the old Second Division at the time.

Bill Shankly, by way of contrast, was building a great club at Anfield. He always used to stop me and talk after we played them and, sure enough, he did it again this time. 'We should've signed ye the night ye scored at the Kop end,' he growled. 'And I shouldn't have listened to anybody else!'

That was right at the end of my time at Bolton. Apparently, their chief scout, Geoff Twentyman, who'd played at Liverpool throughout most of the 1950s, rated me very, very highly. Or so I was told many years later! Geoff had recommended several times that Liverpool sign me. And Manchester City's chief scout, Harry Godwin, used to say every season to their manager, 'You must sign the kid from Bolton!' So, I was getting noticed in a lot of the right places.

Matt Busby, the man who rebuilt Manchester United into a great club after Munich, said to me, 'I should've signed you, because I first bought John Connelly from Burnley and later went back and bought Willie Morgan from Burnley – but you could have come in between!' Morgan was younger than me and Connelly was older. If he'd signed me when I was 20, in 1964, I could have done John's job, and Matt probably wouldn't have had to buy Willie Morgan at all!

I hope you get the drift, here. Leave Bolton? It seemed you'd have to tunnel your way out. If you asked for a move, it seemed the stock answer from Bill Ridding was: 'What? *You*? You want to move? And who do you think would buy *you*?'

As time went by, of course, I'd know exactly who'd have liked to buy me. I knew the directors didn't want me to leave Bolton. When they realised my mind was set on a transfer, director Ted Gerrard was dead set against it; he was nostalgic and regarded me as a latter-day Joe Smith, the old striker whose pal had apparently started the tales of my 'drinking' after a shandy at the bowls club.

My conscience was clear, though. I'd given Wanderers eight years of my life, and they got me for a £10 signing-on fee. I'd paid my dues and I certainly wasn't letting anyone down, especially when they got a £65,000 transfer fee from Manchester City as the return on their tiny investment.

Sure, I'd asked for a transfer before but, by late summer 1967, I was adamant I'd go, despite the club's refusals and blocking tactics. In the end, I'd served my contract out and I'd effectively packed the club in … I was playing on just a weekly contract. I was determined my career wouldn't be stalled at Bolton in the way my mate, Freddie Hill, had seen his hit neutral. He'd become a great friend, and when I first played for Wanderers in 1960 his was the standard I was aiming for. Maybe, just maybe, I never did match it, and I really believe a great football talent was largely lost when that Liverpool transfer collapsed around him. After the medical wrecked his deal, he saw specialists who could find nothing wrong with him and, by common consent, it was reckoned Freddie had got so excited that he built up an artificially high blood pressure for a short while – a tragedy. I played more than 200 games with Freddie at Bolton, and he *made* me. His ability on the ball was superb, and in the mid-60s there was no one to compare him with, in my opinion. I'd include Pelé and Eusébio, by the way, in making that statement. I may have led the Bolton scoring charts for years, but so many of those goals were down to Freddie. Freddie's experience, with that Liverpool deal falling flat in particular, convinced me I was making the right decision to get away.

The 1967/68 season began well – I scored in seven successive games at one point, and I knew there was a lot of interest. Then it was eight goals in nine games, despite my standoff with the club. We'd beaten mighty Liverpool on 27

September in that League Cup replay clash. So it was, in late September, I puffed out my chest, walked into Bill Ridding's office and asked for my cards! This is how it happened …

I knew that Wolves' manager Ronnie Allen was an admirer. He was putting up cash plus his winger Terry Wharton, and Bolton wanted me to go and speak to them. So, I went down out of courtesy, really, to talk to them. Ridding told me to drive to a hotel in Stone, Staffordshire, and meet their manager. I went on my own – there were no agents then, not even a solicitor, just me alone. Ridding and the directors drove to the meeting separately. It looked like a done deal, but it wasn't. That's because I wanted to carry on living around my Bolton base, for a very good reason. Wolves, quite understandably, wanted me to live close to Molineux, and that wasn't going to work for me. Why? The simple fact was that I'd built up a business of my own from scratch and it had blossomed, just as my football career had blossomed. Remember my first 'business' … selling snacks at school? Well, this was the real world and I'd worked bloody hard on the pitch and off it.

I was determined that I wasn't going to give up the lifestyle my dual livelihoods were starting to provide. I'd followed the creed laid down by my father: prepare yourself for life after the game … because it doesn't last forever.

Wolves' condition that I had to move to their area was a perfectly fair one, but it pushed me to the brink of quitting the game, at 24. I'd have preferred that to having to return and play for Bolton again. I felt the only reason Bolton had accepted Wolves' bid was because they knew very well that I wouldn't fancy a move to the West Midlands. I let Bolton know smartish that I was ready to walk away from football and, once they knew I was serious, their blocking tactics wilted.

The Bolton directors got together to discuss this. They weren't happy that I'd turned my back on the Wolves deal and apparently decided that, if I was worth all this money, they couldn't have me on a week-to-week contract. I met with two of the directors plus manager Bill Ridding in the Bolton boardroom. They told me they'd concluded that they had to put me on a proper contract. Bear in mind, I was still on just £35 a week, and we'd just knocked Liverpool out of the League Cup.

'We would like to make you an offer of increased wages,' they said.

'Oh,' I said. 'How much is that?'

'One hundred and fifty pounds a week,' was the astonishing reply.

I said, 'I'm only on £35 now!' They told me that was their offer – a two-year contract. They weren't expecting what I said next: 'Thank you very much, but no.'

'What do you mean?' Ridding shot back.

I said if I was suddenly worth that much now, what about all the years they'd been underpaying me? I also told them they hadn't thought this offer through. I spelled it out. Once it became public knowledge that I was on £150 a week and my team-mates were on, say, £45 or £50 a week, they'd just give me the ball and say, 'Right, there you are – if you're that bloody good, do it on your own!' I wouldn't be part of the team if I was getting three or four times the money the rest were on.

I told them that we weren't going to agree. And, as I was on a weekly contract, if I got injured and couldn't play, they wouldn't pay my wages. They agreed with that, so I told them to give me my cards – my National Insurance cards – and I'd walk away. 'When you find a club that wants to buy me, I'll come back and talk again,' I said. Ridding and the directors agreed with that and, at last, the door was open for me to walk away.

But there were still a few mysteries around Bolton's handling of my departure. The collapsed Wolves deal was valued at £40,000, plus Terry Wharton of Wolves going in part-exchange to Bolton, valued at £25,000. A while later, Wharton did go to Bolton in a separate deal valued at £60,000–£70,000. In the blink of an eye, Wharton's value had more than doubled, and then some!

Add to that a Stoke bid for me, later put at £65,000, lodged a fortnight before Wolves came in. That was the same bid made by Manchester City – yet Bolton turned down Stoke. Why? I knew nothing about Stoke's bid at the time.

But it was over for me at Bolton after eight years and 106 goals in 210 appearances in all competitions. The stats look good, they *are* good, yet Bolton had no real regard for my worth as far as what they chose to pay me, right until virtually the end. When I signed on at 15, I was told I'd be on full first-team pay once I made the first team. Well, I made the first team at 16 – and I wasn't. It was the same story through the years that followed, even though I became their leading goalscorer, season after season. At the very end of my Bolton days, in 1967, I was still on just £35.

Things could have worked out differently. Wolves might have allowed me to travel from Bolton to their training ground; Bolton might have accepted Stoke's under-the-radar bid. As it happened, I had no clue that Manchester City were keen and yet the transfer to Maine Road turned out to be perfect for me in every way.

I'd been on the very brink of chucking it all in and concentrating on my business. Now I was free to see just how far I could go in the game. And that really excited me. My football needed rescuing and, after the Wolves deal collapsed, I had no idea if I'd play for *anyone* again. But when the rescue finally happened, it was another episode cloaked in mystery!

Chapter Three

Another Career … I'm Listening, Dad

HERE I must briefly interrupt my football narrative. Before I get on to the mystery of my transfer to Manchester City, I should explain just why I was so determined not to go to Wolves – and why I was adamant that I wanted to carry on living in the Bolton area. Remember, when I was 18, and forging my career in Bolton's attack, they were paying me pretty miserly wages. That was the backdrop when I first met and made firm friends with a guy called Peter James.

We first bumped into each other at a local cricket club dinner in 1962. I loved my cricket in the summer, so it wasn't odd to find me there. He told me his wife, Connie, had worked with my mother, Millie, on the night shift at the local cotton mill. At the time, Peter had a window cleaning round and he was also a councillor for Westhoughton's Central Ward. After the club dinner, we had a chat about working together.

Fresh in my mind was the row I'd had with Bill Ridding. I might have been the team's leading scorer at 17, but it hadn't counted for much. I told him that if I was good enough to be top scorer in the first team, I was good enough to be on the same pay as my team-mates. These sums seem ridiculous in the 21st century, but I wanted another £5 to make my pay up to £25 a week.

Ridding's reply was cutting: 'What else can you do? You're only a labourer, aren't you?' Within a few, short years I could laugh at those churlish comments. But I wasn't laughing at the time.

After our meeting at the cricket club, Peter and I bumped into each other again on a bus and talked a little more. We spoke about joining forces in some extra work. I wasn't afraid of that, and a bit of side work might push my earnings up a little. I'd done pocket-money jobs as a young lad, working for a while at Dunscar Golf Club, just north of Bolton, and I also worked for my uncle cleaning and fixing gravestones. I enjoyed working and I was happy to do a second job.

And so it began. I started by helping out with Peter's window cleaning business in the close season. If we strayed into the well-heeled posh districts, where the Wanderers' directors had their homes, I went under cover, disguising myself with a pair of spectacles and a flat cap!

Peter was a bit older than me, but we just hit it off right away. He seemed a good lad who wanted to get on and that suited me. I'd help him with his round and then I started a new business with him, far removed from a wash bucket and ladder.

Peter joined me as we started to buy and sell wastepaper and cartons and, through my contacts, we got in touch with the people in the cotton mills in Bolton. Many of them were closing down but there was also the printing industry, too. We became quite successful at it. We were buying paper in and baling it, selling it, transporting it. Nobody thought about 'green' issues 60 years ago, but this was early recycling, plain and simple!

I did quite a lot of the lorry driving myself as I was only training in the mornings at Bolton. This went on for quite some time. Talk about multitasking! I used to drive my lorry during the week. This extended even to Thursdays and Fridays before the weekend games – I'd be in the lorry, collecting wastepaper. I carried on with my old window cleaner disguise of cap and scarf so that I'd not be easily spotted!

The hours were even longer in the summer when there was neither training nor games, and my earnings from the business were already more than I was taking home from Wanderers. I used to do a lot of haulage in the close season's long, sunny days, and we'd make a lot of money – £2.50 a ton. I'd do two loads a day from North Wales to Blackburn. I was making £200 a week at a time when the average working wage would have been less than £30 ... and I'd have been lucky to be making £30 a week from football with Wanderers. My lorry then progressed to an articulated wagon and the business was on the up.

We'd buy, say, two tons of printed shavings and off-cuts from a printer. We'd buy it either baled up or take it to our baling machine at our premises and bale it up to be recycled at paper mills. We did all that and became quite successful at it. And it wasn't my only sideline away from the game. I always remembered my dad's words about football not lasting forever, or not working at all. I always heeded his advice.

I'd already broken the Lee family tradition by escaping working life in the local mill, but I wasn't afraid of hard work. Maybe that's why Ridding dismissed me as 'just a labourer'.

Apart from the paper business and the lorry driving that went with it, often to North Wales, other enterprises were to follow. Both Peter and I were working-class lads who'd started with nothing, but we were rich with ideas. We noticed how a lot of people would trek from the outskirts into central Bolton to use the launderettes, so we opened one up that was on their doorstep. Then we opened a ladies' hairdressers. Later on, there was a menswear boutique – very George Best – which we opened in the middle of Manchester.

With the main paper business, we then started taking some tissue products from a company in Bolton, which had set up making toilet rolls, kitchen towels, handkerchiefs, that sort of thing – plus cooking foil, cling film, Christmas decorations and all sorts. We took their waste and would sell it on.

The lads at Wanderers used to pull my leg about my working life outside football. If Peter and I walked into a pub after finishing work with the wastepaper or whatever, they'd raise a glass and shout, 'Here come Steptoe and Son!' Yes, I'm sure we were good for a laugh at the time, but I was to have the last laugh … eventually.

There were some good laughs along the way, as you might expect. In the early days of the window cleaning round, I put my ladder up to the front bedroom window at one house while Peter walked around to do the back. His ladder went up to the bathroom window, and when he reached the top panes where the glass was clear, he saw the lady of the house desperately clambering out of the bath. I'd just started at the front when she dashed from the landing into the bedroom – only to see my cheery face!

As the waste business was being established, I'd often take one of my lorries to Wales and do a 12-hour shift, including loading and unloading the paper. A 10pm finish wasn't unusual, and we'd end the day with dust in our hair and looking very scruffy and down at heel. But when I raise a fine red wine today, I'm not so sure it tastes any better than the couple of pints we used to enjoy after one of those long stints.

We might have been the butt of the odd joke and a laugh at the bar when we enjoyed one of those pints, but there were few nights after a hard day's graft that we didn't pick up tips about another wastepaper source.

The business expanded rapidly, and we soon had lots of the residue – big half-ton reels of tissue. We were buying these reels that were either off-shade or single-ply and we had a big former railway warehouse that we used to fill up with these things. It was very difficult to cut up to recycle because it got so dusty. We saved it up and soon had something like 200 tons of it.

We were now doing big business and Peter was dealing with one of London's largest paper merchants, who were into wastepaper big time, right across the land. This was one of the biggest – if not the biggest – operators around and they had depots in other cities, such as Birmingham and Manchester. Life was looking good.

And that's precisely the reason I wouldn't be railroaded into a move that meant upping sticks, lock stock and barrel, to Wolverhampton. It's also why the transfer to Manchester City, when it happened, was absolutely ideal in every way. Because our company, James and Lee Waste, was now going places. I was going places – on and off the pitch. Yet I hadn't played much immediately before the mystery of my transfer concluded. I'd been driving my lorries more than anything in the aftermath of getting my cards from Ridding and co. at Bolton.

In fact, my last job had been roping and sheeting a lorry loaded with about 15 tons of paper and cardboard from a mill in Bolton – heading for the Sun Paper Mills in Blackburn – when I got the call from Ridding, on 5 October 1967. I was told to get myself to Burnden!

My transfer was happening at last. I'd finally tunnelled out.

Chapter Four

Manchester City and Feeling Champion

IT'S TRUE; there I was doing the hard yards with my other business, ensuring my lorry's load was safely roped and sheeted, when the telephone call came from Bill Ridding: 'I've got you a new club,' he told me. When I asked who this club was, I was told to get down to the Burnden Park car park and I'd find out more. 'And bring your National Insurance cards with you!' he said.

So, I did, and when I arrived he was waiting for me. 'Get in your car and follow me,' he said. 'Where am I going?' I asked, still with no clue as to who wanted to buy me. It was like I was embarking on one of those mystery tours that Women's Institutes and church groups used to organise at the time!

We set off and headed out of Bolton, going south, so I knew it had to be one of three clubs: Manchester United, Manchester City or Stoke. We got over the Barton Bridge that crossed the Manchester Ship Canal and turned off towards Sale. I knew now it wasn't Stoke and it had to be either City or United. We drove another mile or so and turned off towards Chorlton. That's when I knew it had to be City – my transfer destination mystery was over!

But my nerves were still on edge because, at that very moment, I looked at the gauges on my car – a second-hand Austin Cambridge – and I was showing empty on fuel! *If I run out of petrol now*, I thought to myself, *before I get to the ground and leave Bill Ridding to arrive without me, he's going to tell everyone that I always was an awkward bastard!*

I nursed my car through those final miles, running on fumes, and I made it. Just! And that's when I met City manager Joe Mercer. 'I think you might be the final piece in our jigsaw,' he told me. We could talk immediately as the clubs had agreed a fee. I did think to myself, in honesty, that his jigsaw didn't look too clever just then. They were about fourth-bottom in the top flight and had just been beaten at home by neighbours United, 3-2. But I was keen. I wanted the move to further my career, having seen what Bolton had done to my pal, Freddie Hill. Freddie was a fine player and he would have been a great one had he gone to a good club. I was determined that Bolton wouldn't leave me in the same situation.

I had a good chat with Joe. He quickly warned me not to ask for anything 'exorbitant' in terms of wage-wise, because they didn't have any money. He said they were skint, yet I'd just turned down £150 a week at Bolton! 'So, we're going to offer you £60 a week basic wage, plus your crowd bonus and appearance money and so on,' he said.

'That sounds all right,' I replied. At the same time, I was thinking I must be the only player in history to take a 150 per cent drop in wages offers to further his career! But I was happy to do it; happy to get to a bigger and better club and see just how far I could get in this wonderful game.

To keep fit, in those empty days after I'd got my cards at Bolton, I worked out with Peter Keeling, a sportswriter and athletics coach, training on a university sports field at Fallowfield, and we played an hour's squash daily in nearby Didsbury. I was fit, but not properly match fit.

I also spoke with Joe's right-hand man, coach Malcolm Allison. I didn't give them a final decision immediately at our first meeting, not because I wasn't happy with what they told me, but I simply wanted to make sure I'd made the right move. It didn't take long to decide, and the next day – a Friday – I went back to Maine Road and agreed the deal.

Bolton weren't quite finished with me yet, though. Ridding had already told the City officials that I wouldn't get the usual 10 per cent cut of the transfer fee because I'd asked for the move. And then there was a reaction from the Football League. I had my boots with me and was all set to travel with the team to Sunderland for Saturday's First Division game at

Roker Park when Joe emerged from his office to say, 'It's all off, the League won't accept your registration!'

Well, not quite 'off'. There was a hiccup in the paperwork, and it meant I did miss the game at Sunderland – which City lost – but the deal was finally completed on the following Tuesday. The Football League had put a spanner in the works. The League's secretary was the considerable figure of Alan Hardaker, and he wouldn't initially accept my registration. The League said they were looking into the 'ways and means' of the signing. It did go through, eventually, but the League wouldn't approve my 10 per cent cut of the transfer fee: £6,000, a considerable sum back in 1967. They gave me five per cent instead, so naturally I asked why I'd only got half of what I was entitled to. They said there were 'extenuating circumstances' around the transfer, and they thought five per cent was appropriate. So I said, 'You're 50 per cent right and I'm 50 per cent wrong, am I?' It's a good job I didn't have to go before a Football League committee as they might have hanged me!

Joe certainly wanted me in his team. In that first chat he said in that jovial way that he had, 'I hope you will sign, we feel we've got the start of a good side. We are just one player short – and we think that you are that player. The odd goal or two will turn us into a great team.'

And I knew Malcolm rated me. We'd bumped into each other sometime earlier in Bolton's Empress Ballroom.

Was he tapping me? I'd gone along with a friend when we met another party of big time football names. Apart from Malcolm, there were England World Cup winners Alan Ball and Nobby Stiles, plus my old Bolton team-mate Tommy Banks … it was Tommy who did the introductions. Malcolm told me that he'd seen me play against his previous sides at Bath City and Plymouth Argyle. He said to me, 'I've watched you play and I'm going to make you into a top-notch player.'

I told him not to bother. I shot back, 'I'm a top-notch player now!' That was our earliest exchange … no wonder I thought he was arrogant. And no bloody wonder he thought the same about me!

This was my first taste of the transfer business, so what was I to make of all that? A new manager blowing smoke rings my way? Just selling me the deal with so much flannel? A leading coach making bold promises? Joe Mercer, though, was absolutely sincere and he was proven to be bang on with his judgement.

As it turned out, Malcolm was right, too. He did make me a better player by getting me to concentrate on what I did best. He knew I was quick; I could beat people and he knew I could finish. Malcolm said he wanted me to create havoc in the opposition's half. He didn't want to see me repeating what I'd done at Bolton, chasing back wingers and pressurising people. He also wanted me to keep a high work rate, but he was determined to get the best out of my abilities. 'Your game is about beating people and scoring,' he said. That's what he wanted to see.

My first chance to show what I could do, ironically, was against the team I could have joined just a few weeks earlier: Wolves, on Saturday, 14 September. It was a great start for me, a 2-0 win at Maine Road with goals from Mike Doyle and Neil Young. It was my first game for three weeks and I'd had to get fit quickly. I actually played well, considering my lack of preparation. From that match on, my new life was in top gear, and I realised I'd moved up to the next level.

With my new club there was no chance of easing up in training. My god, we trained and worked hard at City. I was glad that I'd kept ticking over with my private training prior to signing, because City's regime was something else altogether. It was an exhaustive – and exhausting – regime. We'd warm up with a 2.5-mile run, then we had to run 440 yards (imperial measurements back then) in 65 seconds, 220 yards in 30 seconds and 150 yards in 15 seconds. There followed a short recovery and then we did it all again in reverse order.

This was on the Monday after my debut against Wolves! We trained with international athletes as pacemakers every Monday. We were in the gym and on the weights in the afternoon. Other times, we'd also have a fartlek session in Wythenshawe Park, with three miles over the country with speed intervals thrown in. From there it was back to the track for several 50-yard jogs and sprints followed by the 150-, 220- and 440-yard runs. A few breakfasts made reappearances during that lot. I'd definitely moved into another world.

The intense training did me no harm, either, as in my next game – away at Craven Cottage – we beat Fulham 4-2 and I grabbed my first City goal, to go with a couple for Mike Summerbee and another from Neil Young.

After I joined my new team-mates, we went on an 11-game unbeaten run and we didn't lose until around Christmas, when we were in third place. It took me two or three games to get match fit but then I was fine, and I fitted in straight away. One of the highlights was a 6-0 home win over Leicester, when I grabbed a couple of goals to go with a brace from Neil Young and one each from Mike Doyle and Alan Oakes – here I was, in a good team with talented players around me. If you can play the game, it makes slotting into a team pretty easy, and I can never understand players saying it takes some time to bed in. I don't see that.

The team just clicked after I joined, but I was only one cog in a great side with smashing players. The new environment suited me just fine. From a secretary-manager in Ridding at Bolton, I was now with a modern managerial pairing of Joe Mercer and Malcolm Allison. The boss and the coach. It was such a big difference, and when you get someone who's a good coach, such as Malcolm, who was motivating the other players, then I fancied having some of that. I wanted to be motivated, too. It worked both ways because they were pleased to have bought me and I was keen to show what I could do – to give them value for money.

Yet around the time I signed, if you read the newspapers, it seemed I might lose the chance to work with Malcolm, because his name was strongly linked to Coventry City. His big pal from their early playing days at West Ham, Noel Cantwell, a former Manchester United captain, was trying to follow Jimmy Hill as manager. Hill had done a fantastic job at Highfield Road before moving into the world of TV sport.

Press reports claimed that Coventry had made an offer and Malcolm was quoted as saying, 'This is too good an offer and I must accept it, provided the [Manchester City] directors agree to release me from my contract.'

Just a day later, Coventry's chairman Derrick Robins snuffed out the story and insisted his club wouldn't be appointing him. Robins said, 'I stressed that it must be treated with secrecy. The next thing is that it is blazoned across the newspapers. This is not the way we work.' Malcolm complained that the whole affair 'makes me look stupid'.

I think because of his long-standing friendship with Noel, Malcolm had listened to their offer, as his pal's team were struggling. Instead, Robbins entrusted the job to Cantwell, who went on to have a good five-year stint at the club. That was good news for me, and I flourished under Malcolm and Joe Mercer.

Bill Ridding had always said I was an awkward bastard and difficult to deal with. So difficult that after 12 months at City, Joe Mercer said, 'I can't believe what your old manager used to say about you. You're the easiest professional player that I've ever had to deal with.'

Another highlight in my first season, as we chased after the league title, was the kind of match you just don't see these days, a home game against Spurs on 9 December 1967, and selected for the *Match of the Day* cameras – only one or two games were featured in those days. It was dubbed the 'Ballet on Ice' because of the freezing conditions and the game was voted *MotD*'s match of the season. It ended with us winning 4-1, thanks to goals from Colin Bell, Tony Coleman, Mike Summerbee and Neil Young. Our boots had been chosen carefully and modified, and City's players kept their feet pretty well, while Tottenham's lads were slipping and sliding all over. Playing on a frozen pitch like that just wouldn't happen these days ... but we were happy with the result!

There was a bit of a Yuletide hiccup as we lost that unbeaten sequence on Boxing Day, going down 3-2 at West Brom, before the Baggies made the return trip to Maine

Road and won again, 2-0. But we immediately picked things up in the New Year with a couple of 3-0 away wins at Forest and Sheffield United, and just rattled on.

I've said that Malcolm made me a better player and he had an instant effect in that first season at City. I had a four-week spell when I wasn't quite at it, I struggled. I felt low and he responded and asked me to do extra work with him. People thought he was loud-mouthed and bombastic but behind that image he was like a mother hen. He was patient and willed me to get over my dip.

Were we concentrating on the league? Well, yes – and we bloody well had to as Leicester took us to Filbert Street for a replay in the FA Cup third round. After a 0-0 stalemate at Maine Road, they edged us 4-3 at their place. That was the game that my dad went to and got back home very late. Just a few hours later, he died at work. That's when Malcolm investing extra time with me was so invaluable.

Dad had been so important in my early days, allowing me to gamble on my education to go to a football-playing school. His understanding was critical – as were his wise words on having a plan B, something else to fall back on. Dad's influence was massive.

In that era, perhaps because of two points for a win, it seemed that anyone could win the league and we had a scrap on our hands. We were confident and it was obvious that it would mean so much to that City side. For a start, it would be the first time anyone in that team had won anything major. There were also perhaps four or five of our side that had lived in the shadow of United for so long. Malcolm always used to tell us, 'You're frightened of the fuckers. Just go out there and play them – you're as good as them!' Winning the title would lay that to rest.

We were an exceptional side, and we scored a lot of goals. We attacked as a side and defended as a side and, because we were so fit, we could do that. It was a great period and our style at that time was to attack with five forwards – very unusual for the time. We scored 86 league goals in 1967/68 and conceded exactly half that total. After our cup exit, our concentration on the league looked decent as we claimed four successive league victories: at home to Sunderland, Coventry and Fulham, with an away win at Burnley squeezed between. The run was ended by Don Revie's very strong Leeds United side, 2-0 at Elland Road, and then came a huge Manchester derby at Old Trafford, a midweek clash on 27 March 1968, with both City and United going full tilt for the title.

We had to go to our neighbours to try to get back on top of the table. We did – we beat them 3-1 in front of a crowd of 62,243. I scored, with Colin Bell and George Heslop getting the others.

When you run into form like that, no one can stop you. We did have a sticky spell just after Christmas and it was a real contest at the top. Any club in contention taking maximum points over the Easter fixtures had a very good chance – and we did just that, beating both Chelsea and West Ham. After that there was a defeat in the return match at Chelsea and a goalless draw at Wolves, but they were our only slips.

So, we'd gone to Old Trafford and beaten the side that was destined to win the European Cup that same spring, and then, after 38 games, with just four still to play, City were on 50 points (the days of two points for a win, not three, remember), looking up at Leeds in second place on 53 points and United were top on 54 points. Both City and Leeds had a game in hand over United.

City really stepped it up, now we *were* really concentrating on the league. We beat Sheffield Wednesday 1-0 as Leeds fell away, losing all of their final four league games. And in our final home game of the season, we beat Everton 2-0. With United suffering a shock 6-3 defeat at West Brom, it left City and their Old Trafford rivals level on points at the top, with two games left to play. It was so tight, and the boss, Joe Mercer, summed up our task: 'Now we have to climb Everest and K2 in a week, but we can do it.'

We had two tough away games to end our season, first Spurs and then Newcastle United. We passed the first test well, 3-1 winners at White Hart Lane. I got a couple of goals there, with Mike Summerbee getting the other one. We were fit, powerful but also a particularly good footballing side.

One game to go, and that left us with Newcastle United. Going into the last weekend of the season, we were level with Manchester United on 56 points. They'd just thrashed the Geordies 6-0 at Old Trafford in their penultimate game.

We were confident we could do our own business, even though we expected a reaction from Newcastle, who weren't a bad side, despite that United hammering. But Manchester United's last game was at home to Sunderland, who had nothing much to play for. Only United could catch us, but if we won, the title would be ours. Even so, no one expected United to slip, and Newcastle were no mugs at home, so, in many critics' eyes, that made United clear favourites. It was a real Manchester-North East season finale!

I'll never forget that last game, because so much was riding on it. And, certainly by today's standards, it was such an open game considering the high stakes involved. As I've said, Newcastle were certainly better than average, with some good players in their team.

Wyn Davies, my old mate from Bolton, was a very good centre-forward; Bryan 'Pop' Robson, a rising star who went on to have a fine career, was alongside him up front; Bobby Moncur, their Scots skipper, was a composed figure at the back; Jackie Sinclair was decent on the right wing; and a certain left-back, Frank Clark, solid at the back. They would win the Fairs Cup a year later.

But this was our time, and we won the game 4-3 amid a flurry of goals … and we were never behind. It was a fantastic match in front of 46,000 packed into St James' Park, with some great goals. What a way to clinch the title, and I had quite a say in it!

Mike Summerbee gave us the lead in a tense, frenetic first half, after good work from Mike Doyle, but that was cancelled out by Pop Robson's smartly taken equaliser. Then Neil Young swept in our second at the Leazes End, after a good set-up from Colin Bell, only for Jackie Sinclair to rattle in another equaliser.

At the break, Malcolm had apparently thought about reading us the riot act, but he was calm. He just told us we'd had a half to get used to the occasion and now it was time to go out and play. His measured reasoning had the desired effect and any nerves in our play melted away.

Neil Young got his second to put us 3-2 up and we looked well set. Our second-half display was classy and, on 63 minutes, I got the goal that made it 4-2 and proved to be the winner. We were sweeping forward, and Belly spotted my run and played me in at inside-right. I hammered it past keeper Willie McFaul's right hand and celebrated with my arms spread and with a big smile on my face in front of the Gallowgate End.

We finished well on top, even though Newcastle's big, uncompromising centre-back John McNamee headed them a third, just before the end. And that was that. It was incredibly special to all of us because it was the first major trophy any of us had ever won – and it was the league championship! It was pure drama, a game for the ages. The line-ups for that crucial match were:

> **Newcastle United:** Willie McFaul, David Craig, John McNamee, Bobby Moncur, Frank Clark, Jackie Sinclair, Jim Iley, Jim Scott, Tommy Robson, Wyn Davies, Bryan 'Pop' Robson.
>
> (Goals: Pop Robson, Jackie Sinclair, John McNamee)
>
> **Manchester City:** Ken Mulhearn, Tony Book, Mike Doyle, George Heslop, Glyn Pardoe, Tony Coleman, Colin Bell, Alan Oakes, Neil Young, Francis Lee, Mike Summerbee.
>
> (Goals: Mike Summerbee, Neil Young (2), Francis Lee)

And it was an amazing final day because, against all expectations, Sunderland went to Old Trafford and beat United 2-1. The Wearsiders did what the Tynesiders couldn't and beat our neighbours, with George Mulhall and Colin Suggett getting the goals that did the trick, with George Best's United strike no consolation at all.

City won praise nationwide. The newspapers universally applauded our success, hailing a stylish, progressive side as being good for the game. Malcolm had proved himself one of the best coaches in the business, too.

And yet there was no post-match presentation at Newcastle that day, no instant glory. Because the famous old league championship trophy had been taken to Old Trafford on the last day of the season for an expected presentation there. That proved a redundant move!

But we quickly sorted that out. And so it was that City contacted Bury and swiftly arranged a friendly at Maine Road, just three days after our Tyneside triumph, so that a very public presentation could be made! All 11 players who had been on duty at the weekend played, and skipper Tony Book was presented with the trophy before the game, which we won 4-2. It was all lapped up by 34,000 fans and the scoreline didn't matter, of course.

It was fun to see Malcolm come on as a substitute for George Heslop in the last ten minutes. 'Allison for England' was the chant that went up – and Bobby Owen scored one of Bury's goals … he would join City later that summer.

My first, fabulous season with City was over and I'd never forget it. I hadn't arrived until October, but I scored 17 goals in 35 games, making me City's third-top scorer. The Football League champions' medal I grasped in my hand that night at Bury more than convinced me that my career was going only one way.

Chapter Five

The Good Life – City Cup Glory and an England Call-Up

KEN BARNES, the great old City player from the 1950s and later a coach and chief scout, once said to me, 'When you made your debut for Bolton at 16 and scored on your debut against Manchester City, who coached you?' The answer was 'nobody', and Ken said, 'You did not need coaching. You played in the street, with your mates, at school, with the Bolton Boys Federation ... that's why you could go straight into a First Division game.'

Nobody really coached me at Bolton. They might say, 'Don't beat a man – get it and play it,' but there was no coaching. Later, at City, Malcolm Allison made me a better player because he made me play to my strengths. Even before I got there, he'd told me in Bolton's Empress Ballroom that he'd seen me against his previous teams, and he shot me that line – 'I'm going to make you into a top-notch player' – and I'd given it back with interest. But, of course, he was right.

He wanted to see the best of me. Malcolm knew I was quick, that I could beat defenders and that I knew where the net was. He wanted me to terrify defenders and he wasn't really interested in me repeating some of the things I did at Bolton, closing down opposition wingers and suchlike.

After 17 goals in my first season, largely from the wing, they must have thought there wasn't much they could do to improve on that. I'd done well. Now I wanted to ensure I was in the best possible shape for my first full season at Maine Road. But my best intentions – and those of the other City players – were, to an extent, scuppered by a huge mistake the club made as soon as the league championship trophy was secured. And it was a stupid mistake.

We'd qualified for the European Cup and then they took us on a five-week summer tour of North America and Mexico! We covered god knows how many thousands of miles and Neil Young picked up an injury that needed 26 stitches in his leg. That severely affected Neil for some time – and he was a key player for us – so we came back knackered after that trip. It didn't do us any good at all. It was the very worst kind of preparation for the start of 1968/69.

Not only that, Tony Coleman and Stan Bowles got locked up in the States. Goalkeeper Ken Mulhearn and I saved them from getting beaten up by the cops. They could be nutters, those two. Tony liked a drink – and he did like to drink a lot. He had a bad-boy reputation before he joined the club from Doncaster, and he could turn nasty. He only had four teeth in the front, with a palate of false gnashers. He'd quickly turn nasty, but you could shut him up if you fronted him. He wasn't always the bravest.

I'd just joined that season, of course, and I was rooming with Coleman, who – in fairness – contributed his fair share as we won the title. We'd arrived at Hartford, Connecticut during the afternoon and we were playing the next day. Malcolm and Joe told us to have a bite to eat and a walk around – be back at the hotel at half ten. The boss and Malcolm trusted all the players and treated us as adults.

We went for a stroll. There was Ken, Stan Bowles, me and Tony Coleman. We went into this little bar with a pool room. Ken and I ordered beers and Coleman said, 'I'll have a Bacardi and Coke.' The barman refused, saying he wasn't 21. He also refused Bowles for the same reason. 'I fucking am 21!' said Coleman.

The barman then asked me if they were 21. 'Yes, they are,' I said. He asked for ID, but I explained we didn't have ID cards in England. He asked for mine and I showed him my passport – Ken had his, too. But neither Coleman nor Bowles had theirs on them.

'Right, you don't get a drink then,' the barman told them.

'And you can fuck off!' said our dynamic duo – and they started to get really nasty. I told them to calm down while we finished off our drinks and then we'd go. I gave the barman his money and we went off somewhere else.

We had two or three more drinks and were heading back to the hotel and walked past the same bar. With a bit of bravado, the potty pair started having a go at the same barman for not serving them. He was probably well used to dealing with proper thugs and he wasn't too bothered. He went to the back of his bar and quietly rang the police.

We didn't know that, of course, and we casually walked out and into this precinct. I could hear the crackling of radios and, as we walked around the corner, there were about six policemen there. All in leather jackets, gunned up and with truncheons in hand. 'You, you and you – stand by the wall' came the order. They quickly demanded to know who we were and where we were from. I told them, but then they wanted to know which of us had been in the bar. 'All of us,' I told them.

The senior officer asked Stan for his name and Bowlsey shot back, 'What's your fucking name?' He pounced on Stan, grabbed him by the collar and threw him to two other officers, who shoved him straight into the back of their van. Coleman screamed, 'They've got Stan! They can't have Stan, he's one of the lads!' He wanted to have a go at all these coppers, so Ken and I grabbed him by the jacket. He only managed to wriggle out of his jacket, but then he's facing them … and he suddenly realised his hopeless situation. And they just shove him in the wagon, too. Even then, Coleman grabs the door on his way in and one of the officers took his truncheon and smashed it right between his two hands. God, if he'd hit either of his hands across the knuckles it could have chopped his hands off!

And off they went. The police told Ken and me to tell our coach they'd be on bail and could be collected from 8am the next morning. On our way back to the hotel, we started laughing … how the hell were we going to tell Joe and Malcolm that two of his star title-winning squad were locked up – with a game looming the next night!

When we got back, we raised Johnny Hart, City's first-team trainer. We told him the problem. We gave him the police ticket, and next morning they're up and out to get the boys released. Coleman was running his shoes across the bars to attract attention!

I'd gone out for a walk and Joe Mercer spotted me across the road. 'Have you got a minute?' he called. I went over and he asked what had happened. I told him that the boys wouldn't have been arrested had they not turned abusive. Joe responded by saying he was surprised that I'd got mixed up with it. 'Coleman and Bowles,' said Joe, 'don't you know they're mad?'

'I'd no idea – it's the first time I've been out with them,' I reasoned. 'And anyway, who put me in with TC as his room-mate? You did! You must have had something to do with it.' Joe then said he'd thought I'd be a calming influence! I couldn't win. I said, 'Well, that theory didn't work, did it?' Joe had to agree with me – and said he'd change the rooming arrangements straight away.

And Bowles? Well, Stan was a talent, but he was peripheral to that side. He couldn't hold down his place. He did get called into the team over Christmas against West Brom, when we should have won, but lost 3-2. He got a late call and I don't think he expected it – he wasn't in the best shape, shall we say, and he let the side down badly that day. Perhaps a little too much Christmas spirit? I couldn't have much to do with him after that.

He then got sold on for peanuts, to Bury, before swiftly moving on to Crewe and then to Carlisle – all for not a lot of money. In fairness, he did well for Carlisle and moved on to QPR, and then had a good career after that. He finished up playing for England, so he made some sort of recovery, but I know he had a lot of problems with gambling. The old crack was: if only Stan could pass a bookies as well as he passed the ball …

It's a good job Stan didn't have a punt on us to follow our neighbours United and win the European Cup in 1968/69 (having said that, maybe he did!). Because we were in far from the best shape to either defend our title or launch a campaign in Europe after that pre-season trip.

And so it proved, we fell at the first hurdle in the European Cup, sent packing by Turkish champions Fenerbahçe, who in those days were rated by many as being no better than decent Second Division standard. It was therefore a draw that was warmly greeted by the blue side of Manchester when we were paired with the Turks, the first leg to be played at Maine Road on 18 September 1968. By common consent we'd got an 'easy' draw to ease our way into the competition. 'We'll terrify Europe!' was Malcolm's bold prediction as we prepared for the opening round. Well, I guess he might have expected a reaction given what followed … and it duly came.

I knew what Malcolm was doing. He always spoke out for a reason and here he was, keen to avoid any anxiety in our debut European Cup venture. He was trying to fill us with maximum confidence. In retrospect, the nightmare double-header with Fenerbahçe was the toughest of lessons that stood us in good stead, as we went on to more and more success. But losing in the European Cup is a lesson I'd rather not have had to swallow, thanks very much.

In the first leg at City, we were confident all right. Far too confident, as we hogged the possession and the Turks did, indeed, look like second-raters. But we were strolling, it was as if we were in an exhibition game. The backheels, the flicks when a chance beckoned weren't coming off and we played it like a friendly. Belly and Mike Summerbee both missed glorious chances.

Malcolm could see the danger signs and he tore into us at half-time and warned us the game was in danger of passing us by. He urged us in no uncertain terms to go out and grab a hatful of goals. If only it were that simple. Sometimes, when you play yourselves into a pattern, it can become a rut and it's difficult to get out of it. We'd let Fenerbahçe mug us into a goalless draw and now we faced the return in Istanbul. The Turks, on the face of it, were still pessimistic about their chances, although there was plenty of acclaim for their stoic rearguard action at Maine Road. Few in the Turkish media, however, believed they had it in them to emerge from their blanket-defending approach to take the game to us.

We were suddenly apprehensive about the return game, none more so than me because I was a doubt right up to the day of the game, with ice packs on a swollen ankle. But I won't offer any excuse for myself or the team. Collectively and individually, we weren't good enough in either game.

None of us had experienced competitive European football before; we had no idea of what we'd face, especially in the second leg. The shut-out at Maine Road was a hammer blow, viewing it now, in retrospect. We were totally inexperienced, and we had to learn from it.

In the years after I signed for them, City were as good as any team in the country. Our standards were high. Therefore, I won't pull punches about our keeper, Ken Mulhearn, that night in Istanbul. Had City bought a really top-class keeper – and they should have bought Gordon Banks not long before I joined from Bolton – we'd have cleaned up even more trophies. Malcolm was always on to Joe: 'Have you signed him [Banks] – have you signed him yet?' Instead, the best keeper in the world went to Stoke of all places. If we'd got him, we wouldn't have won five trophies, it would have been 15!

You just can't get away with *not* having a really top keeper. That's a factor in why we got knocked out of the European Cup by Fenerbahçe, when Ken had a nightmare. Malcolm gave him a bollocking in Istanbul and told him he'd bottled it as their fans turned up the heat. They were firing rockets from the terraces from the moment we came out of the tunnel. That carried on all match and then they later started lighting bonfires on the terraces. It was literally foreign to all of us – especially poor Ken.

We had a very early scare with a Fenerbahçe goal chalked off for offside after six minutes ... cue much protest, jostling the referee and irate fans. But, when Tony Coleman (yes, the Americans did let him out of jail!) scored after just 12 minutes, it looked as though our worries were misplaced. I sent a looping ball into the box and Ercan tried to overplay it. Tony nipped in to score. We could see this through, couldn't we?

We held that lead through until the break. Job done at that stage, but then almost immediately after the restart there was a calamitous defensive mix-up and they equalised through Abdullah, who pounced on a good through ball from Ogün.

The second and decisive goal came 15 minutes from time. A clever flighted free kick by winger Can was prodded into the net, too easily, by Ogün – who'd been flown in from Washington, where he was in talks with an American franchise – and the spotlight fell on Ken Mulhearn again. Yet it was by no means the only factor. Perhaps the main reason for our exit was the way we fooled about in the first 45 minutes of the first leg at Maine Road. We were both naive in our overconfidence and not wise or savvy enough to respect a side that had played in this competition over five seasons. We may have had the class of English champions, but we were European Cup greenhorns, and it showed.

This was a rare black mark in my years at City as we closed out the 1960s, riding a blue wave of glory like a surfer on a perfect point break. But it was symptomatic of our start to the season after that nightmare summer tour. It had all looked so good in the season curtain-raiser, the FA Charity Shield (as it was then called) when we thrashed FA Cup winners West Brom 6-1. I bagged a couple of goals in the process, but it was a false dawn.

In the league games leading up to the first leg with Fenerbahçe, we started our league title defence with a 2-1 defeat at Liverpool and lost three more, at Leicester, Arsenal and Stoke. Not only that, we could only draw at home to Manchester United, away at QPR, and at home against Ipswich and Southampton. Our only league win during that period came at home to Wolves.

Three days after our return from Turkey, we got back on the horse with a 4-0 win at Sunderland but followed that up by getting knocked out of the League Cup, 1-0 at Blackpool. We needed two games with Huddersfield to get that far, drawing the first tie 0-0 at Leeds Road. So, not to put too fine a point on it, this was a bloody awful start to my first full season at Maine Road. I'd made such an impact the year before, after joining in October, but this felt like a false start by anyone's standards.

And yet it wasn't supposed to be this way. Before the season started I was like a fitness enthusiast at New Year, with resolutions aplenty about improving my habits. I don't know if this had anything to do with sharing a room with Tony Coleman in the summer, but I was determined nothing would halt me on City's glory road: as pre-season started I decided to stop drinking and stop smoking. I had the sweet smell of success in my nostrils and nothing was going to stop me.

My clean living may have been partly inspired by the forward-thinking Malcolm Allison. Decades before Arsène Wenger's fastidious approach to curbing players' bad habits, Malcolm had said in pre-season that he wanted a curb on player drinking: 'They'll have to drink lemonade,' he said. 'There is no point in me working on their fitness during the day, for them to go drinking at night. To be the best team in the world you have to sacrifice things. We are aiming for higher targets now, so we have got to work to higher standards. And that means no booze at all in the season!'

Whatever the motivation, I certainly felt on top of the world as the season began with our thumping Charity Shield win, but when the real action began we were far from brilliant. Me included. I was doing okay, I thought, but it seemed others had reservations. Newspapers were niggling away at me as our early results disappointed. When we travelled to Newcastle for the first time since our title-winning triumph on the same ground just a few months earlier, the speculation was that I was about to be dropped. The whispers increased as the party that set off north included young forwards Bobby Owen and Ian Bowyer.

Our results had continued to fluctuate and, before the Newcastle game on 16 November, we'd lost two on the bounce, at home to Sheffield Wednesday (1-0) and at Chelsea (2-0). Even so, I wasn't impressed by the speculation that I might be dropped ... was this my reward for dedication and abstinence? After two months without a drink or a smoke, I looked at the papers on the morning of the game and even the local Tyneside media reported that I was likely to be axed. I put my papers down, slipped out and bought myself 20 of the finest Virginia tipped. If reserve-team football was the best I could look forward to, why not have a little of what you fancy?

Having said that, the packet of fags was still unopened as I slipped into the pre-match team talk. I sensed a little unease in our group; certainly I was far from happy, even though I knew I wasn't in top form. The tension was broken as Mike Summerbee caught Malcolm's eye: 'Wouldn't it be best,' he asked, 'if a player was told he is being dropped before he reads it in the papers?' Malcolm barely blinked or showed any emotion. He looked around us all, the entire group, and said, 'Who do you think picks the team? Is it the press, the public, or the boss and me? When we've picked it, we'll tell any player if he's out. And, this week, there's no need to – because nobody is out. Okay?'

Those freshly bought cigarettes stayed in my pocket and, although we lost 1-0, at St James' this time, I was delighted that Malcolm and Joe kept faith with me that day. For I really recaptured my best form the following week against West Brom, as we romped to a 5-1 victory at Maine Road. It was then I decided my normal habits were just fine and dandy. I don't think any side trained harder than City in that era – a very different age to the Wenger-inspired regimes of strict diet, calorific checks, dietary supplements and goodness knows what else. I believed then that a couple of pints never did anybody any harm.

I was never one for smoking heavily, so I returned to my usual behaviour – but it was everything in moderation. Yes, I enjoyed myself and put a little weight back on, but I'd slipped to about half a stone below my best weight. Now I returned to a normal diet and that included a moderate amount of beer and fags – and I still hit a high pitch in training.

The West Brom game was followed by a loss against West Ham, but we hammered Burnley 7-0, I picked up a goal and it was about this time I heard that Sir Alf Ramsey, the England manager, was watching me. Before I knew it, I was selected in the squad for the Wembley game against Bulgaria, on 11 December 1968. I could have put it down to my new (old) regime, but I couldn't help but smile that only a few weeks earlier my place in the City team had been apparently at risk. I wasn't nursing any great expectations about my place in Sir Alf's thoughts, though. This was my first England call and I reckoned I was going along just for the experience.

I had no delusions of grandeur and convinced myself I was simply being bedded into the squad, giving me time to get used to Sir Alf's team systems in case I was picked to play in future games. Then Alan Ball was hit by flu and wasn't fit to play, but I still thought nothing of it. The game was taking place on Wednesday, and before that we trained at Highbury on the Monday. Next day we trained at Roehampton before watching a film and then went by coach to the FA's HQ at Lancaster Gate, where the manager was to announce his side to the media.

Alf, of course, would first tell the squad who was playing – and he did this on the coach ride to Lancaster Gate. He began the roll call of names and I wasn't paying much notice, gazing out of the coach window as we drove towards central London. He'd got through the defenders and then he announced 'Lee'. *What*, I thought, *who's Lee?* That was my first, split-second reaction ... then, of course, the realisation hit me!

So, Bally's illness had a dividend for me. Maybe Sir Alf also thought that he wanted another all-out attacker rather than a schemer, as England had drawn 0-0 with Romania in November. The team for my England debut included fellow debutants Gordon West, in goal, and Leeds' right-back Paul Reaney would come on as substitute to replace Keith Newton. Sir Alf clearly wanted to assess his options with the 1970 World Cup on the near horizon. As the defending world champions, we had no qualifying games, so these friendlies took on real significance.

This was the England team for my debut against Bulgaria:

> West (Everton), Newton (Blackburn), Labone (Everton), Moore (West Ham), McNab (Arsenal), Bell (Manchester City), Mullery (Spurs), Charlton (Manchester United), Peters (West Ham), Lee (Manchester City), Hurst (West Ham). Sub: Reaney (Leeds United).

Sir Alf deployed me largely from the right flank and I think I had a reasonable game – but it ended in another friendly draw for England, 1-1. I put in a real shift in the first half, perhaps doing too much chasing, and Sir Alf told me at the break to stay upfield more, alongside Geoff Hurst. The Bulgarians took the lead through the impressive Georgi Asparuhov – a fine strike after 32 minutes. That lead was quickly rubbed out by Geoff Hurst's goal just four minutes later.

So ended my first taste of international football and it was an eye-opener. I wanted more. Nothing was left to chance with Sir Alf, every bit of preparation was considered. The opposition was thoroughly vetted with no detail overlooked. You can read what happened next with me and England in Chapter Seven but, for now, we had a league title to defend at City and it was not going to plan.

We drew at Spurs, beat Coventry at home but then Everton arrived on Boxing Day and beat us 3-1. We beat Chelsea, could only draw at Wednesday and then, amid a flurry of FA Cup ties, we lost 2-1 in the league at Burnley … the same Burnley we'd recently hit for seven at our place. We wouldn't be winning the league title this season!

But those FA Cup ties … this was a time when the FA Cup was as big as the league, and arguably more glorious. Could this be our route to success in the New Year? Well, it looked like a comfortable draw when we were pulled out of the hat in the third-round draw at home to Second Division Luton Town. We didn't exactly set Maine Road alight with this first match of 1969, though, swiftly following on from Everton turning us over.

Luton gave it a right good go. We now had Harry Dowd in goal and he had to be in pretty good form. He tipped a good header from Keith Allen on to a post and a young Bruce Rioch had a typically meaty drive well saved, too. I had the distinction of winning the penalty and then converting it to get us ahead after 26 minutes. I was fouled in the box by John Moore and then I smacked the penalty inside the keeper's right-hand post. Our blushes were spared, and Joe Mercer summed it up: 'Luton scared us to death.'

We took three points from league games against Chelsea (won 4-1) and Sheffield Wednesday (drawn 1-1) before our fourth-round tie away at Newcastle United. St James' Park again! I'd notched in that Chelsea win and then, in a hard-fought draw at Hillsborough, I smacked a free kick against the bar and had a shot blocked ... it fell for Neil Young to strike an equaliser and ensured we claimed a point.

Then it was up to Tyneside for the FA Cup. We battled out a 0-0 draw in front of close to 58,000 packed into their ground, so we had another crack at them at Maine Road four days later. There was an even bigger gate for this one; almost 61,000 saw us dominate the first half but we only had an early goal from Neil Young to show for it. A Bobby Owen overhead kick had sent Neil clear, and he tucked it away. So, we still had a lot to do, especially as we had to overcome the loss of Mike Summerbee, who was sent off.

I played well and had one shot cleared off the line and then I hit a free kick beyond the wall, but it bounced off the post. Newcastle roared back at us after the break but a well-taken goal by Bobby Owen, 20 minutes from time, saw us safely into the next round.

Then followed an enforced winter break from the league with pitches unplayable, which meant it was almost a month before our next game – in the FA Cup again. This was the rearranged fifth round at Blackburn's Ewood Park, on 24 February 1969. We could have been excused had we been rusty, as could Second Division Rovers, given they'd overcome a flu epidemic, but we were more than ready. I raced on to a cracking pass from Colin Bell after 13 minutes to open the scoring and, as I did, I had Malcolm Allison's game plan ringing in my ears. He reassured us that Rovers' defence was far too square and we'd beat them with through balls. He couldn't have written a better script.

Their striker Jim Fryatt headed them back on terms early in the second half but there was only one outcome on the night. Another good pass from Belly set up Tony Coleman, and he made it 2-1 with a fine shot. Next, Neil Young slipped a few challenges to find me, and I finished my run with a good shot past keeper Adam Blacklaw. Five minutes later, Coleman got a second goal, too, to wrap it up 4-1.

Our next game, remarkably, was yet another FA Cup tie, a quarter-final at home to Spurs, and it meant we played four FA Cup games on the spin without a league game in sight. The game kicked off our March programme and we were confident. Spurs had given City few problems since I'd joined, but this turned out to be a very different Tottenham side. They set up against us very differently, with much more accent on defence and containing tactics. They may have had good footballers such as Jimmy Greaves, Alan Gilzean, Terry Venables and Alan Mullery in their side, but their tactics were to press us, chase us, harry us and defend doggedly.

It was a slog in the Manchester rain. It looked like Spurs might scrap for at least a replay but my solitary second-half goal settled it. It was not much more than a half-chance when Mike Summerbee forged an opening and I got a volley away, not the cleanest strike, and it squeezed past Pat Jennings's right hand and into the net. Mike Doyle thought Spurs provided our toughest cup game and he may be right – but my verdict would go to our next opponents.

Meanwhile, we at last we caught up with some league action. First came that miserable result at Burnley, losing 2-1, before we edged the Manchester derby at United, 1-0, but lost 2-1 at Ipswich before bouncing back with a 3-1 Maine Road win against QPR. We were consistently inconsistent leading into our 22 March semi-final against Everton, at Villa Park.

It's bonkers looking back at how a big, glamour game like that – an FA Cup semi-final – impacted the wallets of our fans back then. Even allowing for inflation, it seems remarkably good value: a place on the Villa Park terraces would have cost just 7s 6d. in old money (37p or so in decimal cash). A souvenir match programme was 2s or the princely sum of 10p.

This game, in my view, was the toughest of our cup run. Everton were one of a clutch of clubs battling for our league title and they were a good side, boasting their fine midfield three of Alan Ball, Howard Kendall and Colin Harvey. They had a good, young striker in Joe Royle and a very solid rearguard with Brian Labone, who had just replaced Jack Charlton in the England team, and John Hurst in central defence.

They were a tough nut to crack but I was surprised by their negative approach. I got a caution for my pains, though goodness knows why – I'd fallen in a heap with Bally and Tommy Wright, the Everton full-back. We all got to our feet with a bit of pushing and shoving but nothing more. Bally said something and I shot back, 'Don't be daft,' and I was promptly booked by referee Bill Handley.

Both sides had chances. Gordon West did well to deny Neil Young with a reaction stop as the final whistle approached. I'm not sure he knew much about it, but it cannoned away for a left-wing corner. Neil took it, and when Mike Summerbee headed it down, one young lad – in his first season of first-team action – emerged from the ruck to rifle in the winner: Tommy Booth, our young centre-back, had gone up for the flag kick, and this was his first senior goal for the club.

I recall Tommy's first senior appearance at Huddersfield, and my first impression was that he was very raw. But never judge anyone too soon and Tommy was allowed time to settle in and eventually made the first-team place his own. He played in 36 games in 1968/69, restricting George Heslop, who'd played throughout our title-winning season in 1967/68, to just 21 games. George, however, would be an important squad player for a few years to come. Tommy's time had come that day, though, and I knew he was going to become a top, top defender. The young lad had just helped us into the FA Cup Final!

There was a month between the Everton semi-final victory and the Wembley final against Leicester. Into those four weeks or so we had to squeeze *eight* First Division games, thanks to that mid-winter run of postponements. We conspired, thanks to some away-day blues, to lose five of them: Nottingham Forest, Leeds, Wolves, West Brom and Southampton all beat us. There were no draws during this month of playing catch-up as we won our home games against Stoke, Leicester and Sunderland.

Tommy's semi-final heroics meant a Wembley showpiece and the clamour for tickets from fans, friends and family was on. For me, that meant a party of 40 or so joining me from my Westhoughton stamping ground. There were plenty of folk in the Bolton area who didn't think I'd make a success of myself in the game at Wanderers, never mind City, but for those closest to me this was a chance to have a big day at the home of English football. They could finally see what the lad from Westhoughton was all about.

One of them was a pal of my partner Peter James's father, a chap called John Morris. He was a down-to-earth bloke, a council road sweeper. He headed for Wembley in style, driving down with a friend in a new Rolls-Royce. When they checked into one of London's plushest hotels he was asked for his occupation. He filled in the form, writing: 'In local government.'

But the serious side of the equation was a certain football match, and Leicester City stood in the way of a second major trophy for Manchester City in successive seasons. They'd been to Wembley in the FA Cup Final six years earlier, losing to Manchester United. I'd never been to one as a player and I'd only seen one as a fan, three years previously, in 1966. Then I'd stood behind one of the goals with my business partner, Peter, and watched one of the best finals of the era, as Everton came from two down to beat Sheffield Wednesday 3-2. I'd said to Peter, 'I'd give a year's wages to play in a cup final!' Now here I was, about to do just that. I'd realised one of my big football ambitions.

These were the teams that contested the 1969 FA Cup Final on 26 April:

> **Leicester City:** Shilton, Rodrigues, Woollett, Cross, Nish, Fern, Roberts, Gibson, Glover, Clarke, Lochhead. Sub: Manley.
>
> **Manchester City:** Dowd, Book, Doyle, Booth, Pardoe, Summerbee, Bell, Oakes, Coleman, Lee, Young. Sub: Connor.

Although the result gave our season the happiest of endings, the game itself wasn't one of my personal favourites.

I was a little disappointed in the final, if I'm honest. I'd looked forward to it, anticipated the occasion and was desperate to play well but, in truth, my own performance was just about okay, and our 1-0 win wasn't as convincing as it could – and should – have been. Perhaps the pitch didn't help, as Wembley's lauded legendary turf was now in a dreadful state after the grass was mangled by a show-jumping event some months earlier. The decision to hold that equine shindig there really backfired, with the most famous real estate in world football simply desecrated. Joe Mercer wrote it off before the game as 'a cow pasture'.

We all seemed a little tense before the final. I turned in early, at about 10.30pm, at our Weybridge hotel. This was my usual preparation on the night before a game. I'd swapped rooms with defender Arthur Mann – he had a single room and wasn't in the side – as he was staying up later to play cards. No one told Arthur's girlfriend, who rang my room and woke me after midnight! I had to see the physio at about 2am to get a sleeping pill to send me off to sleep again.

But if we needed relaxing ahead of kick-off, Malcolm and Joe had the answer as we got changed in Wembley's famous dressing rooms. If Arsène Wenger's reading this, look away now. For the boss and Malcolm got the brandy out and we all got a tot just minutes before kick-off! That's not in the 21st-century coaching or nutrition manuals!

And as the buzzer sounded to call us out on to the Wembley pitch, Malcolm called us back from the door and made us sit back down. 'Let Leicester go out there in the tunnel first,' he urged. 'Sit down and relax for a few more seconds. I want you all to go out there and play your normal games. It's just another game – do your best!'

Both sides had a few chances to score but when we did grab the goal, I had a hand in it … literally. You rarely saw me take a throw-in, but this was one occasion when I did. The ball had gone out of play on the right wing, midway in Leicester's half, and I could see space ahead of Mike Summerbee, so I hurled the ball beyond him, aiming towards the penalty box. Mike got there and saw off a challenge from defender Alan Woollett before angling the ball back from the byline. It was perfect for Neil Young to send an elegant drive from 14 yards past a young Peter Shilton.

And that was it, the FA Cup was ours and the success was so very sweet. Remember, this was pre-Premier League and pre-Champions League. This was also years before the advent of satellite TV and the Sky Sports era of saturated televised coverage of the game. It was the era – still fondly recalled by many older fans – when the FA Cup Final was just about the only club game guaranteed to be televised live in any season. Winning the FA Cup was really massive.

The blue half of Manchester certainly thought so. It was reckoned more than 200,000 fans turned out to watch our procession as we displayed the famous old trophy through the streets of the city to the town hall. Life was good, but the holes in the fixture list after the winter weather wrecked the league programme meant we had three home games still to play to finish the campaign.

There was no hangover from our high-spirited post-Wembley celebrations. We drew 1-1 with West Ham, then beat Newcastle and Liverpool, both by 1-0, to finish the season a disappointing 13th on just 40 points. I scored the winner against Liverpool to end the season as top scorer with 18 goals. Leeds took our league title, with 67 points, six points clear of Liverpool. Leicester, beaten by us in the cup final, had their misery compounded by being relegated, along with QPR.

Elsewhere, Derby County were runaway winners of the Second Division, and they had a young, brash manager making a few waves … a certain Brian Clough. And away from the game, the Americans would realise John Kennedy's dream – spelled out at the start of the decade – by putting the first man on the moon, Neil Armstrong, in July.

It doesn't rival the Apollo 11 mission in the history books, but I also had dreams at the start of the 1960s when I made my Bolton debut as a 16-year-old and scored past Bert Trautmann. Nine years later I'd aimed high and reached for the footballing stars; I'd become a league champion, an England player and now I had an FA Cup winner's medal, too. That meant we were back in Europe, with a chance to exorcise the nightmare of Fenerbahçe.

We were ending the swinging 60s on a high. Now we were heading for a new decade and the 1970s in great shape. I couldn't wait!

Chapter Six

Into the 1970s … and City's Dream Double

WHEN I look back on the 1969/70 season, I view it as though it should be marked with a double signpost: one arrow pointing back to an incredible three seasons that coincided with my joining the club, and the other arrow indicating a future where we just failed to consolidate and continue the remarkable success from 1967 onwards. The season itself was fantastic, with a domestic/European cup double, the first time any English club had achieved that feat.

It's worth putting that into context because Manchester City had endured dark days not too long before I joined them. Many remembered the times within the past decade when angry fans had hurled stones and bricks at the boardroom windows. The fans who were hugely dissatisfied as the club languished in the Second Division were now hailing the players in light blue as the greatest team in the land.

I'd fully back up that claim. City were to win the 1970 European Cup Winners' Cup, UEFA's second-ranked trophy, exclusively reserved for domestic cup winners – and that followed winning the League Cup, just weeks earlier. So, we'd bagged four major trophies in just three years and, in my view, that put us out on our own as the outstanding side in the English game.

It was another campaign that found us inconsistent in the league, though we started well enough, defeating Sheffield Wednesday 4-1 at Maine Road. I finished the scoring with a penalty. But after that we lost home and away to Liverpool and came away beaten at Newcastle, before a home draw with Everton gave us a reprieve. We then beat Sunderland, Spurs and Coventry, those results bookending draws with Burnley and Chelsea ... only for us to lose 2-0 at Stoke. It felt similar to the year before in the First Division, but a new focus was just around the corner.

In the first week of September we made the short trip to unfashionable Southport on a miserable, wet night, for a League Cup tie. Our spirits were low, owing to our mixed fortunes in the league. You know the old saying about big teams not liking it on a cold night in Stoke? Well, just insert 'Southport' so far as we were concerned. And Southport, who had an old Bolton team-mate of mine, Eric Redrobe, up front, gave us a fright all right.

Redrobe was a lad who could have gone further in the game with a little more development at Bolton. He almost put them ahead with a thumping 20-yard drive in a fiery opening. Joe Corrigan, who'd now come into goal for us, twice made smart stops. I helped settle our nerves with the opener after five minutes and we weathered the early battering to run out 3-0 winners. The City fans chorused 'easy, easy' after my goal, yet it was anything but. We certainly needed Alan Oakes's second goal, just after the hour, before Colin Bell wrapped up the scoring late on.

This was the start of our League Cup run that, remarkably, would see us never have to travel outside the old Lancashire County boundaries to meet our opponents until we got to the Wembley final. The next club out of the draw were a far cry from Southport – Liverpool, at home, in the third round. There wasn't much in it. I set up our first early on – a 30-yard snorter from Mike Doyle, after I'd slipped a few challenges and laid it on. Then Liverpool equalised when George Heslop's clearance clattered in off young striker Alun Evans. Our second came shortly after the break when my shot from Belly's free kick was blocked – it fell to Ian Bowyer, who slipped it on to Neil Young and he shot past Tommy Lawrence. We went further ahead through Bowyer, only for Bobby Graham to quickly claw it back to 3-2. Our defence held firm after that as Liverpool looked to level in a cracker of a tie. I enjoyed this night on what was my favourite away ground.

As we savoured the win, I recalled thinking how I'd always fancied playing for Liverpool. I'd done well at Anfield for Bolton and you can't help but admire their fans. They adored 'Shanks', the boss who built modern Liverpool's first great side. As I've said, I know Bill rated me and the admiration was mutual. His side that night was a good team, but one in transition. It included players who'd form the rock of their side through the 1970s: Emlyn Hughes, Tommy Smith and Ian Callaghan, plus bright young striker Evans, who looked a real prospect at the time. But there were also stars coming towards the end of the road at Anfield: keeper Lawrence, inspirational skipper Ron Yeats, winger Peter Thompson and World Cup winner Roger Hunt.

Roger was one of England's most underrated forwards and, though no one knew it that night, he was in his last season of a wonderful career at Anfield. He totalled 244 league goals and more than 280 in all competitions – a wonderful record. He went on to bag a few more for Bolton after Liverpool let him go. He was a great athlete, a wonderful runner up front and, in my opinion, always a great player.

What followed in the next round couldn't be made up … we'd seen off Liverpool, only to draw their Merseyside rivals Everton at Maine Road! They had a few injury problems, with five regular players – Colin Harvey, Alan Ball, Jimmy Husband, John Hurst and Johnny Morrissey – all declared unfit. Even so, we took nothing for granted.

Two goals settled it, both in the first half. Just five minutes in, I got the ball up front and passed it on to Colin Bell, who smacked a great 25-yarder beyond Gordon West. West kept us out for a while with several good saves, but Everton full-back Sandy Brown handled in the area just before half-time. I took the penalty, smacking it past West's left hand, and Everton had no way back.

Everton's patched-up side perhaps told a tale. Their boss, Harry Catterick, was making a real bid for the league title and I think he'd decided not to risk some of his players who'd picked up knocks. It was all pretty routine for us, and we didn't pile on the pressure after the break. We'd had more trouble dealing with Liverpool and Southport! I don't decry Catterick for that, he knew what his priority was and, in that 1969/70 season, it paid dividends for him.

We now thought this League Cup run could pay dividends for us, especially as the next draw, the quarter-final, saw us at home again – this time to QPR. The furthest we'd had to travel in the competition so far was Southport, on the Lancashire coast … we were certainly saving a few quid on coach travel, as were our fans! It was a 3-0 breeze against QPR but, in fairness, we were particularly good in a blistering first half.

The *Daily Mirror*'s Derek Wallis wrote: 'Colin Bell and Francis Lee had produced some enthralling performances in the past, but rarely a combined effort of such merciless splendour.' I won't argue with that. Belly scored two goals early on, both assists from yours truly, and then I laid on the third for Mike Summerbee. Just as in the Everton game, all the damage was done before we went in for half-time.

We got some stick afterwards for taking our foot off the pedal but, in fairness, we also had our league programme and Cup Winners' Cup campaign to consider and it's okay to take a breather when you can. And we needed to take a breather considering who our semi-final opponents were – city rivals Manchester United over two legs!

We had a good omen in our locker as the first leg at Maine Road loomed in early December. Just a couple of weeks earlier, we'd thumped United 4-0 at home as we sought some consistency in our league form. It was a bitter pill for United, the European champions just the year before, but now clearly in decline. It was good for us to put down such a marker, with many critics noting a gulf in class between the sides on the day.

For the first leg at Maine Road, United welcomed back a key player, midfield tiger Nobby Stiles, on the comeback trail after a nasty knee injury. He obviously wasn't match fit, but Nobby was nothing if not a competitor. He'd missed that 4-0 thrashing but now he was back, and I certainly felt his presence a couple of times!

This match was much tighter than our league romp, but I set up our early opener for Colin Bell. I got free, cutting in from the left to try a shot and it broke for Colin to finish smartly. It was nip and tuck, but we then faced a real fight after the break when Bobby Charlton, running into the box, saw a Brian Kidd cross break his way and he hammered it into the net from eight yards.

That could have flattened us but instead it inspired us to play our own game in a classic cup tie. There was great, late controversy as I both won and scored the 88th-minute penalty that gave us a precious 2-1 win. Not for the first time I was accused of diving, but that was nonsense; I was clearly caught and brought down by defender Ian Ure as I knocked the ball past him.

I got up and put my penalty firmly inside Alex Stepney's right-hand post. We had the advantage, a slim one, going to Old Trafford. United's George Best found himself suspended for four weeks after knocking the ball out of referee Jack Taylor's hands at the end of the Maine Road game. I thought he was unlucky, in that this match was televised, and the incident was blown out of all proportion. The effect of TV on the game would only increase as the decades rolled on after that!

But the ban wasn't in effect when the second leg was played a fortnight later, so George was playing. We, on the other hand, were without Colin Bell, who was injured, while United made the unwise decision, in my view, to drop young Brian Kidd and bring back Denis Law. I'm a huge fan of Denis, one of the greatest players in the world at his peak, but in the middle of the 1969/70 season, he was no longer at the top of his game. United brought him back into their side even though he'd suffered a string of injuries and had no hint of the form he'd possessed at his best. Young 'Kiddo', however, was certainly in form but, for the semi-final second leg, he was named as substitute. In our dressing room, we were more than happy about that.

Mike Doyle, who was rabidly anti-United, never missed a chance to wind up the boys from Old Trafford and, when he heard about United's team, he offered to buy all the United players dinner if they beat us! He was so often a standout performer in derby clashes, and the League Cup semi-final games were no different. The first game was a thriller and the game at Old Trafford continued the drama. We had the perfect start with a goal on 17 minutes, after I'd combined with Mike Summerbee on the right. His cross was neatly controlled by Neil Young, who found space, but his shot was blocked near the line by Ian Ure, only for Ian Bowyer to poke it in at the second attempt. We were now 3-1 up on aggregate and looking good.

United were always in it, though, and when they scored midway through the half, there looked to be a hint of good fortune about it. Pat Crerand laid on a good ball for their promising young full-back, Paul Edwards, who nudged the ball forward and let fly from 18 yards. It bobbled as he hit it and he seemed to strike it at least partly off his shin – it didn't matter, it flew past Joe Corrigan to make it 3-2 over the two legs. The tie was still very much up for grabs and United must have fancied their chances when their gamble on Denis Law seemed to pay off. Denis pounced on a Corrigan error when he spilled George Best's shot, following a typically impressive 50-yard run, and the master forward smacked it home to make it 3-3 on aggregate.

Then the roll of the dice on Law suddenly backfired. Just as United scented blood, Denis seemed to want to go off with a niggle. Kidd actually walked on as substitute, but Crerand bundled him off again and pulled Denis back on to the park because Nobby Stiles was receiving treatment. It was total confusion in the United dugout and Law stayed on. All this nonsense seemed to affect United's momentum and we wrestled back the initiative. I thought about coming off myself because I thought I'd tweaked a muscle or had cramp – and I never got cramp! But trainer Dave Ewing convinced me to play on. I'm glad I did!

With time running out, Ian Bowyer was blocked off by Willie Morgan about 28 yards out. Referee Jim Finney raised his left arm for an indirect free kick but, to be honest, I didn't even notice that. United lined up their wall on the 18-yard line and I just ran up and let fly with my right foot. It flew straight through the 'wall' (they must have forgot the cement!) and Alex Stepney instinctively went to save it. He may have been unsighted as the ball zipped through the wall but, anyway, it bounced off him and Mike Summerbee pounced to knock the ball in. Had Stepney stepped aside, my shot wouldn't have counted as the dead ball was indirect ... but he didn't, and we drew 2-2 on the night, winning 4-3 on aggregate. We were at Wembley for a cup final for the second year on the bounce, this time to play West Brom.

Stepney, who got a lot of criticism in the papers afterwards, really had no choice but to try to save it. It could have taken a deflection off the wall, and he had to make his decision in a fraction of a second. We were all relieved, none more so than Mike after he'd tucked in the rebound: 'I had to score,' he told me as we ran to the Stretford End to celebrate, 'I'd just missed a sitter from three yards before that!'

I'd played my part with a disputed (but correct) penalty in the first game and then my decision to go for goal with an indirect free kick in the second leg. And we could point to Best pushing Tony Book just as Charlton got their goal at Maine Road, so all in all the result was absolutely fair.

This was United's best chance of silverware this season and that had now gone. They did get some small consolation a few weeks later when the clubs were drawn together again, in the FA Cup fourth round. Brian Kidd scored twice as United beat us 3-0.

At that stage our concentration was on the League Cup Final on 7 March 1970. It proved to be a Wembley classic in front of a 97,000 full house, paying then-record receipts of £123,000. Cup finals can often be anticlimaxes and I didn't have the best memories of our FA Cup win the year before. No complaints this time, with a cracking game going the full distance of 90 minutes, plus extra time to boot!

We pitched camp in London, a little late after a troubled plane trip back from one of our Cup Winners' Cup ties in Portugal, on the Friday before the Sunday final. The day before the game, I recall we went to the cinema to see *Butch Cassidy and the Sundance Kid*, starting Paul Newman and Robert Redford – their superb banter reminded me a little of the wisecracking in our dressing room! There was a post-breakfast walk on Saturday, followed by a lunchtime team talk. In typical City fashion at this time, it developed into a chat about us more than the opposition.

It would be the first time we'd played 4-3-3 in England in a major game, although we'd trialled it in the European game against Academica, 125 miles north-east of Lisbon, in Portugal. Malcolm talked us up, insisting we had too much in our locker for Albion: 'Forget the hard week we have had, it's all in the mind. You can recover from anything in 36 hours. The Albion back four is not good enough to hold our front three. And Doyle, Pardoe and Oakes will grab hold of midfield.'

He was showing his faith in us while talking down a very good Albion defence, but this was Malcolm, this is what he did. And he always did it very well. With Arthur Mann now drafted in at left-back, it allowed Joe and Malcolm to put Glyn Pardoe into midfield in their 4-3-3 system, but that meant there was no place for our FA Cup winner, Neil Young, in the Wembley line-up. This was our team in 4-3-3 formation:

> Corrigan, Book, Booth, Heslop, Mann, Pardoe, Doyle, Oakes, Summerbee, Bell, Lee. Sub: Bowyer.

Another change Malcolm made was to restore George Heslop at the back, alongside Tommy Booth, to play against Albion's big centre-forward, Jeff Astle. George was thrilled to be back; he was really chuffed and he played so well. His delight was understandable as he'd been rather sidelined due to the emergence of Tommy. Now, after almost joining Middlesbrough earlier in the season, he was back and in a cup final at Wembley. He even had the nerve to ask Jeff at the start, 'How do you want to play the game?'

We were banking on our cup magic in both the League Cup and the Cup Winners' Cup, because our league form had been patchy, to say the least, following our thrilling December ties with United. From 20 December through to the end of February we lost five of our league games, at Chelsea, Everton, Coventry, Stoke and against our Wembley opposition, West Brom. Our only wins during this time were at Wolves and home to Ipswich, though these came immediately before Wembley. Three other games were drawn.

We didn't have the best of starts at Wembley, falling behind after just five minutes. We gave away a needless left-side corner and it was only half cleared to their Scottish left-back, Ray Wilson, who sent in a cross. It looked comfortable for big Joe Corrigan, but he was outjumped by Astle, who headed in from five yards or so out. It was 1-0 to Albion at half-time but it didn't reflect the half. We'd created so many chances but failed to put them away. Albion had a few of their own and this see-saw action continued after the break.

It looked a little ominous for us when Mike Summerbee struggled to run off a knock, and he was moving rather shakily when he played his part in our equaliser after 65 minutes. Glyn Pardoe's right-wing corner found Mike, hobbling 16 yards out. He managed to flick it over his head and Colin Bell climbed to head it towards the far post, where Mike Doyle fired in low from ten yards. Shortly after, Mike, his job done, was helped off and Ian Bowyer replaced him. Albion stayed with us when it looked like we had the wind in our sails, but I was always confident we'd win this one. Even when the final whistle went and we were heading for extra time, I fancied us. And I still fancied us after a stand-up row with Malcolm before we restarted!

My dander was already up because I thought we should have wrapped up our cup win in normal time. Then Malcolm called on me to drop back deeper and leave the fresh legs of Ian Bowyer up front. What? What did he say? I felt fresh. I wasn't tired; in fact I felt good ... and I told Malcolm so! We might have had a gruelling week, travelling to and from Portugal, but I reckoned we were more up for another half hour than Albion.

Malcolm was an absolutely brilliant coach, but I never took everything he said as gospel. That's not my nature. We were drawing 1-1 and we'd been the better side. At full time he said, 'Come on, right, this is what we're going to do!' And when he told me what he wanted, I said, 'Hold on, just a minute. This is what we should do – give the fucking ball to me and we'll win.' Everyone went quiet and I told the lads it was simple. They all said, 'All right then,' and that was that.

So, there was much pointing, arm waving and heated words before we got into extra time. And I did stay up front! Four minutes before the turnaround in extra time, we got the goal that won the League Cup. It was a good job I insisted on staying in attack, because I laid it on.

It happened when I got the ball from Mike Doyle at outside-right, 40 yards out, with Albion defender John Kaye in front of me. I feinted and dummied, showed him the ball and then took it on the outside and dinked it towards Colin Bell. He again won a decisive header and Glyn Pardoe reached it ahead of keeper John Osborne to poke a right-foot shot into the net. We'd done it, the League Cup was ours.

Well, I enjoyed that! From a personal point of view, I enjoyed it more than the FA Cup win the year before. Because this game was one of my personal career highlights and I was ITV Sport's man of the match. The ITV crew brought me to speak to Jimmy Hill afterwards. I told him:

> They had us in trouble early on with the high ball when Jeff Astle scored, and I thought they played very well, but I thought we were just too strong for them. It's the mark of a good side when you can come from behind to win.
>
> I thought we monopolised a lot of the play, but Albion played very well. After we equalised, I always thought a second goal was on the cards. I've never seen us create so many chances without knocking them in. Although Albion had one or two chances, I've never seen us create so many.

> For the winning goal, I hoped John Kaye would commit himself against me, but he didn't. So, I had to try and outrun him and I saw Colin Bell and chipped the ball for him at the near post. He rises above John Talbot and knocks the ball on for Glyn Pardoe to jump and volley it into the net.

What ITV and Jimmy Hill *didn't* get into was the running battle I'd had with Albion's Scottish right-back Doug Fraser, who was an old-fashioned tough defender, and he decided he'd leave his mark on me at Wembley. I had the bruises to show for it afterwards, and he got a reprimand from referee Vic James for a punch he aimed at me ... but never landed. I admit I feigned taking the blow because it was the only way I could stop him – if I'd reacted by punching him back, I could have landed in real bother.

The bruises I got were real, though, and not earned by play-acting. I had to protect myself and I had every right to because a player can be sent off for intent, whether his punch lands or not, and plenty of Fraser's digs did land. I didn't moan, though, and I understand why Fraser did what he did. He was a good defender and I think he just lost his rag because we had them under the cosh.

Meanwhile, that row with Malcolm at the final whistle might seem like indiscipline, but it wasn't. What it was, in fact, was very typical of City at this time where everyone's view was encouraged and respected. We all knew who was in charge – and that was Joe and Malcolm – but everyone had a right to make their point. It meant that at times our dressing room could be a verbal jousting area, and no one pulled their punches. We all signed up to that and there were no shrinking violets.

At the same time there was no room for hard feelings or sulking and, when everyone had their say, the verbals were forgotten, and we were pals again. It was open, it was healthy and it made for a successful side.

The success was now flowing with the League Cup ours, and that meant guaranteed European football whatever happened with our Cup Winners' Cup campaign. Our Euro journey actually began months earlier in September against Athletic Bilbao in Spain, managed by Ronnie Allen, the boss who'd wanted to sign me for Wolves back in 1967. It was a year since our nightmare in Fenerbahçe and we needed something to exorcise our horrible showing in the European Cup.

It wasn't to be a good start, though. We were two down inside 12 minutes and it says a lot for our team spirit that we wouldn't be steamrollered. José Maria Argoitia put them in front on nine minutes, and just three minutes later Javier Clemente doubled their lead. It was time for us to retrench and ensure we stayed in the game.

Fortunately, we halved the deficit just a few minutes before half-time when Neil Young scored. That gave us a platform going into the second half, but it was a bit of a false dawn as 12 minutes after the restart Fidel Uriarte made it 3-1. So, were we going to settle for a defeat and a mountain to climb in the second leg? Were we hell! Those memories of Fenerbahçe burned in the back of our brains and I have to say Mike Summerbee had a corking game. The atmosphere in the San Memes Stadium was crackling and those Basques made it tough for us.

It was a hard, physical match, but thanks to Tommy Booth on 68 minutes and an own goal from Luis María Echeberria, four minutes from time, we got the goals to emerge with honours even. The raucous crowd gave us quite an ovation after the 3-3 draw and I don't think they were accustomed to seeing six goals. Their usual ration was one or two a game!

We should have known it was never going to be easy when we endured what became customary travel problems whenever we ventured on to the Continent. The flight to Bilbao was hours late, thanks to the original plane needing an engine replacement. We'd reported at Manchester Airport at 9.45am and were in the departure lounge at 10.30. Then came the plane trouble with no further information available until noon. We finally got on the replacement aircraft and we took off ... just before 3pm!

When we finally arrived in Spain, our hosts seemed to have it in for us as the coach laid on was a disgrace. I don't know who'd used it before us, or when it had last been cleaned, but it was a dirty, unkempt vehicle and smelled of sick. We weren't at all keen on that and ended up making the ten-mile trip to the hotel in a fleet of cabs. We completed our training session in semi-darkness, hardly ideal preparation.

We had no such worries back home ahead of the return leg on 1 October. In the league we'd beaten Coventry but lost at Stoke before we rolled out the welcome mat for the Spaniards. I don't know how the game was goalless at the break – probably down to the heroics of their keeper Iribar and the packed defence in front of him. I was still sure we'd crack them. We kept the pressure on but had to wait until 12 minutes after the interval before the breakthrough came.

Alan Oakes picked the ball up on halfway and he ran forward, and ran, and ran … they just backed off and Alan tried his luck, brilliantly, from 25 yards, and it absolutely flew in. Our second one seemed to end up in the back of the net in slow motion. Iribar dashed out to try to block Mike Summerbee on the edge of the area, but the ball squirted out to Neil Young and his shot was half blocked, the ball looping high towards the goal. When it finally dropped, Colin Bell was able to nod in from almost under the bar. We wrapped it up five minutes from time when I played an angled ball through to Neil Young. When he again had a shot blocked by keeper Iribar, Ian Bowyer pounced to despatch the rebound. That was it, 3-0 and our first success in European competition.

The Fenerbahçe monkey was off our backs and the 6-3 aggregate victory sent us through to a second-round tie with Lierse SK of Belgium. The Belgian game has come on in leaps and bounds in recent decades but, back in 1970, this was the poorest side we would face in the Cup Winners' Cup. We faced them in November and we certainly let off a few fireworks in their defence. We went to their place first and beat them 3-0. It was all over by half-time, in truth, and I bagged myself a couple to put us two up in 35 minutes. Colin Bell set me up for the first and the two of us would have some fun in the opening 45 minutes. My second came after Neil Young had intercepted a poor pass and sent me clear for an easy finish. Then, a minute from half-time, I escaped some close attention on the touchline and crossed for Belly to hit a low drive through a crowded area and beat keeper Engelen. It was too easy and, frankly, we eased up after that.

Then we went to town at Maine Road, walloping them 5-0 in the second leg. It sounds ridiculous, but they actually started the game quite well, throwing caution to the wind as they had nothing to lose. Striker De Nul had one attempt cleared off the line and then he hit a post. They had the half-capacity Maine Road crowd's full attention and we needed to start applying ourselves. Mike Summerbee settled us down with the opener and then Belly and I bagged a couple each to give us a 5-0 victory and a record aggregate score of 8-0. We were pleased with that, and then European games took a winter break until the New Year.

So on to the league, and our form continued to fluctuate. The first match after our cruise against Lierse, we lost 2-1 at home to Leeds. Into December, and we thrashed West Ham at Upton Park, 4-0, but then drew at home to Spurs before losing two on the bounce, at Chelsea and Everton. We managed a home draw with Burnley before crashing 3-0 at Coventry, 1-0 at Stoke and 3-0 at West Brom. Inconsistent? You might very well say that! We'd started the defence of our FA Cup in the New Year with a 1-0 win at Hull in the third round only to lose our grip on it in that 3-0 defeat to United in the next round.

Our league form picked up in February, with a couple of draws, and then wins against Ipswich and Wolves immediately before our League Cup success against Albion. But there was definitely a Wembley hangover because we then lost three successive league games, against Palace, West Ham – getting quite their revenge with a 5-1 thumping – and Derby County.

That West Ham game still lives in the memory of all who watched it on *Match of the Day* at the time – or the clips of the quintessential 'sucker punch' goal we conceded on our way to slumping to our worst defeat in five years.

Believe it or not, we played pretty well in the first half but found ourselves 3-1 down at the break. The Hammers had found a spark, and that was the signing of goals legend Jimmy Greaves from Spurs, who had a record of scoring on his debut at every one of his clubs – and for England. This was his Hammers debut and Jimmy obliged again.

I'd already had a penalty shout turned down when a West Ham break saw Pat Holland – who looked well offside – cross for Greavesie to score after ten minutes. But we levelled three minutes later when I tried my luck from well outside the box and it zipped across the sodden, pudding of a ground and past keeper Peter Grotier. Although we were looking more than okay, a terrible mix-up at the back presented Jimmy with an absolute gift and he bagged his second on 36 minutes. Worse followed, as midfielder Ronnie Boyce – more of him in a trice – flighted a good ball for Geoff Hurst to dive full-length and head their third on the stroke of half-time.

We tore back into them at the start of the second half and I hit the post before a Glyn Pardoe shot bounced off Grotier's chest. We just couldn't get a goal, and then, in the last ten minutes, they finished us off. Their fourth was the stuff of dreams ... or nightmares for Joe Corrigan. Eight minutes from time, Joe cleared upfield from the right side of his penalty area and he turned to head back towards his six-yard line. But it was a poor kick, and with Joe's back still to the ball, Ronnie Boyce – 40 yards or so out – volleyed the ball first time and, as the crowd erupted, it sailed past our bemused keeper and into the net. Joe knew nothing until it flashed past him, and he had to take the justified criticism on the chin.

Joe said later, 'I took a lot of stick over that incident for a long time afterwards. But now I can look back and laugh myself, even though it is at times still shown on television. However, there's one point I would like to make: no one at that time gave Boyce any credit for seeing his chance and volleying such a tremendous goal.'

Geoff Hurst wrapped it up just before the end when a half-cleared Billy Bonds cross fell nicely for him to thrash a 15-yard volley high into the net. I played with a heavy cold that day and I was certainly feeling under the weather at the end of that one! Our league performances were strangely mixed … we'd won the League Cup but we needed something else to add gloss to our season.

Some came with our first league 'double' over United for 15 years. We took the bragging rights, 2-1 at Old Trafford, with all the goals in the first half. I got us underway after ten minutes with a penalty after Stepney fouled Neil Young, now restored to the side. Stepney dived right, I put it to his left. But our lead lasted only ten minutes or so, with Joe Corrigan unable to hold Willie Morgan's shot. It fell to Brian Kidd, who scored. Our second goal wrapped it up,

Neil Young forced an error from David Sadler and it broke for Mike Doyle. Our United-hating hero took great delight in firing past Stepney.

This was just a couple of weeks or so after our League Cup win. This period also saw the resumption of our Cup Winners' Cup campaign with a double-header against Portugal's Academica of Coimbra in the quarter-finals. It was a hectic schedule for us, with Coimbra on the Wednesday before the League Cup Final just three days later. To make matters worse, our travelling jinx struck again as we needed more than 13 hours to make the trip home after a 0-0 draw. Why? A fireman's strike at Heathrow.

It had been quite a game, with Coimbra not much interested in playing. They'd been written off before the tie as just a bunch of footballing students. The small ground, a very late kick-off and a crowd of under 9,000 seemed to fit this theory but it was way off beam. It seemed they just wanted to stop us from scoring. They practised all the dark arts associated with the Continental game (not the English one!) back in those days. Shirt-pulling, hacking, you name it, and they'd have a go. Yet as soon as you touched them, down they went, crying for a foul. They succeeded, though, claiming their goalless draw. We thought, well, if that's their approach at home …

Sure enough, they absolutely doubled down at our place on 18 March. Mike Doyle later reckoned it was the first occasion he encountered a massed defensive system with all 11 men behind the ball. He had it right and they were so blatantly cynical. We just couldn't break them down and, goalless again, the game went into extra time. I'd missed a close-range chance but, finally, we found a way to win with a goal four minutes into the second half of extra time. Young midfielder Tony Towers, who'd come on at half-time for George Heslop, reacted when keeper Cardoso palmed out a cross ball and he hit it first time through a packed area. It was scrappy but, in the end, enough to win.

This was our chance to add that further gloss to our season. We'd just won the League Cup and now we were defying quite a hectic schedule to go for more cup glory, in Europe. We were now drawn in the semi-finals to face the Germans FC Schalke, and the camp was buoyant. The way we'd beaten Coimbra indicated how Joe and Malcolm were developing the squad with young Towers being our match-winner. For we certainly had good young players coming through. We had 18-year-old Tony, Ian Mellor, Ian Bowyer, and Arthur Mann had been bought in from Hearts to add defensive cover. We nicknamed Tony 'Growler' because he had such a deep voice, especially for a young lad, and he'd very nearly scored in normal time against Coimbra with a fizzing 20-yarder that forced a great save from the keeper.

Tony established himself in the City side the following season and went on to win England caps while at Sunderland; Ian Bowyer later won the European Cup with Forest, but he couldn't get into our team on a regular basis at that stage. We had Willie Donachie, also 18, breaking through. And the goalkeeping situation was on the way to being solved by the development of Joe Corrigan. He became a very good keeper later in his career, although at this time, in 1970, he had potential but was still learning. He forced his way ahead of Ken Mulhearn and Harry Dowd, but Joe did struggle early on. Goalkeeper at this point was an unsettled position for us, and there was no continuity until Joe eventually made it his own.

You can't afford to give goals away but that's what happened in a spell from, I'd say, 1968–72. That's why Malcolm was right all the way back to 1967 when he wanted Joe Mercer to sign Gordon Banks. We specialised in leaking soft goals … yet we were still good enough to win the league, the FA Cup, European Cup Winners' Cup and League Cup.

And next up in that roll call was the Cup Winners' Cup semi-final double-header with Schalke. The clashes with Bilbao and Coimbra taught us that this European football lark was no easy street. We knew we had to be on our mettle. Yet again, we were drawn away first (as was the case throughout) and set off for the Rhineland and the city of Gelsenkirchen. This was the Rhine's industrial heartland, and for Gelsenkirchen read Sheffield, and our foreign hiccups struck again with the Germans providing us just one ball with which to warm up before kick-off. Malcolm sorted this by assuring our hosts that if we had one ball in Germany, they'd find none at all in Manchester!

We came out of the traps flying early on, dominating the early exchanges, but a goal eluded us. We did struggle to fathom their sweeper system and Schalke ensured they'd take an advantage to Maine Road when right-winger Reinhard Libuda struck 12 minutes from time. He cut in from the flank to fire past Joe Corrigan and into the corner of the net. He played quite a few games for the West Germany national side and was nicknamed 'Stan' after England's own Stanley Matthews.

Ahead of the second leg, we'd lost at home to Sunderland and away at Palace before drawing with Southampton, at The Dell. Those results were disappointing, but training was good, and we were ready for Schalke, with both Mike Summerbee and Colin Bell passed fit to play after niggling injuries. We worked hard in training with tactics to counter their sweeper and it paid off when the game got underway. Malcolm wanted lots of movement from our forward players in and around the box to isolate and confuse the man sweeping up. This involved our forwards pulling the defence to our right side before switching play to Alan Oakes on the left, exploiting the space.

It worked a treat when Alan pounced to set up Mike Doyle, breaking forward to give us the lead on nine minutes. Alan repeated the trick five minutes later by providing the pass to Neil Young, coming in from the right, who rattled in our second. Incredibly, Alan did it again by threading the needle with another pass to Neil, who notched with a 16-yard ripper of a left-foot drive on 27 minutes.

So, it was 3-1 at half-time and we'd got the game plan just right. It was even more comfortable when I chipped in with our fourth, moving from the left towards the box. I collected Mike Doyle's pass and crashed a right-footer in from 14 yards. Our fifth wrapped it up when Neil Young's left-wing cross was met by Colin Bell at the near post, and his deft flick shot inside the keeper's left-hand post. Virtually our only fault on the night was allowing a last-minute consolation, with 'Stan' Libuda poking in after big Joe had parried Erlhoff's shot.

A big semi-final win, 5-2 on aggregate, and we were absolutely over the moon with that. We were all pleased for Neil, whose devastating first-half brace was so vital. We all sensed he was firing again after a sticky season when his form variously rose and dipped. Here, on the night, he was really top class and our plan to pin Schalke back and pressurise their defence worked a treat. But while we were delighted for Neil, we were gutted for Mike Summerbee, who'd been struggling post-League Cup Final with his injury – and here it struck him down again. Mike would miss the Cup Winners' Cup Final.

This semi-final win, I reckon, was on a par with the best performances during this golden three-year spell for City. It was up there with the brilliant 4-3 title-winning triumph at Newcastle in 1968 and the 3-1 derby win over United in the same season. Now we faced the Poles of Górnik Zabrze in the final after they overcame Roma in their semi-final. Malcolm let us know in no uncertain terms that our accent on attack would be to the fore again. He anticipated another tussle with a Continental club utilising the sweeper system, and we planned for this in our training ahead of the final.

'The biggest fault in Continental football is that it's defensive, and often they don't know what to do when a team attacks them,' he told us. 'They cannot believe it when we take the play to them. So, pressurise them and do not give them a chance.' This was serious stuff, of course, but even amid the planning at City there was time for laughs. And it came when my business partner, Peter James, was watching us train at Cheadle, and Malcolm got him kitted up and he joined in an attack-v-defence session! He even had the cheek to tell our illustrious coach that even he, a one-time window cleaner, could have made a decent player in that City line-up. He might have been right – but only his total lack of ability, stamina and courage stopped him!

The other thing we were cautioned about ahead of the game was the atmosphere we could face in the ground. Or rather the lack of it. When we arrived in Vienna – the neutral venue for the 29 April final at the Prater stadium – we knew we'd have the backing of 4,000 travelling City fans. But we were told by Malcolm that not many Polish fans, then living in a communist republic, would be at the ground because of problems with visas. Malcolm warned, 'The hardest thing will be overcoming the lack of atmosphere – you will have to create your own atmosphere and forget about the gaps on the terraces.'

At least we blazed a bit of a trail with our own support. There has been much made of WAGs (wives and girlfriends) in football since the turn of the millennium. Well, back in 1970 we had our own prototype version: WANGs – wives and *no* girlfriends. I thought it showed we were extremely serious about the job in hand when the club decided to invite our wives. They thought it was the right thing to do and it certainly cut out a lot of the larking about!

And no, there were no girlfriends (this was 50 years ago, remember) and the cracks from the single lads started on the plane: 'Oh, so and so's a bit quiet, isn't he? Oh, yeah – he's got his wife with him!' The young lads loved that. And that came just after we'd averted another travel disaster at

Manchester Airport – we got on our aircraft just before a strike by ground-staff got underway!

On the night, we knew our fans would make themselves heard, but they had to do it in the worst possible conditions as the rain was torrential. But hopefully we cheered them up by making a blistering start and putting the Poles under siege. I shrugged off a foul by one of their defenders, Olek, flicking the ball over my head to hit a rising shot from eight yards that keeper Kostka tipped away, diving high to his right. And then we were ahead on 12 minutes, when I beat two or three men on the left and let fly. It smacked off the keeper's legs as he dived to his right and the ball fell to Neil Young, who calmly picked his spot and flicked the ball into the net.

We lost Mike Doyle, such a key player for us, just four minutes later. He'd damaged a nerve in his leg, and we had only ten fit men for quite a few minutes before we could get Ian Bowyer on. But we got the second on the stroke of half-time and it was the Lee-Young double act again. There was no doubt about our penalty award when Kostka charged out to flatten Neil as he bore down on goal. Call it a rugby tackle, call it a body check … Neil later likened it to German keeper Harald Schumacher's assault on France's Patrick Battiston during the 1982 World Cup!

I remember striking the spot kick pretty hard. I got plenty of meat into it and, although it struck Kostka's legs, he couldn't keep it out. Strike it hard and the keeper has far less chance. So, the keeper's legs had indirectly played a part in my contributions to both goals!

The City fans were in party mood as we carried on in the same attacking vein after the break, but a goal for Górnik on 68 minutes meant it was a little more tense in the closing stages. Their goal came from good play from their very good striker Włodek Lubański, and their skipper Stanisław Oślizło scored. But we were never unduly troubled, and we saw out a fantastic win as our fans went nuts in the rain.

My, were we happy. I'd been a little wary before the game as we'd lost Mike Summerbee and then, early on, we also lost Mike Doyle. But once again 'Growler' Towers came into the side and played his part, doing a top-class job in place of Mike in midfield. These were the teams on duty in Vienna:

> **Manchester City:** Corrigan, Book, Heslop, Booth, Pardoe, Towers, Doyle, Oakes, Bell, Lee, Young. Sub: Bowyer for Doyle.
>
> **Górnik**: Kostka, Gorgoń, Florenski, Olek, Oślizło, Latocha, Wilczek, Szołtysik, Banaś, Lubański, Szaryński. Subs: Skowronek for Wilczek; Deja for Florenski.

And so our season ended with a then-unique double. We partied that night in Vienna, and it was champagne all the way. We were the first side to win a major English cup and a top European trophy in the same season. City had come of age in the late-60s era when there were some good rival sides about: neighbours United with their 1968 European Cup win; Don Revie's Leeds had won the league in 1969 and the League Cup 12 months earlier; and Everton, the 1970 champions ... these were all top teams. But for my money, no one matched the Manchester City side in that three-year stretch when we claimed the Football League title in 1967/68, followed by the 1969 FA Cup and then our domestic/European cup double in the spring of 1970.

It was a long, hard season and I'd played 55 games in all competitions, joint top-scoring with Colin Bell, on 22 goals. And yet I was so happy that night and I looked forward to the summer, England, and the 1970 Mexico World Cup!

Gladstone Street today: Franny's first home – No 5, with the white door – was on this street in Westhoughton.

Cup winner aged 14: Franny, seated far left, bottom row, next to a teacher, with his Horwich and Westhoughton School team.

Young Franny, aged 16, lines up for his debut for Bolton Wanderers, 5 November 1960. He scored after 15 minutes – against Manchester City!

Sparking another attack: Bolton top-scorer Francis Lee beats Fulham full-back George Cohen to a through ball, September 1963.

Bolton legend Nat Lofthouse, nearing the end of his playing days, checks his boots at Burnden Park in 1960.

Joe's final piece of the jigsaw: Manchester City manager Joe Mercer chats with Francis Lee.

Fittest team around: Francis leads a City touchline sprint in training.

Champions in the making. City line up ahead of the 'Ballet on Ice' with Spurs, December 1967. Francis is sixth from left.

The goal that clinched the title: Firing past Newcastle's Willie McFaul to put City 3-1 up, 11 May 1968.

Lee vaults McFaul as his shot heads for the back of the net.

Pure joy: Francis Lee celebrates at St James' Park's Gallowgate End after scoring.

Dress to impress: Great pals Franny and 'Buzzer' Summerbee prepare to emerge from Newcastle's dressing room as champions.

Lee (1 pen) – that was the craic. Here's why, as Francis blasts in a spot kick, sending Leeds' Gary Sprake the wrong way.

Toasted in pop! Five-year-old Gary Lee drinks to Dad's success in the Maine Road dressing room as Francis and team-mate Bobby Kennedy look on.

Son Gary takes on Francis at Higher Landedmans, their thatched home in Westhoughton.

England calling: Lining up ahead of his first cap, December 1968, with (from left) Arsenal's John Radford, West Brom's Jeff Astle and manager Sir Alf Ramsey.

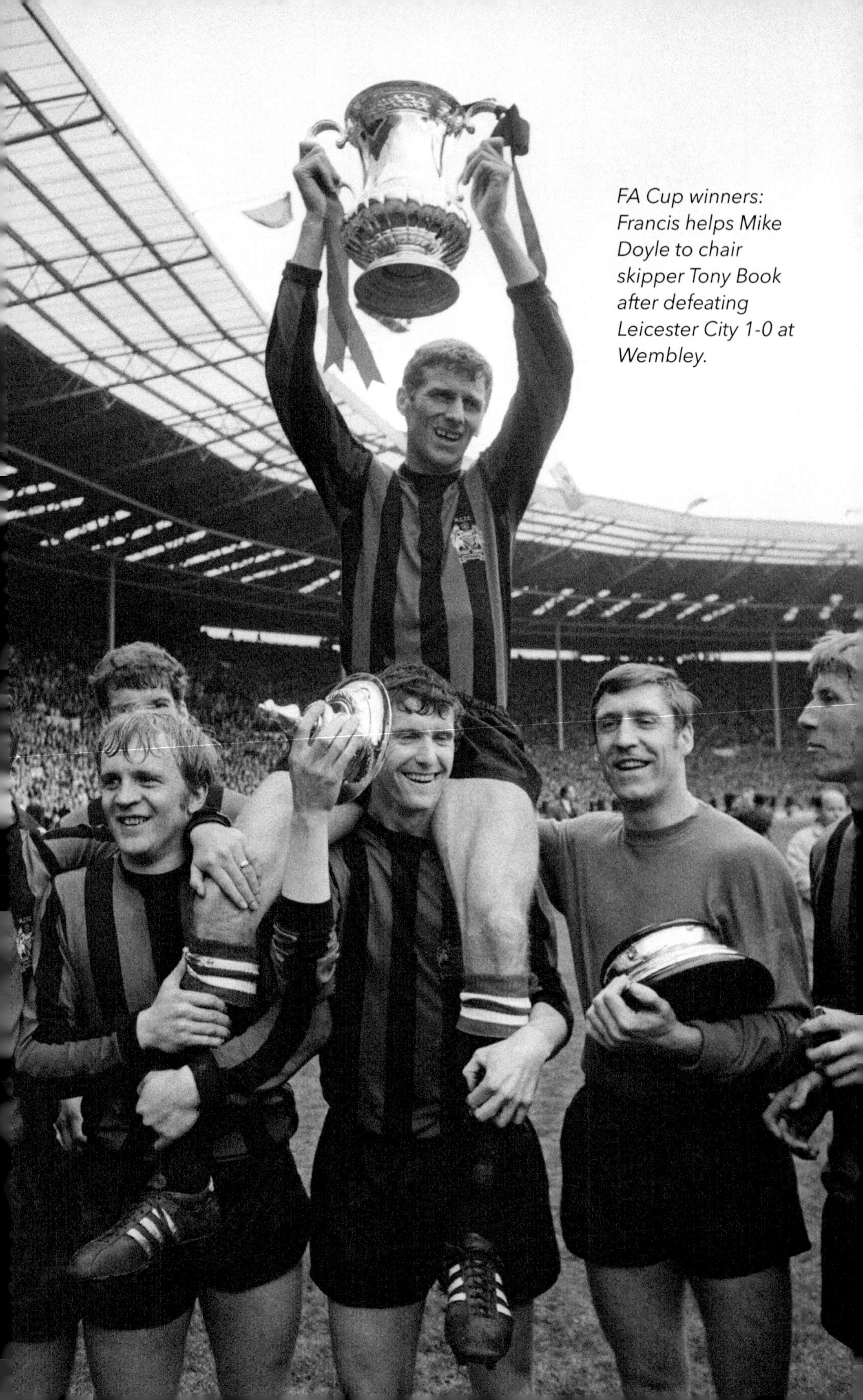

FA Cup winners: Francis helps Mike Doyle to chair skipper Tony Book after defeating Leicester City 1-0 at Wembley.

Top of the Pops! Performing the World Cup song 'Back Home' at the BBC. Francis is pictured, far right.

Mercy mission: Francis and coach Malcolm Allison are joined by Tony Book, Mike Summerbee, Alan Oakes and Mike Doyle in a visit to 15-year-old City fan Nigel Shadbolt as he awaits a kidney transplant in St Mary's Hospital, Paddington.

Training, 1969-style, on City's club car park! Franny heads for goal (and a rough landing) as Tony Book and Mike Doyle look on.

Winners again: The 1970 League Cup is City's as Francis and George Heslop carry skipper Tony Book after beating West Brom.

Francis, his first wife Jean and son Gary welcome baby daughter Charlotte, born on Boxing Day, 1969.

Late departure for the Mexico World Cup: Francis, travelling alone, heads for his trans-Atlantic flight from Heathrow Airport, May 1970.

Acclimatising: Francis works up a sweat during Mexico World Cup 1970 preparations.

England v Romania, 2 June 1970: Francis lines up, fifth from left in Guadalajara ahead of the World Cup Group C tie.

Stamina sapping: a full-length study in the heat of Mexico.

Losing his marker and losing pounds! Francis turns to lead another attack against Brazil, 7 June 1970.

Who, me? Francis pleads innocence but he's booked for clattering into Brazil keeper Felix.

Quarter-final heartache: Francis Lee takes on West Germany's Wolfgang Overath (left) and Karl-Heinz Schnellinger.

Francis takes on familiar foe Schnellinger one more time.

Chapter Seven

England's World Cup Dramas and Beyond

I WAS relaxing in my holiday home in Portugal's Algarve – a place I grew to really love – in the summer of 2021 when I heard that City were to commission statues of the most recognisable trio in the club's history: Lee, Bell and Summerbee. Well, about time, I thought. We didn't do so badly for them, did we?

The club had already unveiled tributes to Vincent Kompany and David Silva, with another for Sergio Agüero in the pipeline, to rightly recognise the new era at the Etihad Stadium. I thought a commemoration of the three of us was a really nice idea, especially as Colin had passed away earlier that same year. It also reflected a different, simpler era for the English game because we were all home-grown England internationals. Colin was from County Durham, I was from Westhoughton and Mike was born in Preston.

We delivered on the pitch together and we were great team-mates, but off the pitch it wasn't always fine and dandy – as I discovered when I first got the call from England.

I really enjoyed playing for my country, especially to begin with. In my early days at Bolton, it was always my ambition to go as far as I could in the game and, when I first got the call, having moved to City, I knew it was a great chance for me to show what I could do. And I was playing for the reigning world champions!

When I got that call, in mid-season 1968/69, it was the season after I'd made my mark at Manchester City and helped us win the league title. Manager Sir Alf Ramsey – he'd been knighted the year before to recognise his part in the 1966 World Cup triumph – decided to put me in a room with my City team-mate Colin, who'd made his England debut earlier in the year against Sweden. That seemed to me like good thinking. We were both pretty new to the international game and we were from the same club.

This was for the game against Bulgaria at Wembley, in December, that I mentioned a chapter or so back. And when we got together, I said to Colin, 'Look, Belly, we're playing in a team with Hurst, Peters and Moore, who know each other so well. There are others who know each other very well so, when you get the ball, first, look – look for me! Play it into my feet and don't worry, I'll get it. Just like we do for City.'

I was amazed when Colin turned and said, 'Oh, I can't do that. You'll have to play your game and I'll play mine.'

I said, 'Hang on a minute, I'm your mate. If you see me, even if I'm half-marked, don't worry – pass it and I'll get it.'

But Belly didn't want to know. 'No, no, I've got enough on my plate without thinking about you.'

Thanks very much, I thought, *at least I know where I stand*. But I couldn't believe it! We seemed pretty close in the line-up; I wore No. 7 and Colin had No. 8 but we clearly weren't on the same wavelength. I just couldn't understand that.

It wasn't a great result, either, as we drew 1-1, with Georgi Asparuhov's fine opener for the Bulgarians after 32 minutes quickly cancelled out by Geoff Hurst's strike, just four minutes later. Geoff struck after Belly and Bobby Charlton had seen successive shots scrambled away. We should have won but, in fairness, their keeper, Simeonov, pulled off several top-class saves. But I did okay, making several darting runs from our right side. There were other debutants, too, with Everton's Gordon West getting a rare opportunity in goal and Leeds' right-back Paul Reaney introduced as a substitute to replace Keith Newton, the fine Blackburn full-back, who would soon be off to Everton.

That strange pre-match exchange between myself and Colin doesn't mean I was worried about cliques in the England set-up. It didn't figure in my day, as far as I was concerned. It took me all of five minutes to settle down and feel at home and I didn't feel as though any of the players with fellow club-mates in the squad were freezing me out. And if I was 'on' and anybody did *not* pass the ball to me, then I'd be sure to let them know! I might say something along the lines of 'the game is hard enough with you lot not playing me in when the pass is on'. Crikey, I'd even play cards with the Leeds United lads … if anyone deserved not to be included in anything, it was those guys!

It very rarely happened to me – certainly not with England – but watching games, I can see situations at times, when very good players in a side may bypass someone they may consider not to be in their class. They're looking for the better player first. That does happen.

With Manchester City arguably – and I would argue this – the outstanding club side in the country in the seasons leading up to the 1970 World Cup, I was delighted to be involved for my country. It was those initial two seasons of success at Maine Road, winning the league title and then the FA Cup, that launched my international career. That Bulgaria game, on a chill December night, was a friendly, and friendlies were the order of the day as England, as champions, didn't have to qualify for the Mexico finals in 1970. With no competitive qualifying games, we needed these friendly matches to prepare us for when we defended our world crown.

My next game was in another friendly, against France – again at Wembley. We won that one 5-0 on a pudding of pitch (Wembley was then close to its late-60s worst, thanks to hosting the Royal International Horse Show some time earlier on the hallowed turf). Pudding or not, I scored my first goal for my country to make it 4-0. That was a milestone, a proud moment, on a night when Geoff Hurst bagged himself another Wembley hat-trick. Leeds' Mike O'Grady had volleyed the first to make it 1-0 at half-time and the floodgates opened after that.

My goal came after I'd made a decent run through at inside-left, jinked my way into a shooting position just inside the area and finished with a right-foot shot inside the keeper's right-hand post as he advanced. Geoff bagged himself two penalties and another with a deflected shot that looped in. What a feeling! I felt great, as good as it gets. It was my first strike for England and one I've never forgotten.

I was apparently regarded as the player who broke up the famous Geoff Hurst-Roger Hunt 1966 World Cup partnership, but that was none of my doing … I wanted to play for my country, and I had the highest regard for Roger, a fantastic finisher and someone who'd run all day up front. In short, he was a great player. Roger had played in the international sandwiched between my debut, against Bulgaria, and my second cap, when I scored against the French. That was a 1-1 Wembley draw against Romania, notable for Bobby Charlton captaining the side and his brother Jack scoring our goal.

The game against the Romanians was Roger's last cap and – reportedly frustrated by a London press campaign to have Jimmy Greaves reinstated at his expense – he retired from international football soon after. Within months, Liverpool controversially sold him to my old club Bolton, who were in the Second Division. He played on for three more seasons before retiring from club football, too, but he'd enjoyed a fantastic career.

Once I was in for England, I seemed to be well in. I played in all three Home Internationals in 1969, scoring in our 3-1 win over Northern Ireland at Windsor Park and also in a 2-1 victory over Wales, at Wembley. My display against the Northern Ireland lads was well received by the media and I was a bit concerned when Sir Alf pulled me aside at one point and I wondered if he thought the rave notices had gone to my head. He warned, 'I don't know whether you are a player who gets big-headed, but if you are, I will drop you like a stone!' He told me to forget my last game, which had been a good one, and concentrate on the next one, reminding me of the old saying: you're only as good as your last game, so forget it and move on. That summed up Sir Alf; he covered all the angles, and I wasn't going to get above myself.

We finished the Home Championship with the big one, a Wembley date with Scotland on 10 May 1969. The Scots were up for this one. They'd relished being the first side to beat the world champions on the same turf in 1967. But they were rarely in with a serious chance of repeating that feat, even though the atmosphere was electric. This was the first sell-out international I'd played in since making my debut. The old West Ham one-two of Hurst and Peter settled us down nicely with a goal apiece inside 20 minutes, but Rangers striker Colin Stein eased their half-time team talk by pulling one back just two minutes before the break. The Scots did okay, with the Leeds duo of Eddie Gray and Billy Bremner on song, but Geoff and Martin repeated their first-half double in the second half as we ran out comfortable winners of the Home Championship crown.

During these first few months as an England player, I could see how Sir Alf moulded these disparate club players into a real team – and that's the key aim of any international boss. They only have limited access to the players and then must weld them together into a proper team. I'd seen the value of that in my first couple of seasons at City, where the team spirit and togetherness were fabulous. Now I was seeing it with England as, in the summer of 69, we set off on a trip to South America to rehearse for the conditions and styles we might face in Mexico in a year's time.

Players I'd usually play against and chat with only twice a year were now my international colleagues. Now I got to know their quirks and personalities. It brought us all together, but four days wasn't long for us to acclimatise for our first game in the heat, humidity and altitude of Mexico – but that's what we were there for. Before a crowd of more than 100,000, we were undercooked but sweltering, if you get my drift. Even so, we managed a 0-0 draw, not bad in the circumstances. It took at least three times longer to recover from a run, so this was a steep learning curve. Gordon West deputised for Gordon Banks but afterwards he announced he no longer wanted to be considered for England as he suffered from acute homesickness … a big call. We squeezed in a 'B' game against a scratch Mexico line-up, and our FA XI won it, 4-0, emphasising our strength in depth.

Then we were off to Montevideo to face Uruguay, the first winners of the World Cup back in 1930. We won the game 2-1 in the Centenario Stadium, and I got us in front early on. Belly found me with a lofted pass (perhaps he was now taking my advice to look for me!) in a bit of space and I pulled it down to shoot. The ball got away from me a little, but I got it back under control on the stretch and nudged it home.

It wasn't an easy fixture, so it was ideal preparation. They had the usual array of Latin-American talent but backed it up with a fair bit of backbone. Shortly after the interval, Mujica's long free kick was flighted to the far post where winger Luis Cubilla, a good player, beat Banksy with a diving header. The Uruguayans then put us under pressure, but we eased ahead again ten minutes from time when Alan Ball found me on the right. I crossed for the on-running Geoff Hurst to turn it in. This was a real test and the win gave us all great satisfaction.

We were to play just as well against Brazil in our final game – only to lose by the same scoreline. Colin Bell scored after quarter of an hour and we did play well, only to be hit by two goals in the last 11 minutes. The match was played in stifling heat in the famous Maracanã Stadium, in Rio, and we tired in the last 20 minutes, not surprising as this was the 16th day of our tour. We'd all remember the names of their last scorers, a certain Tostão claiming their equaliser, followed by Jairzinho's winner two minutes later.

Before we ran out of gas, it looked like Banksy's penalty save from their skipper, Carlos Alberto, would secure us victory. Whatever the result, we emerged tired but confident that Brazil weren't going to be a particular problem in the World Cup. We felt we'd more than matched them. Edu, touted as a boy wonder, did little against Tommy Wright; for all his wonderful talent and achievements, Pelé looked to be a faded star on this showing. When they were behind, they struggled, but, at the end, with their noses in front, they looked good and started taking the mickey. Even so, I'd have taken anybody's money on them winning the World Cup!

We jetted home and I could relax for what was left of the summer, content with another great season with City and delighted to have fulfilled my ambition of competing at the very top of international football. Twelve months later, it would be the World Cup itself.

The following season, as City embarked on what would be that League Cup/Cup Winners' Cup double campaign, it was all about preparation and experiment for Sir Alf and England as he tinkered with his line-up in a succession of further friendlies – plus the Home Internationals – to put to bed the squad he wanted to take to Mexico.

The first outing came on bonfire night 1969, in Amsterdam, when we beat a tidy young Dutch side, which included the aspiring Johan Cruyff and Rudi Krol, 1-0. It took 85 minutes to get the goal; Bobby Charlton didn't mishit many shots but he skewed this one and it fell for Colin Bell to hammer it in.

Next up was Portugal at Wembley, just a month later, and I had the chance to chalk up another penalty, after a foul on Jeff Astle, but having missed one against Wales earlier in the year, I fluffed my lines again … and I didn't miss too many penalties. Perhaps the antics of the Portuguese played a part as they went ballistic when the kick was awarded. First someone grabbed the ball from my hand as I went to put in on the spot; then several of their team jumped and trampled on the spot itself as they protested. I was determined this wasn't going to rile me but, as I ran up to take it, I slipped, keeled over and almost hit the corner flag. So, I was pleased that Jack Charlton's goal, heading in brother Bobby's corner midway through the first half, proved to be the winner.

Into World Cup year and we had another date with the Dutch, in January, this time at Wembley, and I remember it well because the fans gave us a slow handclap as we were held to a 0-0 draw. Perhaps few in the crowd knew this Dutch side was emerging into one of the teams of the new decade. Nor, I reckon, did they appreciate that Sir Alf was still looking, learning and experimenting with the players at his disposal. He gave a one and only cap to Nottingham Forest winger Ian Storey-Moore and brought back Leeds' striker Mick Jones to lead the attack after four years' exile.

I was subbed in the second half as Sir Alf brought on Alan Mullery to stiffen midfield, and Mick Jones gave way to Geoff Hurst late on. The media were unimpressed and asked Alf about the slow handclapping, but the manager wouldn't be drawn into criticism. He had a classic, measured reply: 'Slow handclap? I thought it was the Dutch they were slow handclapping.'

The Low Countries were certainly in our sights. Next stop was Brussels and a rain-lashed 3-1 win over Belgium. The pitch was a gluepot, but Alan Ball had one of his non-stop nights and grabbed goals either side of half-time before

Geoff Hurst made it three. Jean Dockx's solitary reply was a mere consolation. The newspapers that crucified us for drawing a blank with the Dutch were now full of praise. Fickle? You bet. It always happens in football; one match you're king of the hill, the next you're rubbish. I refused to ever be seduced by all the praise or be too downcast when any criticism came.

After this, we broke our run of friendlies and set about the Home Internationals, so this meant competitive football, even if it was against players who would hardly surprise us as we knew them so well. In April it was away to Wales at Ninian Park, and I notched our goal in a 1-1 draw. West Brom's Dick Krzywicki caught us a little square to shoot in Alan Durban's through ball at the end of the first half. But, if I say so myself, my equaliser was some hit! Alan Ball passed it to me near the left touchline and I cut in six or seven yards and, when I saw the angle of the penalty area, I just let fly from about 28 yards – I simply let it go – and it exploded into the net like a rocket.

We then beat Northern Ireland in Belfast, 3-1, with Bobby Charlton captaining the side on his 100th cap. Belly and I sat this one out as Sir Alf gave game time to Ralph Coates and young Brian Kidd. We were in cruise control when Bobby's corner was headed in by Martin Peters on eight minutes. George Best briefly pegged us back after the break – but Geoff Hurst restored our lead with another header just a minute later. Ten minutes from time came the perfect finish … a 48th international goal for man-of-the-hour Charlton. That set up a final Home International with Scotland, at Hampden, before England headed for our World Cup preparations.

But I was to sit out the Hampden trip, too. The Scotland game was on the Saturday before City's Cup Winners' Cup Final with Górnik, in Vienna. Manchester City had requested that Alf overlook me so that I'd be fresh for the final. In fairness to Sir Alf, he was going to have me as just a substitute against the Scots, but he was minded to accept the request from Joe Mercer and I wouldn't play. He also left out Colin Bell for the same reason. Brian Kidd took my place in the squad and both Jeff Astle and 1966 World Cup squad veteran winger Peter Thompson were picked in the side. Another 0-0 shut-out – the first goalless draw between England and Scotland since the first official international in 1872. It brought more brickbats from the press, but Sir Alf didn't care; the results didn't particularly bother him, it was all preparation for the big tournament to come.

So, I'd got established in the national side as 1970 rolled on. England were world champions, something that not all modern players are truly conscious of. Perhaps Alan Shearer, for one. I know he and my old mate Mike Summerbee don't rub along too well, and on one occasion they had words. Shearer pointedly asked Mike, 'Did you ever play for

England?' Mike shot back, 'Yes, I did … when they were world champions! Something you never did!'

True. And we were extremely proud reigning world champions when I played for England in defence of our title in the 1970 tournament. The core of the legendary 1966 side was still around, front and centre in the Mexico squad: Gordon Banks, Bobby Moore, Bobby Charlton, Martin Peters, Alan Ball and Geoff Hurst were all still key men. Nobby Stiles and Jack Charlton, while no longer first picks, were also in the squad, along with Norman Hunter and Peter Bonetti – also 1966 squad members.

But the fresher names in the squad, sprinkled around those veterans of 1966, arguably made the squad as good as, if not better than, the 22 who triumphed four years earlier.

Full-backs Keith Newton and Terry Cooper, of Everton and Leeds respectively, were rightly highly regarded. Alan Mullery, of Spurs, was a quality midfielder. Everton's Tommy Wright was a useful defender, and his team-mate Brian Labone had supplanted Jack Charlton alongside Bobby Moore. Liverpool's Emlyn Hughes was good, either in defence or midfield, and fresher names up front or midfield included my City team-mate Belly, Chelsea's charismatic Peter Osgood, Leeds' Allan 'Sniffer' Clarke and West Brom's robust No. 9, Jeff Astle.

And then, of course, there was me. I was there – and I deserved to be!

We had a very fine team in Mexico, no doubt about it, with strength in depth across the positions, but it was not to be. The title of world champions slipped from our grasp, even though many good judges thought we were decent enough, certainly with enough playing quality, to win the title again. So, what went wrong?

I've lost count of the number of times I was asked that question once it was all over and we were back home. As ever, it wasn't one single thing but a combination. It seemed the dice were loaded against us. But on the pitch, on the playing side, very little was wrong. All I know is that trying to make sense of what conspired against us – when I mostly felt totally numb in the sweaty, desperate aftermath of that 3-2 quarter-final defeat against the West Germans in León's steaming stadium – is far from easy.

From that day – Sunday, 14 June 1970 – until my dying day, I'll feel that something was left unfinished, unwritten and undoubtedly unfathomable on that rotten occasion. Despite the heat of León, the memory of it still chills me. It gives me the shivers.

As I said, on the pitch, very little was amiss. But we ran the gauntlet off it, let me tell you, and as reigning champions we were there to be shot at. The Mexicans and more besides made sure they lined up to have a go. Throughout our build-up games in Columbia and Ecuador and on into the Mexico tournament itself, there seemed to be jibes and much worse constantly aimed at England. Worst of all (off the pitch) was the deliberate attempt to frame Bobby Moore, our skipper and the world's premier defender, after an alleged jewellery theft. As for Gordon Banks's absence against West Germany in that key quarter-final – after he suddenly became 'ill' – that's another story with definite ramifications *on* the pitch.

All of this made the players think there was a deliberate effort to destabilise England. With the Moore affair, it said much for the character of our skipper that he stood up to it all, ramrod straight, and played brilliantly in the tournament. He was one of the best players on view in the four matches we played. So, what happened?

After a fortnight of training in Mexico, we'd climbed an additional 1,500ft from Mexico to Bogotá, more than 8,000ft above sea level, for the first of our warm-up games, against Columbia. We'd been in our hotel, the El Tequendama, for less than an hour when it all kicked off as we padded around, getting used to our new billet.

The two Bobbys – Moore and Charlton – were in the jewellery shop in the hotel foyer. They were looking around at the items on display and chatting to a salesgirl at the counter. After leaving the shop, the girl followed them and accused Bobby Moore of stealing a bracelet. It quickly emerged that the 'evidence' was, at best, conflicting and, at worst, transparently untrue. The shop girl – later named as Clara Padilla – apparently claimed Bobby Charlton had distracted her while the other Bob took the bracelet. Both players immediately returned to the shop and asked her to call the police. Instead, she called her manager, and when the boys asked him to search them, he said it didn't matter. And that seemed to be that, matter resolved. We all expected them to discover the jewellery had been bought earlier from another member of staff.

So it was that Bobby Moore was free to play in the game against Colombia, at the Estadio Nemesio Camacho, on 20 May. I was again paired with Geoff Hurst up top in a 4-4-2 and we won comfortably – a real 1966 vintage show with two strikes from Martin Peters plus goals from Bobby Charlton and Alan Ball in a 4-0 win. All good then, so we believed.

What we didn't appreciate at the time was that the Mexicans had form, so far as the jewellery shop business was concerned. We discovered that Brazil's Botafogo club side had got mired in something very similar a few years before. And, lo and behold, the Moore affair flared up again the following week …

We were on our way back from the second warm-up game, in Ecuador, where I'd put us ahead after just five minutes and a Brian Kidd goal wrapped up a 2-0 win. There was no direct flight back to Mexico, so we called into Bogotá again en route. With time on our hands, we called into the hotel to watch a film – *Shenandoah* – and while we were there, the police, armed with guns, strode in and asked Bobby Moore to go to the police station to 'sign some documents'. It was assumed this paperwork was a formality to close the case and tie up the loose ends. Instead, when we took off from Bogotá, our skipper was left behind with the Colombian boys in blue – he'd been arrested!

The farce rumbled on, with the main 'witnesses' contradicting one another; the stolen item was variously a £600 bracelet or a £100 ring! It finally ended with Mooro released and able to eventually join us in good time to prepare for our first World Cup tie, against Romania. But not before Bobby had been held under house arrest, detained at the home of Alfonso Senior, the director of the Colombian FA. Bobby then appeared before a judge and was cleared, after a crime reconstruction discredited the claims and undermined any prosecution.

There was still time for another 'incident', with publicity throwing a potential spanner in the works. In Ecuador, Jeff Astle had played in a 'B' international game and scored a hat-trick, just at the point Sir Alf was cutting his initial 28-man squad to 22. The unlucky six? They were Bob McNab, Peter Shilton, Brian Kidd, Ralph Coates, David Sadler and Peter Thompson. Bob dashed back to take a spot in ITV's World Cup panel of pundits … the age of punditry began there and then with that tournament. The straight-talking quartet was my Manchester City coach Malcolm Allison, Wolves' talkative striker Derek Dougan, the forthright Pat Crerand, of Manchester United, plus the departed Bob McNab.

Jeff reckoned he was *spared* the axe because of those 'B' team goals in Ecuador. Yet his hat-trick didn't make flying any easier for him. Jeff was a dreadful traveller, and we'd flown through a storm to get back to Mexico. Jeff had taken anti-sickness pills to settle his stomach, and when we left the plane he was still drowsy ... and poor old drowsy Jeff became 'drunk' Jeff, according to the local press. Incredible.

So, did we feel that events were conspiring against us? Damned right we did! Apart from the chicanery that seemed to be going on, the conditions were something else. When we'd played in Ecuador to help our final acclimatisation, that was 10,000ft above sea level. We looked out of our hotel and the clouds were below us, they really were! The conditions were astonishing. In the Mexico Olympics, held two years earlier, the thin air undoubtedly helped the likes of Bob Beamon, in the long jump, create records that couldn't be matched for decades. It helped in dynamic disciplines such as that, but not when you were sweating buckets and struggling for breath in matches lasting 90 or 120 minutes. I noted in my diary that I'd lost 10lb after the 7 June game against Brazil. Yes, 10lb in one game!

That fateful game against West Germany, a rerun of the 1966 World Cup Final, was at the quarter-final stage, and a win would have put us within striking distance of retaining the Jules Rimet trophy. It came after we'd made it through the group phase.

We were drawn in Group Three and played Romania, Brazil and Czechoslovakia. I played up front again with Geoff Hurst, and my partner's goal, a neat far-post swivel and shot, was enough to beat Romania in our first World Cup finals game, in front of 50,000 fans in Guadalajara. We finished the group with another 1-0 win against the Czechs – in the same stadium – thanks to Allan Clarke's second-half penalty. Alf rotated the side for the Czechoslovakia game, with Brian Labone, Geoff Hurst and me dropping out for Jack Charlton, Jeff Astle and Allan Clarke. It was Allan's first cap, and he took his penalty well – and this game turned out to be Jack's last cap for his country.

Sandwiched between the Romania and Czech games, we played the mighty Brazilians, Pelé and all. I felt privileged to play in it; not so privileged that we didn't get some sort of result, because we deserved it. The match is rightly remembered for Gordon Banks and his wonder save from Pelé … and the fact we were possibly unlucky to lose it 1-0, going down to a goal from Brazil's latest sensation, Jairzinho, just on the hour mark.

Before it got to that stage, it was some save by Banksy. We were only about ten minutes into the action when Carlos Alberto, their skipper and right-back, fed Jairzinho, who ran past Terry Cooper and stood up an inviting cross from the right. Pelé's run was perfectly timed, and he climbed above the ball and thumped his header down – coaching-book perfection – only for our No. 1 to turn and then spring low to his right to somehow turn the ball over the crossbar. Wonderful from Banksy.

Yet I look back on the Brazil game with an element of regret. Because I could have had a big effect on the scoreline before I gave way in the heat of the second half – substituted by Jeff Astle – just after Brazil had taken that slender lead.

Yes, when Jeff came on, he had the best of all our chances within moments of joining the action, but he could only shoot wide, when he looked a certain scorer with the goal wide open. But before Jeff fluffed his lines, I'd had my own chance, too, and I also reflect on what might have been. Keeper Félix saved from my big opportunity, as I ran in to meet the ball ... if that had gone in, I'd have been a real World Cup hero. I was going to hit it on the volley, but my studs caught in the grass. So, I decided to head it instead, but that didn't matter, because I should still have scored. Félix saved it, and he deserves credit for getting something in the way – and that's that.

When I was replaced by the boss, Sir Alf Ramsey, he took off Bobby Charlton, too. He was replaced by Belly. Bobby had run himself to a frazzle, as I had, and the conditions were brutal. I'd also been booked for catching Félix in the first half, but I was more concerned about playing in that heat. Guadalajara is 5,500ft above sea level and the game kicked off at noon for the benefit of European TV viewers … it was 7pm back home when we started the game. In that heat and altitude, I ask you!

Norman Giller, a Fleet Street stalwart, wrote of the match: 'Only mad dogs and footballers would have gone out in such sweltering 98-degree conditions.' Mad dogs and Englishmen, eh? It was a thin-air climate that made walking, let alone running, a challenge. Remember, this was the game in which I recorded a weight loss of 10lb.

After 1970, I didn't think they should ever hold the finals in Mexico again, because of the altitude, but, in fact, England did it all over again in 1986 when, with Bobby Robson as boss, they eventually ran into Maradona and his Hand of God. I wouldn't have held it there again, though. The altitude and the heat meant that the world's best players couldn't express themselves as they should.

Back to the West Germany match; we should have won it. Looking back now, Alf made a mistake in bringing Bobby Charlton off when he did, just after the Germans pulled a goal back through Beckenbauer to make it 2-1. Alf had done the same thing against Brazil, and I think Alf was saving Bob, 32 at this time, for the semi-final, bearing in mind the conditions we were playing in.

Belly certainly played all right when he came on as sub and took Bobby's place in midfield, but he could have really made a name for himself. The stage was there for him to come on and stamp his personality on the game. Colin was a great player so he was good enough, but he didn't quite manage that.

I played throughout the 90 minutes and the extra-time period. We'd gone one up through a neat near-post finish by Alan Mullery (I had a front-row seat for that one as I was just a few yards to Mullers' left when he smashed in Keith Newton's pass). Then we made it 2-0 not long after the interval when, in typical fashion, Martin Peters ghosted in from the left to convert another right-wing cross from Newton. We were two to the good and, though there were chances at both ends, we had it under complete control.

The loss of Gordon Banks in our goal also inevitably came to haunt us. He was ill, so in came Peter Bonetti to deputise. This is *my* opinion: we'd have been better off with Alex Stepney in goal. He was a big-match keeper and people still remember the way he'd kept out Eusébio in the Manchester United-Benfica European Cup Final a couple of years earlier. To me, Alf pandered to the London press by picking Bonetti. In fairness to Alf, we weren't concerned by Peter's inclusion before kick-off. He'd had a good season with Chelsea, won the FA Cup, and no squad was as well equipped in the goalkeeping department. Stepney was top class, and even fourth-choice Peter Shilton, who was cut from the final 22, would have made most of the finalists' teams assembled in Mexico.

But let's call it right. Peter should have saved the drive from Franz Beckenbauer that brought the Germans back to 2-1 … he could have thrown his cap on it, to use an old-fashioned saying. Beckenbauer had been trying his luck from distance all game, but his 22-yarder was there to be saved. Instead, it went under Peter.

And Uwe Seeler's back header to equalise was just an effort to get the ball back into a good area. It was a fluke. I've never, in all the years since, seen a goal like that one. Those go in when it's not your day.

So, 2-2 at the final whistle and we all really needed another 30 minutes in that heat! Another sweltering day and another 12 noon kick-off. But we were now without Bobby Charlton *and* Martin Peters, who'd made way for an extra defender, Norman Hunter, to help Terry Cooper deal with tricky substitute Jürgen Grabowski. Our two most-experienced midfielders, who'd controlled the middle of the park, were now withdrawn from the heat and saved for a semi-final that would never come our way.

After the extra-time turnaround, Grabowski was at it again. He beat his man and his cross from the right was knocked back for Gerd Müller to bundle it past Bonetti from almost under the bar: 3-2 to the Germans.

I'm not sure how Banksy found out what was going on back at the hotel, whether he was throwing up, or what. But if he'd asked for the score, he might have been told we were leading 2-0, which of course we were. I can see Gordon going back to bed with a smile on his face. Only to wake up and discover …

Nobody said anything to Peter afterwards, so far as I recall. The disappointment was too great. I always used to say to players – when they'd row in the dressing room after a poor performance – 'Hey, you've had your chance out there on the pitch.'

The loss of Gordon, rightly regarded as the world's best goalkeeper, has long been speculated upon. So, he was ill, was he? So, he had an upset stomach? Or was it food poisoning, or another type of poisoning? There was speculation right from the off that our No. 1 had been 'got at'. I guess we'll never know. But I do know this: until Gordon had his stomach trouble, just before our quarter-final, not one member of the England squad in Mexico had missed a day's training through illness. That's because we were so careful.

Let me explain: I'd actually joined the party later than the rest of the boys as Sir Alf kindly allowed me to stay behind as my then wife, Jean, had to be rushed into hospital and I was given compassionate leave. After eventually taking the 14-hour flight from Heathrow – via Bermuda and the Bahamas – I was in Mexico. I recovered from the trip quickly, taking a sleeping pill to get some good rest on my first day, and then I quickly had the England doctor around, checking on antibiotics and salt tablets. In my first 48 hours with the squad, I felt like I was a guinea pig, with so many tablets inside me. The precautions were worth their weight in gold because I – and the rest of the squad – was in tip-top condition.

The regime was tight; we watched what we ate and drank and didn't take silly risks. There was a brooding anti-English feeling in most of Mexico (there usually is a wave of bad feeling against reigning champions) so we were in no mood to do anything to harm our own preparations. So, considering what would befall Banksy, it wouldn't have been surprising had his stomach problems been the work of a crank, trying his luck to rob us of the world's best keeper. Gordon had felt unwell ahead of the West Germany game, but he seemed to be on the mend. He was well enough to attend our pre-match team talk but then had a relapse.

It was the latest episode that struck our campaign. Throughout the trip, the warm-up games and then the tournament itself, there had been a smear campaign against England. We were labelled 'arrogant', 'rude', 'drunk' and 'scruffy'. There had been the incredible attempt to involve our skipper, Bobby Moore, in that alleged jewellery theft and to discredit the world champions. And when the squad set off from our Guadalajara Hilton Hotel HQ for the coach trip to León to face the Germans, we did so without Gordon. He'd been in high spirits in the days before, too, having just found out he'd been made an OBE. But now Banksy felt decidedly unwell, and he stayed behind.

We all know that other top sports performers – athletes, boxers, even racehorses – have been got at or nobbled to neutralise them before a big event, especially when the stakes are high. Yes, it's a long shot, but it may have happened to Gordon. A high-rolling gambler who wanted to see England lose may have thought their best chance at tipping the odds their way was to KO our goalkeeper. How? Organise a friendly staff member to slip something into a plate of food or a drink? Gordon, like the rest of us on that trip, would have done everything by the book, but no one can rule out the possibility, however outlandish, of an outside force getting up to no good.

With Banks absent, in essence, there had been 20 minutes of that game that changed all our lives dramatically. We were there as world champions only to go down to the West Germans in dramatic circumstances – so we left Mexico as losers. There were ramifications. It was the end of Bobby Charlton's glorious England career;

after a record-breaking 106 caps, he never played for his country again.

It was a turning point for Alf, too. He remained manager for a few more seasons but he was never quite in control, it seemed, the way he had been before that World Cup. It was noted by the media that his substitutions were ill-timed and costly. This element of the game was relatively new to everyone, but an eye-opener for Alf, who'd never made a single substitution in his club management career with Ipswich. They weren't introduced as a part of the game until after he'd been installed as England manager.

But I won't have that as an excuse. I will *not* blame Alf, although – as I said – his decision to pull Bobby Charlton out of the game could be seen in retrospect as a mistake. When we left the field in León, dejected and beaten, I was prepared for the mother and father of a rollicking … that's what I'd have expected from Malcolm Allison at City. We'd have been bawled out by Mal after letting slip a 2-0 lead, and justifiably so.

Anyone who says now that Alf's tactics, worked out in advance, were wrong is way off the mark. Alf's policy, his blueprint, had put the Germans on the floor and the game was all but over after 50 minutes. But Alf couldn't step over the white line, he couldn't play and finish off the job – that was up to us, his players. We'd screwed it up for him. Was it a lack of professionalism? I don't know, but we'd conspired to let slip a lead that most Third Division clubs would have clung on to. If we'd got a bawling out in the dressing room, we'd have deserved it.

Even after Müller made it 3-2, we could have salvaged it late on. I still don't know why Geoff Hurst, the extra-time hero of 1966, had a goal chalked off after I'd crossed from the byline for him to 'score', nor why we were denied a penalty after Belly slipped the ball past Schulz only for the German defender to chop him down. But that's just after the fact. There should have been no need to debate the merits of those late efforts. We were in a daze in a changing room that resembled a mortuary, but instead of a deadly diatribe from the manager, Alf simply said, 'Bad luck, lads.' That was the character of the man.

Those 20 minutes that followed Beckenbauer's goal were so costly. I do think every England player in León died a little that day. No story is complete without the dark shadows to contrast with the brighter, better days. We'd shown for almost 70 minutes against the Germans that defeat to Brazil wouldn't define our World Cup defence; that we could and would beat the Germans once again.

It almost seemed we were too comfortable, too much in control, that it was so much within our grasp. And yet we lost … and I just couldn't fathom it. I couldn't believe it. After the game ended, it felt like I was dreaming, and experiencing a really brutal nightmare.

My attitude to defeat is usually pragmatic. That's it, it's over. Move on. I'm not one for inquests, so much so that by the time I get home, any defeat is forgotten. Not this time. This time the taste and manner of defeat lingered and festered. All I could think was this: come 1974 we can go again and have a chance to win back the World Cup.

Chapter Eight

What Can Possibly Go Wrong?

IN 1970, life seemed so very, very good … if you take away the gut-wrenching England defeat against those West Germans. I was on top of my game with City, a recent league champion and FA Cup winner and I'd just cleared space for two more medals, the League Cup and European Cup Winners' Cup. I'd represented my country in the World Cup finals and, on top of that, I'd built a thriving business of my own alongside my partner, Peter James.

I wasn't an especially lucky guy, because I'd made my own good fortune, through bloody hard work as a footballer. In addition, before I'd even started to earn a half-decent living at Bolton Wanderers, I'd established and grown a business that was going from strength to strength. I'd started other businesses, too, and by World Cup year 1970, I'd moved into a luxury £20,000 thatched cottage home in Westhoughton – Higher Landedmans – that, with inflation, might be worth something like £1 million at 2022 prices.

I was settled there with my first wife, Jean, and my children, Gary and Charlotte. Gary had come along back in 1963 when I was first truly hitting the goals trail with Bolton, and little Charlotte was a Christmas baby, arriving on Boxing Day 1969.

And then, oh hell, it all started to go wrong for me. Big time. The rug was pulled from under me, and I didn't see it coming. This had nothing to do with Joe Mercer; nothing to do with Malcolm Allison nor my team-mates; nothing to do with my football at all. It was all to do with my friend and partner, Peter James.

He started to fiddle me. I'd gone away for the World Cup, for the time of my footballing life, and then came back and my business suddenly didn't seem so good. We'd moved into an old spinning and dyeing mill called Deakins Mill, in Bolton. We had a secretary, Moyna Moorcroft, a dear old girl who was initially like a clerk, I suppose. She came in and wanted to know what her role was … I told her to look after the Pay As You Earn and answer my fan mail – she often reminded me, in later years, that she only came to me to do the fan mail. Bless her, she ended up doing the wages for 240 people! I trusted her implicitly.

It's a real heartbreaker as I write this, because this guy, at this time, is supposed to be my best mate. Peter was older than me, but we went everywhere together; he went on City trips, to away games and suchlike and got friendly with Malcolm and the lads. As I've already detailed, Big Mal even got him kitted out to train with us in one light-hearted session. He had a good personality and was quite amusing and fun to be with.

But he didn't like working! I knew that. He got into this association with a guy at one of the biggest wastepaper merchants we dealt with, and they got this fiddle going between them. So, I'd returned from the excitement of Mexico and life went on as normal, at least for a while, but things weren't quite right, I knew that for sure, and around 1972 things changed massively.

Peter said to me, 'I'm going off to America, to Las Vegas. I'm going to see Elvis!' I asked why the hell he wanted to go to Vegas. 'My wife's always wanted to go,' he said. 'We have some friends out there and we could stay with them.' I told him I was going to South Africa to play football to earn some extra money. I also told him I needed to … because I couldn't afford *his* standard of living.

So, his brother Michael would keep an eye on the business, and my own brother, Trevor – one of our first employees – would be on hand, so we knew it would tick over in our absence. But I wasn't happy at all. How could Peter afford this? I confided in my secretary, Moyna, that I also wanted her to keep an eye on things because I was concerned. I then went away for four weeks to South Africa.

I came back from my African trip, and Peter returned from his jolly to the States. I quickly found out that he'd travelled first class on the plane. He was only officially taking £200 to £250 a week out of the business – a fair amount of money back then, it must be said – but you don't go buying first-class tickets to Las Vegas on that money. My radar was up, and I started looking for answers.

One morning Moyna came into the office at the mill and said that she was perturbed: somebody had been into the office and been through the filing cabinets. She told me someone had been looking at the wages details and bank statements. I could sense her anxiety and she asked if I had any idea who it might be.

'Yes,' I said, 'it was me.' She naturally wanted to know what I'd been looking for. 'Things are wrong at the bank,' I told her. 'Because our cash flow is good, we shouldn't have any debt, but we've got into debt at the bank, which we've never had before. I'm not happy with how things look.'

She looked at me and said, 'I know what you mean.' And so began the process of trawling through our affairs and dealings. I discovered we owed some £60,000 to the big wastepaper firm that Peter had got close to. Peter had been drawing the money from this company in cash … you could deal in our commodities, a bit like scrap metal, in this way. You send in the material and draw out what it's worth in cash. There was a big shortfall.

I asked Moyna if she would check it again, because this was Peter. This was supposed to be my best friend. She said she would, but she indicated straight away that she knew what was going on.

It all came to a head, and I faced him up. I said to him, 'I can't believe this, you're living like Frank Sinatra and I'm playing football and working my balls off while you're here, there and everywhere spending money like water. I can't afford to do what you're doing. My wife can't keep up with your wife and keep on spending. On top of this, the bank is going daft because we're teetering over our overdraft limit.'

Because he was my 50-50 partner in the business, the bank wouldn't give us a big overdraft, anyway. There were other problems mounting and I told him we owed this company he'd been dealing with up to £60,000. 'We can't pay them,' I told him straight. 'Don't worry,' he tried to assure me. 'We'll get around it.'

'No, we won't get around it,' I said. 'Because you don't work hard enough to get around it.' I then told him what I was going to do. I was going to see Alf Gill, our accountant – he'd been Peter's accountant from way back, when he had the window cleaning round.

And that's exactly what I did. I gave Alf all the books and I said I wanted all the news – the bad news. Alf was very upset because he'd introduced me to Peter. When he came back to me, he said, 'It is a dire situation, especially with this particular firm, because you're dealing with them all the time and not bringing down your debt with them.'

I told Alf there was money coming out of that company, but it hadn't been coming my way. It was Alf who told me that Peter must have been taking the money in cash. I asked Alf to stay with me until Peter got to the mill – and I wanted Alf to explain it all to him. He did exactly that.

'Peter,' I told him when he arrived, 'Alf has been through the books, and he'll tell you what's happening.' So Alf went through it all. There was a lot of cash missing that should have been in the bank and we wanted to know where it was.

'Well, I've never been good at accounting,' he said.

'No, Peter, you've had the money. Haven't you?' I demanded. 'You've taken it!'

'Yes, yes … but we can get it right,' he offered by way of reply.

'No, we won't – there's no way we'll get that right,' I told him. I offered him a piece of paper and told him that James Lee Waste, our company, was finished. 'You sign over your shares in James Lee Waste, right now, and I'll take it on from here and see if I can put it right.'

I'm sure he thought I was going to hit him. He took the paper and signed the shares over to me there and then. 'Right, you can go now,' I told him, 'and I don't want to see you ever again in my life.'

He then asked for a private word, so I went outside with him. I told him he had a nerve to ask for a private chat. He mentioned a couple of personal things but that was it and I sent him on his way – and he was gone from my life from that moment.

I left the mill and I drove down Deansgate, in Bolton, with tears streaming down my face. Here was a guy who'd been a window cleaner and had gone on to have a smashing standard of living – off my back, really – and he'd taken my business away from me. I was absolutely dumbstruck.

Two or three mutual mates had to know what had happened. I had to warn them: don't invite me to anything or anywhere where Peter James might be. At least one told me he wasn't surprised because of the lifestyle Peter had been leading. He'd bought himself a big, brand-new Austin Westminster car, the old Austin brand's answer to a big Jaguar. It was used by all the top police chiefs. Yet he already had a James Lee company car! Peter just wanted to be a millionaire overnight.

I then went to see the big company that James had been in cahoots with. I saw Peter's contact at their place just outside Manchester, and he greeted me by saying he knew exactly why I'd asked for the meeting. 'It's about this huge debt you've run up with us, isn't it?'

I told him I hadn't run up any such debt. Indeed, *he* had done it with my partner. 'He's had the cash,' I told him. 'And I don't know what *you* might have done with some of it.'

I'd worked it out that we owed them £40,000. He asked if I was going to pay up and I countered by telling him that I could ring his father-in-law, the very top man in his firm, and tell him the books had been fiddled, but that wouldn't get anyone anywhere.

I asked for six months to pay back the money. He wondered how I could possibly do that, but I already had a plan – involving those massive reels of waste tissue that had been stored in our mill area for months. By that time we had around 300 tons of the stuff. I'd bought a converting machine and, when the waste was converted, it could be sold on at £1.50 a case to the cash and carry businesses in Manchester and Leeds.

I learned a valuable lesson when dealing with the Jewish businessmen who owned these cash and carry places at the time: charge them all the same price. They'll do anything if they think they're getting a better deal than their opposition.

I shifted all 300 tons of the stuff and eventually that translated into about £90,000. It paid off all my debts and I was also able to buy a fully automated tissue rewinding machine from a firm called Satinex, in North Wales. I got my brother, Arthur, who worked in the cotton mill, to oversee this. He brought another of the cotton mill lads, who was particularly good with machinery, to look at how best to set it up. I needed to do my homework because I'd heard that Satinex were never very happy with it.

He got it running so well that we were making 1,500 cases per shift. I then had to sell it, and started selling to people such as the cash and carries and the old VG Foodstores. After the nightmare of discovering Peter's betrayal, we were at last doing well again, but the pressure of all this business stress while I was playing football at the highest level had to take its toll. I have to confess that Peter's antics and the pressure of the debt had me drinking more than usual to take the stress away. There was certainly a lot of stress.

It all led to me becoming ill. In fact, I had a nervous breakdown, and the stress inevitably had a knock-on effect on my football. It led to my precious England career being snatched away from me forever.

The 71/72 season, when City should have won the league title, was probably my best season. Playing was my only release from all the shit that was happening off the pitch as I uncovered what was going wrong with my company. I kept playing, playing, playing, and at the end of the season, when I finally knew we weren't going to win the league after all, it was as though the world had fallen in on me.

I couldn't cope with it all and it hit me big time in the following season. I was having psychosomatic heart attacks, I couldn't breathe; I had nervous tension and panic attacks – just about everything. I was rushed into hospital and everything was going wrong. Anyway, somehow I got through it. I was determined that Peter James's betrayal wasn't going to beat me. I managed to get things sorted out and eventually got back on to an even keel.

It was perhaps luck that we came through it – that *I* came through it! But, again, I'd made my own luck. We came out with more money than we'd owed, and I was now my own man, James Lee Waste was history and the company became F.H. Lee Ltd. I had big blue-and-white striped lorries for the new company; City colours, of course! And I used to park them on the Mill Square parking ground, in Bolton, so he had to pass them every morning on his travels. I wanted to show him that I'd got out of the horrible mess he'd left me. But it was a close-run thing.

It impacted my football, big time. And then Malcolm Allison left City. There was some story behind that.

In 1970, when I returned from Mexico, City were poised to continue their glory years, consolidate and improve. Instead, we *threatened* to do just that but stuttered and faltered. There was a warning sign when Italian giants Juventus spotted Malcolm Allison's undoubted ability in 1969, just as we were about to win the FA Cup. Malcolm might have been barely tempted by Coventry City, but Juventus? They were serious operators in European football.

We'd heard that Malcolm had been over to Turin to talk over a move – it was even said he travelled there in a sky-blue suit – but he stayed loyal. The firm hint was that he did so because he'd been promised Joe would step aside and leave him in charge but, with two more trophies collected in 1970, Joe was in no mood to go anywhere fast.

So we played out the 1970/71 season against a backdrop of a takeover battle, with boss Joe in the camp of the existing board, led by chairman Albert Alexander, and Malcolm supporting a wannabe rival group led by a double-glazing tycoon, Joe Smith. Smith was promising that Allison would be the manager in his own right. Not the best time for me to come to terms with my own business under serious stress and a football club tearing itself apart.

Malcolm later recalled it this way: 'I didn't want to clamber over Joe, I wanted recognition for my work with the team. I wanted to be a team manager. Joe could have any title he wanted. He threw me a sprat – I could be called team manager, but he would still make the final decisions. I realised, bitterly, that Joe was hanging on …'

In the end the Alexander camp discovered that director Frank Johnson, who was selling his shares to Smith, had broken a covenant by not offering them first to existing directors. The feud dragged on and, in late November, Malcolm was 'sacked' after a 1-0 defeat against Leeds, at Elland Road. But the decision was immediately reversed after

Joe threatened to leave with him. It was a reprieve and the duo limped on, but the damage seemed to have been done.

Our season was also handicapped by injuries, lots of them, with Mike Summerbee again hit by a leg fracture; Tony Book dislocated a shoulder; Alan Oakes suffered cartilage damage to a knee; and Glyn Pardoe was the victim of a shocking tackle from our neighbour's star man, George Best, at Old Trafford.

These setbacks hit us. Alan was, of course, an incredibly good player and, until his leg was broken, Glyn Pardoe was a lovely player – and a bloody important player, too. In December 1970 we thrashed United 4-1 in the Old Trafford derby and I scored a hat-trick – some described it as a perfect hat-trick, because it was first goal, left foot; second goal, right foot; and third goal, header. But that was a dreadful day because of the tackle that badly fractured Glyn's leg. Despite the rest of the action looking good for us, the mood was sombre, because it was a truly shocking tackle by George. It was really terrible.

Glyn was never the same after that and he has always wondered what might have been, but for that break. He did manage to play on, but the injury wrecked his career. It happened at a time when George was starting to attract some bad publicity for his off-field behaviour and maybe he was hungover from the day before, who knows? He lost his rag and leapt in.

So, it was a stop-start season with some occasional top performances and results, such as that win at United, but plenty of inconsistency and lows. We ended the campaign 11th, bang in the middle of the table, and exited the League Cup at the first time of asking (Blackpool) and the FA Cup in the fifth round (Arsenal). We had a good run defending our Cup Winners' Cup crown, defeating Górnik again along the way, but fell to Chelsea in the semi-final when we fielded a scratch team at Stamford Bridge in a 1-0 first-leg defeat. The return ended with the same result and, although we had Mike Summerbee back, he was far from fit, and young Ron Healey, an inexperienced keeper, conceded the solitary own goal.

Our goalkeeping problems were back to haunt us. Young Joe Corrigan had come in and seemed to be the answer as Harry Dowd was allowed to go to Stoke on loan before he left permanently for Oldham. But Joe was raw and prone to the odd error himself. It was in February that Joe was dropped and young Ron came into the side. I hate to bang on about it, but a top-class keeper then could have helped the honours board tick over.

One thing I was delighted about was the fact I'd persuaded Joe and Malcolm to sign my old mate, Freddie Hill, who was allowed to finally leave Bolton in 1969. His career then seemed to be drifting away when he ended up at Halifax. But I never forgot him. Alan Ball's father, Alan

Ball Snr, was manager at Halifax, and he was able to buy Freddie for only £8,000. His career had career slipped so badly. I said to both Malcolm and Joe that we could do a lot worse, and I recommended Freddie for our squad.

Joe Mercer said, 'Oh, he's too old.' But I reminded him that they'd signed Tony Book when he was close to 30, and Freddie was much the same age.

'He's an excellent player for our squad,' I told them, and they got him for a snip, about £12,000 – he went on to play close to 40 games for City. Alan Ball Snr said that Freddie was a far more skilful player than his own son – and that was praise indeed, because Alan would never hear a word said against his boy.

My mind may at times have been consumed with other things but, on the park, I always gave my best and top-scored again with 20 in all competitions. On to 1971/72 when my on-field performances looked rarely better, but, again, off the park all hell was going on – in the football boardroom and in my own business life.

By the start of the 1971/72 season I was close to finally fathoming exactly what had gone wrong at James Lee Waste. But at Maine Road it was a bun fight, with Joe Smith now on the City board and, as the season got underway, Malcolm was looking for his chance to take full control of the side. Even so, looking back, this is the season we should have regained our Football League champions title. It was there for us to take, and we knew it. In the summer I was reunited with my old Bolton strike partner, Wyn Davies, bought for £52,000 from Newcastle. I was pleased about that. I spent most of my career at centre-forward or playing off the right wing but I was happiest when playing off a big striker, such as Geoff Hurst with England, or big Wyn at Bolton and City.

By the time I left Bolton in 1967, I'd scored 106 goals in 210 appearances, mostly from the right wing. But these included a cracking few years with Wyn. I actually preferred operating off him. In one season, before he joined Newcastle in 1966, I scored 23 league goals and Wyn got his fair share, too. Now I was hooking up with him again at City, it was déjà vu. I got hold of him when he joined City, and I told him that he'd been used as a battering ram at Bolton and the same again at Newcastle – players just lobbing the ball up for him. I told him not to bother with that at City, just join in with the play and then make your way to the far post because someone will find you there, don't worry about that. Apart from his fantastic heading ability, he had tremendous speed, but didn't always make the most of it. But he was a great foil and, at Newcastle, must have been one of the best centre-forwards in the land. In the end, his value to me and the City side was underlined because he played up front with me most of the campaign and I had my best-ever goals return.

At first results were patchy. We lost our first game 1-0 at home to Leeds but then pulled things around a bit and by the 11-game mark in the league we were handily placed in fourth, having just beaten West Brom 2-0, with Dave Connor and myself getting the goals. Then Malcolm got the big prize. He was made team boss on 7 October, with Joe stepping aside and taking the 'general manager' role. Malcolm said it would mean he'd lead the side out at Wembley, and he promised to be 'ruthless'; Joe, sounding resigned, said, 'Malcolm has always been the man handling the team. Now he gets all the worries and will call me Joe instead of boss.'

Joe's final match in charge came 48 hours earlier, irony of ironies, an away tie in the League Cup at Bolton, my old club. We fielded a decent-ish side, with me, Wyn and Freddie Hill, all Bolton ex-pats, returning to Burnden. And they whipped us 3-0. Whether that gave Joe and Malcolm a final nudge, who knows. Probably not, as the die was cast. That night, Wanderers snapped at us at every opportunity and their quick striker Garry Jones claimed a hat-trick. No complaints, we were well beaten, and it was not the sign-off we'd have wanted for Joe.

We gave Malcolm a better baptism, winning his first game, at home to Everton, 1-0. I put away a penalty on the hour to wrap up the points, but it was no classic. Malcolm got us on to a run and it won him the Bell's Manager of the Month for November, while, off the pitch, Albert Alexander's son, Eric, replaced his old man as chairman. Joe Smith, whose takeover had been stalled, was the new vice-chairman. A chap called Peter Swales, who'd made money in the record shop and TV rental business and a football name for himself at Altrincham, was now a City director and in the Smith camp.

Then we embarked on a nine-game unbeaten sequence to underpin our title aspirations. We beat Ipswich (h) 4-0; drew with Leicester (h) 1-1; beat Stoke (a) 3-1; drew 2-2 at home with Forest; and 1-1 away at Spurs; followed by a 2-1 victory at Palace to take us level on points with league leaders Leeds United. We then thrashed Wolves 5-2 at Maine Road, followed by a 3-3 draw at Sheffield United. City were now top of the table, two points above Leeds, and another win against Huddersfield, 1-0, left matters looking very rosy indeed as February rolled on.

A 3-0 defeat at Liverpool was compensated by three straight home victories, against West Brom (2-1), Arsenal (2-0) and Chelsea (1-0), with a 2-1 away win at Everton sandwiched in between on 11 March. The title was within touching distance. Slap bang in the middle of all this, Malcolm signed Rodney Marsh from Second Division QPR for a club-record £200,000, with City four points clear at the top. When he first arrived, he came into the side in place of Wyn, and I was moved to centre-forward.

What happened next is well known and it's there for all to see. Signing Rodney, on 8 March, cost us the league title in 1972/73. I know it, Rodney knows it himself, and I think Malcolm must have known it, though what could he say? Truth is, Rodney wasn't fit when he arrived ... not to the standard that the rest of us were, anyway. His debut came ten days later against Chelsea, but he was clearly off the pace. His signing disrupted things, really.

Colin Bell, Mike Doyle and Alan Oakes could be a bit of a clique – insofar as we had anything like cliques at City – and if you went on a bit of a run and didn't give them the ball, they could get peed off. Well, Rodney would be up to his tricks, selling dummies and the like, and it didn't go down too well with some. Rodney is a good mate of mine, but he admits himself that his arrival cost us the league. From being a free-flowing and swift attacking side, the play would stop when it reached him.

Later, he confessed, 'No beating about the bush, I have to hold my hands up, I cost Manchester City the title ... for City, I played the same way I had at Rangers, as a free spirit if you like, and that's what the team wasn't used to. It wasn't that I was playing badly ... it was just that the other lads weren't used to my style and I confused them.'

No doubt, though, he was a very talented player. Malcolm had asked me my views on Rodney when I was on England duty. I told him that he was hugely skilful –

Brazilian-type skill, really. I also told him he had no real acceleration. Malcolm loved players with pace, and I told him that Rodney didn't have that.

After his debut at home to Chelsea, when we won 1-0 to take us five points clear, the hiccups began with a goalless draw at Newcastle. Even at this early stage in Rodney's time with us, the *Manchester Evening News*' Peter Gardner saw problems, writing:

> If Manchester City do take the league championship it could be in spite of Rodney Marsh and not because of him ... Malcolm Allison maintains City will not benefit fully from Marsh until next season, but like the man who buys a Rolls-Royce to enjoy an immediate improvement in his motoring standards, a club paying so much to boost its ranks has every right to think along similar lines.

Even so, we were clear at the top going into Easter 1972. It was a four-way battle, with the chasing group being Leeds, Derby and Liverpool. But we then lost twice, 2-1 at home to Stoke and 2-0 at Southampton.

I got us level against Stoke after a Mike Doyle own goal had shocked us in a match we should easily have won. Instead, Gordon Banks kept us out and, against the run of play, John Ritchie got their second-half winner. Suddenly, we were off the top, replaced by Brian Clough's Derby.

We did our best to recover lost ground with a brace of 3-1 victories, against West Ham and our old foes United, but we then took only one point from away games at Coventry and Ipswich. That left us with just one home game, against title rivals Derby. We won it, too, 2-0, with Rodney and I scoring (mine from a penalty after Rodney was bundled over by Terry Hennessey) but it was too little, too late. Anyone who saw my muted celebrations that day will know what I thought: we'd blown it. The result took us top with 57 points, but we'd completed our programme. Both Derby and Liverpool were a point behind, with County having a game in hand on Bill Shankly's men with two to play. Leeds were two points behind us, also with two to play.

In the end, Brian Clough's Derby won the title that year – on the beach in Majorca! They'd already finished their games and went off on their end-of-season break. Leeds could have pipped them to it but then a scandal broke about them allegedly bribing other teams. Leeds went to Wolves for their last game, on 8 May, and the Wolves manager Bill McGarry said there was only one result possible that night – otherwise Wolves would always be known as the team that 'threw' the game and gave Leeds the title. And Wolves only went and beat them 2-1!

There was always talk about Leeds, their boss Don Revie, and their dubious tactics both on and off the pitch. Years later, Wales international defender Rod Thomas became my big pal at Derby – and his big mate, while on international duty, was the Leeds United keeper Gary Sprake. Rod told me that Sprake had said to him, 'There's not one thing our manager wouldn't do to win a game … lie, rogue, cheat or bribe.' Whatever the truth, or the impact it had on that season, it left the 1971/72 campaign with the most thrilling conclusion to any top-flight season. This is how it finished, with us so near, yet so far from glory:

Pos.		*P*	*W*	*D*	*L*	*F*	*A*	*Pts*
1	Derby County	42	24	10	8	69	33	58
2	Leeds United	42	24	9	9	73	31	57
3	Liverpool	42	24	9	9	64	30	57
4	**Man City**	**42**	**23**	**11**	**8**	**77**	**45**	**57**

It was a huge disappointment not to take the title that year – a year of bitter disappointments in my football, personal and business life. My stats for City looked good, though. I took all the penalties that season and I got 35 goals – 15 from the spot. It was the first time a City forward had topped 30 goals in a season for 30 years.

Not long after the season ended, the great partnership of Mercer and Allison was formally broken up. It had already been ruptured by Malcolm's elevation and Joe's move to general manager but, in June, it ended in acrimony when the board, tilting Malcolm's way, tried to both reduce Joe's wages by a third and remove the word 'manager' from his title. He left, declaring he'd been humiliated, to take Noel Cantwell's job at Coventry.

'He [Allison] has got to start listening to other people again,' Joe cautioned as he departed. 'When you stop listening – as Malcolm has done in the last few months – you stop learning.'

With the Joe Mercer brake no longer being applied and an indulgent board firmly backing Malcolm, he could now drive on City his way, at full throttle.

Chapter Nine

Goodbye to All That

I DIDN'T know it fully at the time, but our bittersweet final victory of City's 1971/72 season and my goal against Derby was the start of a series of goodbyes. It was cheerio to our chance of winning the title, farewell to the period of our club's trophy-winning success and, just a week later, a sad farewell to my England career.

Since returning from Mexico in 1970, I'd remained an integral part of Sir Alf Ramsey's England set-up. I'd scored in a 3-1 win at Wembley over the East Germans in a November 1970 friendly; scored again in a 3-0 European Championship qualifier home win over Greece the following April. The next month, back at Wembley, I scored our second in the 5-0 hammering of Malta in a very one-sided game, but we still got the slow-handclap treatment!

After that we wrapped up the 1971 Home International title with wins over Scotland, then Northern Ireland, plus a draw with the Welsh. I then played in all the European Championship Group Three qualifiers in the autumn of 1971, but I'd failed to score in any of those games that followed our Malta stroll. We first beat the Swiss, 3-2 in Basel, drew with them 1-1 in the Wembley return a few weeks later and then, in December, we beat the Greeks, 2-0 in Athens.

We were now into City's should-have-been 1971/72 season, when I was scoring goals for fun for my club yet, as I've detailed, I was not – overall – in the best of shape. Did Sir Alf spot something others couldn't see? Hard to say but I know now that I was struggling badly, stressed out in the aftermath of a business that had been dealt a hammer blow. My goals and apparent good form were a perfect mask for the horrors I'd been dealing with off the field. Essentially, it led to me losing my England place and, ultimately, my international career. As the 1971/72 season came to an end and City fell at the final hurdle, I collapsed under the strain of my company in crisis – my perilous business life and football world collided and I know now that what I suffered was a nervous breakdown, right in the middle of my best-ever form for City.

So, as I lined up against those pesky West Germans in the Euros quarter-final, on my birthday, 29 April 1972, I was secretly in bad shape but about to bag my next – and final – goal for England. I'd also pocket what turned out to be my last international cap. Of course, I didn't know that at the time. I knew the Germans would be tough opposition, they always are, but few were prepared for how much they'd kicked on from Mexico ... when we certainly should have beaten them.

This was different, very different, and the Germans arrived with attacking intent, bolstered by a talented, new-look midfield of Günter Netzer, Uli Hoeneß and Hacki Wimmer across the middle of the park. There were warning signs even before they got a fortuitous first-half opener, when Hoeneß let fly from 20 yards and the deflection off Norman Hunter left Gordon Banks with no chance. Shortly after, I sent in a flying volley, hit low from the edge of the box, but Sepp Maier made a good stop. In fairness, it was sometimes hard to lay a glove on the Germans, but I managed to get us level 14 minutes from time. Franz Beckenbauer, immaculate mostly, misplaced a forward pass and Colin Bell was away, playing a wall pass with Martin Peters, before driving into the box at inside-right and sending in a shot from 16 yards. Maier dived right, but could only parry it, and I knocked it in from three yards. We were level – but not for long.

We'd had to gamble in defence, with Derby's Roy McFarland pulled out of the squad, leaving Bobby Moore and Norman Hunter – both defenders who preferred playing next to an orthodox big centre-half – paired together.

Bobby, straining to contain the onrushing Siegfried Held, pulled him down just inside the box. Penalty! Netzer went left, Banksy spotted it but, unluckily, his diving push on to the post spun back over him and into the net.

Two minutes from time it was game, set and match and we were effectively out of the Euros. Held mugged Emlyn Hughes and Hoeneß took it on to find Müller, flirting with offside, but he swivelled brilliantly and swept the ball home. We'd be knocked out in the quarter-finals, thanks to the Germans again, unless we could turn it around in the return game in Berlin, in mid-May. Otherwise, my ambition, fired by those flickering World Cup ashes in León, to avenge our 1970 defeat wouldn't be realised.

Yet I had to be honest with myself and to those who were looking for me to perform. I was suffering from stress, phantom heart attacks, panic attacks and had been rushed to hospital. With that second leg looming, I asked Manchester City to write to the FA to ask for dispensation to miss the summer Home Internationals so that I could take some time to rest, recuperate and restore myself to something like the professional condition I needed to be in. The result is in the records for all to see.

That 3-1 West Germany win at Wembley came right at the end of April. The Berlin return was set for 13 May and then we were swiftly due to play those Home Internationals: Wales on 20 May, Northern Ireland on 23 May and

Scotland on 27 May. Someone at the FA heard my request all right, so did Sir Alf. I was excluded from the lot, and I never got the call again. My England career was finished.

I'd not be going further in the 1972 European tournament (we could only draw 0-0 with the Germans in Berlin, so England were out), nor achieve my target of making the 1974 World Cup. My England days drew to a sad end after close to four years, 27 caps and ten goals. Yes, that strike against the Germans proved to be my tenth and final England goal. Still, not a good way to celebrate what could have been a special day ... my 28th birthday!

I never stopped thinking I could still be in with a chance of a call-up. And as the months rolled by, there came a time when I seriously thought I was in with a chance. England may have lost out in the Europeans, but we had a 1974 World Cup qualifying campaign, getting underway in late 1972, with Group Five having us drawn against Wales and Poland. We know now that this would be – disastrously – the first time England failed to qualify for the finals, but it got off to a decent start when a Colin Bell goal gave us the points in Wales. We could only draw the return at Wembley, 1-1, before we were due to finish the group with away and home games with the Poles. And that's when I fancied I could be of some use to Sir Alf. We were due to play them in Katowice, in June, before the Wembley finale in mid-October.

I was still in my 20s and I thought there was a very good reason for pushing myself forward. I had ample experience of playing against Polish defences, because of my experience with City against Górnik in the 1970 Cup Winners' Cup Final. None of their defenders liked me, I knew that. And it wasn't only that one game – I'd been at it again the following year in the same competition, when we drew them in the quarter-final.

We went to Katowice in the middle of the Polish winter for the first leg. On a freezing night, when I spotted the Górnik players wearing sweaters under their shirts and ladies' tights on their legs, they beat us 2-0. I'd heard they'd enjoyed a warm-weather break in Spain, but their legs looked *too* tanned … until I spotted they were tights! The return match was played out in the Maine Road mud and ended 2-0 to us. So, all square on aggregate and in those days, after extra time, it meant a third meeting. This was in neutral Copenhagen, and we won it, 3-1. First-half goals from Neil Young and Tommy Booth put us clear before that fine forward Włodek Lubański pulled one back on 57 minutes. But I then got our third, to finish them off, midway through the second half. We were very good value for the win.

I remember saying at the time that it was – considering the relative inexperience in our side that night – one of the best results I'd enjoyed with City. Frankly, they were scared of us, even though we had kids such as Healey in goal, Towers in midfield and Willie Donachie and Derek Jeffries at the back. To counterbalance that, it was nice to have my experienced old pal Freddie Hill alongside me.

But it was my perception of fear among the Górnik side that I recalled as England prepared for their two World Cup qualifiers with Poland in 1973. In the first game, away in Poland, there were three players in the Poland side who were in the Górnik team we'd beaten in Copenhagen ... Jerzy Gorgoń, Jan Banaś and Lubański himself. They'll remember me all right, I figured. None of them liked me, so I seriously considered telephoning Sir Alf and offering my services, intending to press him on my knowledge of the Poles and how they played. I could do my old boss a turn, couldn't I? In the end, I didn't make that call ... what might have been, eh? Perhaps I should have done.

As it happened, England went to Poland and lost rather limply, 2-0, with a Bobby Moore error – turning directly into Lubański – gifting the decisive second goal. Their first was initially credited to my old Górnik foe, Banaś, though Moore later admitted he'd got the final touch. That game virtually ended Bobby's illustrious career, although he won a few more caps before it all ended shortly afterwards in a friendly defeat against Italy. Moore never wore the three lions again. It all put great pressure on England to win the return at Wembley if we were to qualify. We didn't –

England 1 Poland 1 doesn't tell the story, but it's a story that has been told too many times for comfort.

Errors by both Norman Hunter and Peter Shilton enabled Jan Domarski to put Poland ahead in the second half; an Allan Clarke penalty eight minutes later levelled it. We had 35 goal attempts to Poland's two. And they had goalkeeper Jan Tomaszewski, branded 'a clown' by Brian Clough on TV ahead of the game, performing heroics. So Poland qualified for the 1974 World Cup finals while we stayed at home. The wonderful era of Sir Alf Ramsey drew sadly to a close.

In the meantime, I wasn't exactly pulling up trees at City. We'd had an easy pre-season and won the Charity Shield against Aston Villa (this was before it became a Wembley showpiece and, on this occasion, neither side were champions nor cup winners!) and it boded well. Yet, when the real action began, we started with defeats against both the Merseyside giants – 2-0 at Anfield and 1-0 at home to Everton. We stopped the rot, beating Norwich 3-0, when I grabbed a couple, but then three more away defeats followed, at Derby, Chelsea and Crystal Palace. After six games, City were rock bottom of the First Division.

Wyn Davies had been playing up front with me and had just made his 50th City appearance when he was suddenly sold across the city to United, for £65,000. City bagged a £13,000 profit on a 30-year-old, but I wasn't pleased to see him go. Our league form continued to fluctuate, not helped by a raft of injuries, and a 5-1 mauling at Stoke hardly improved the mood as we lost to Valencia in Spain in the first round of the UEFA Cup. Having drawn the home leg, it meant we'd fallen at the first hurdle.

But the odd result promised more … a 4-3 win over West Ham compensated a little for an embarrassing 2-0 League Cup exit at Bury and a 3-2 league reverse at Coventry. We thrashed Derby 4-0 at Maine Road, beat Everton 3-2 at Goodison and then put three past our neighbours, United, without reply … only to fall down by the same margin at Leeds. We were all over the place. And so was Malcolm Allison!

Now in sole charge, with Joe installed at Coventry, he was flexing his muscles. He made a public push for George Best and that was an accident waiting to happen, given George's behaviour in recent times, both on and off the pitch. Wyn's move was quite a rare direct cross-town move between the Manchester clubs. But going for George – outstanding talent though he may have been – would have been a huge mistake. He wasn't flavour of the month with United manager Frank O'Farrell, who confirmed City's interest. Thankfully, the City board were pulling hard on the purse strings and they wouldn't sanction a formal bid.

Thank god for that. It proved to be very much the right decision as George's days as a world-class player were numbered. He'd been suspended by his club and transfer-listed at a then whopping £300,000, but he shunned Old Trafford for the London nightclubs and the company of beauty queens. His sad decline was accelerating.

I was nowhere near George's condition, but I still had the odd problem of my own. Back on 26 August, during the season's early weeks, we'd gone down 2-1 at Chelsea. Malcolm, me, Mike Summerbee and a few of the other lads went to a club in London. We'd lost four of our first five games and drowned our sorrows – we also drowned out the playing of famous musician James Last with our own carousing. It was not good behaviour, but Malcolm simply ordered more champagne. Without Joe's steady hand, the brakes were off. And no one was stopping our excesses.

Not too long after that, Rodney Marsh and I joined Malcolm – after a Sunday morning training session – at the Brooke House Hotel, on Wilmslow Road. Sunday lunch wasn't a roast, but two cases of Bollinger champagne. It's been said that only one of the 24 bottles was left unopened, and I won't dispute that. I also can't dispute the fact that I then tried to drive home and crashed my new Mercedes into the back of another motor. This was me at the time, close to rock bottom.

In the background, Malcolm's position seemed to be strengthening, after the death of club president Albert

Alexander, our old club chairman. Joe Smith took over the presidency and Peter Swales, now on the rise, took Smith's place as vice-chairman. The old guard was being sidelined but the board seemed united in keeping money tight; the brakes being applied on Malcolm's move for Best was testament to that. Then I got dragged into it …

The new year was only days old when Malcolm was instructed to help 'balance the books', and then the *Sunday People* posted a story that I was for sale – and that City wanted £150,000 for me. I knew that John Maddock, the reporter who wrote the story, had good contacts at City so there must be something in it. I told the *Daily Mirror* that if City were so hard up, I could lend them a few quid! A couple of months later, Malcolm had his wings clipped again when the board said no cash transfer deals were on the cards as the manager made a move for QPR goalkeeper Phil Parkes. At about the same time, young forward Ian Mellor was sold to Norwich for £65,000.

On the pitch, it wasn't improving. We were regarded by many as likely 1973 FA Cup winners, especially after knocking out Liverpool after a replay. We were massive favourites when we drew Second Division Sunderland at home in the fifth round. But they gave us a massive scare, even though Tony Towers had given us an early lead. First Micky Horswill and then Billy Hughes scored to put them 2-1 ahead, but we forced a replay after keeper Jim

Montgomery, under pressure, punched Mike Summerbee's left-wing corner into his own net.

It looked like we'd won a reprieve, but on a freezing February night on Wearside, we were bundled out, 3-1 in the replay, my second-half poacher's goal not enough to silence 51,000 at a bouncing Roker Park. Then we were in trouble in March, with a run of four defeats on the bounce – the last one 1-0 at home to Chelsea in front of 23,973, our lowest gate of the season – meaning we'd taken just two points from the previous seven games.

It seemed Malcolm was losing impetus as he failed to refresh our struggling squad. I couldn't see the logic in trying to buy Best – unless he wanted a new partner for his Bollinger parties – though I could see the need to bolster the squad. He hadn't been able to bring anyone in since the controversial signing of Rodney Marsh, and that was a deal that did City no favours in 1972. But now we were into 1973 and I could understand him looking at Parkes, who was a fine young keeper ... it struck me that Malcolm's desire to have the best possible No. 1 was still gnawing away at him. It didn't happen but, even so, I wasn't expecting the bombshell that was about to be dropped.

During that Chelsea defeat at Maine Road, the sparse crowd got after Rodney, giving him the slow-handclap treatment and more than a few jeers. Just four days later, on 31 March 1973, Malcolm Allison was appointed the new manager of relegation-threatened Crystal Palace. It was utterly sensational.

Two days earlier, City chairman Eric Alexander took an evening phone call from Palace chairman Ray Bloye, who wanted permission to speak with Malcolm. Alexander agreed. Just 24 hours later, tempted by a then-massive £13,000-a-year contract, the verbal agreement was in place, and it was signed and sealed the next day. Club president Joe Smith, in at the start of the pro-Allison takeover bid, made a desperate bid to ward off the move but to no avail … Malcolm was gone. And the great City era of the 1960s and early 70s went with him.

Rodney Marsh said he just couldn't believe it. Little more than a year earlier, Malcolm had signed him, and the future for both men at City initially seemed bright. Then, one night after that Chelsea defeat at Maine Road, he got a phone call. 'Malcolm said he was thinking of going to London,' Rodney told me. 'I thought he was ringing to invite me there for a drink! Instead, he was telling me he was leaving – to manage Palace. I couldn't believe it.'

I felt a bit for Rodney. He'd made his City debut the previous March and we'd won that game – another against Chelsea – 1-0. Roll on to March 1973, and his last game for Malcolm was also against Chelsea and ended in a 1-0 defeat, with him getting the bird from the Maine Road crowd. There's a certain sad symmetry to that.

Before the ink was dry on Malcolm's Palace contract, City placed their old inside-forward Johnny Hart – the man who cleared up our Stateside mess with Tony Coleman and Stan Bowles, and a real one-club man – in charge of the team. We had seven games to reverse our fortunes and we were unbeaten in the first six, winning four.[1] We'd finish a solid but unspectacular 11th in the table.

Years later, Malcolm reflected on those final few months at City:

> Inevitably, a coach loses his edge with a certain set of players. In the last period at Manchester City, I sensed that we had all become too familiar; a kind of complacency had taken hold of both myself and the players. It is at such times that a man should either move on – or radically change the emphasis of the work.

Unable to change the emphasis via the transfer market, Allison left for the smoke, for a new football challenge and with a new lady in his life, Serena Williams (no, not

1 Yes, we lost just one of our final seven games after Malcolm left … the very last game of the season, at home to Malcolm Allison's Palace! Palace couldn't avoid the drop under their new boss, but they overcame our quick start (I got a fifth-minute penalty) to go 2-1 up, courtesy of a couple from Don Rogers in the second half. Then I put away another penalty late in the game to equalise – only for John Craven to get the winner two minutes from time. Malcolm was smiling.

that one), the London Playboy Club's public relations girl. We'd not see his like again at City. In more recent times, of course, the good times have returned in the modern era with a vengeance, especially with Pep Guardiola, who's a special talent. But Malcolm Allison was a brilliant coach and also a tremendously charismatic figure. He was both *ahead of his time*, with his methods, and *of his time* – because his personality perfectly suited the cutting-edge era of the late 1960s and early 70s. He was so different from fellow coaches and managers of the era. Think Bill Shankly, Sir Matt Busby, Bertie Mee, Don Revie – Malcolm was cut from a very different cloth, a more modern weave ran through him. Only Brian Clough, who was a few years younger still, was of similar material.

As I've said, when I first met Malcolm, he told me he would make me an even better player and I initially scoffed ... but he kept his promise. He'd work very hard on those players who needed to be worked, who needed coaching. Of course, the flair players, the naturally talented ones, would be praised and he'd encourage us to use our skills. But the boys who really needed developing, he could and would lift them even more. I saw everything in football, in terms of vision, on the pitch. I've a good analytical brain and, at City, Malcolm would often ask me for my opinions. I appreciated that as he was such a fine coach – and I think he appreciated that I wouldn't take everything as gospel from him, either.

Malcolm would often say we should do this or that and I'd openly question him, saying that's okay, but why don't we try this? That was symptomatic of the open dressing room we had at City under Joe and Malcolm, and the results speak for themselves. But, and there's always a but, you know the old song? You never know what you've got till it's gone.

Chapter Ten

County Lines – It's Swales In, Lee Out!

WHEN I was at my lowest ebb, with the very real threat to my business, I needed a break from playing and I did ask Malcolm for one … but it barely came. I was top scorer throughout my period at City after I returned from Mexico, with the exception of 1972/73 when my seasonal total was bettered by Rodney Marsh.

I played in 52 City games in the season after the 1970 World Cup, scoring 20; I clocked up 47 appearances in our cliffhanger 1971/72 season and hit my career-best 35 goals in all competitions; in 1972/73 – when I was close to being consumed by my off-the-field problems – I grabbed 17 goals in 45 games (Rodney got 19), and in my last full season, 1973/74, I notched 18 goals from 44 games. So, I make it that I was averaging 47 games per season and bagging an average of more than 22 goals … not bad for someone who, for some of that time, was having a nervous breakdown while battling with business problems and taking the odd drink.

The new season began with a significant boardroom change. Eric Alexander, the son of the former chairman, stood down, with vice-chairman Peter Swales set to take the chair in October. Johnny Hart led us into the pre-season, with United legend Denis Law – who'd played for City back in 1960/61 – welcomed back to Maine Road from our neighbours. Johnny insisted Denis hadn't been signed as a stand-in and, as things turned out, he played 30 times and got himself a dozen goals, so I guess he was right. But Johnny was not right in taking the job and it was not the right move for the club to put him in the frame. It wasn't long before his health began to suffer.

I didn't seem to be flavour of the month when the season began under Johnny Hart. I started in the team, but I was then hooked in a 1-1 draw at Stoke. I was then on the bench for the visit of Coventry and came on for the injured Alan Oakes and won us a penalty. I stepped aside for Rodney – who'd been on the transfer list, then off again after Malcolm's departure – to wrap up the points from the penalty spot.

That was followed by a 2-1 win over Norwich with goals from myself and Colin Bell, but then we went down 2-1 in a swift rematch with Coventry. Inconsistency again. We rode our luck in a 1-1 draw at Leicester before I bagged a couple (one a pen) in a better performance at home to Chelsea, winning 3-2.

Then followed an awful 3-0 away defeat at Burnley, after which Johnny decided we needed a new goalkeeper. Big Joe had a sticky night in goal at Turf Moor and, years later, he recounted the experience that night:

> Mike Doyle controlled a cross and played the ball back to me, but the pass didn't have enough pace and, as the Burnley striker slid in, the ball went under my body … I didn't see Mike Doyle run to the manager's dugout, where he let it be known in no uncertain terms what he thought of me as a keeper and as a man.
>
> Afterwards, Ken Barnes told me Doyley had asked, 'What's that fat bastard doing in goals for us?' It left me feeling cold towards Mike for a number of years.

Harsh? Perhaps, but I've made my own feelings plain about the cost City paid for not having a really top-class keeper in those key years. Joe still had time and eventually he would truly emerge, although he'd already been in and around the team since 1970. Anyway, Johnny splashed £100,000 on Keith MacRae from Motherwell, after Ron Healey had initially been drafted in to deputise again.

Our first home defeat of the season came on 27 October, with a 1-0 loss against Leeds United. It was a good battle, in front of 45,000, but we could find no answer to a late Mick Bates goal. And that, as it turned out, was that for Johnny Hart. He stepped down for health reasons and Tony Book, with new chairman Peter Swales backing him, stepped up as caretaker manager on the understanding that Johnny may return after a spell of recuperation. Tony was still part of the playing squad at this point, though he'd turned 40 that September. Now he was in charge ... at least for the time being.

Walsall had been a bit of a League Cup nuisance but, after Tony took over, we finally put them to the sword 4-0 in a second-round, second replay at Old Trafford. The country was in the grip of power cuts with energy workers and miners on strike, but we finally found a spark. All the goals came in the second half, and I helped myself to a hat-trick, including two penalties, with Colin Bell getting the other. We made further progress in the League Cup, winning at Carlisle, but in the league we then lost 2-1 at Ipswich and that signalled the end of Booky's spell in charge.

Johnny Hart, however, wasn't returning. Instead, chairman Swales announced the appointment of Ron Saunders as our new manager, plucked from Norwich City. To say it was a change from the tactical acumen of Malcolm would be an understatement. Ron's approach was, shall I say, much more basic, and it didn't win many admirers in the dressing room. Even so, we immediately beat York in a League Cup fourth-round replay. Ron had ordered extra training on his appointment, and I wonder if that struck a chord with Rodney Marsh? Anyway, Rod responded with a hat-trick and I tucked away a penalty in our 4-1 win. I then scored in a 2-1 defeat in the league at West Ham, offset by a 2-0 win at White Hart Lane.

We bagged a 2-2 draw at Coventry in the League Cup and then, welcoming old boss Joe Mercer back home for the replay, we romped it 4-2 in the Maine Road mud – all our goals in the second half coming courtesy of a couple from yours truly (one pen!) and one each for Mike 'Buzzer' Summerbee and Denis Law. The midweek match kicked off at lunchtime because of power rationing and we had to be at our best to overcome opponents who were twice in front. That put us into the semi-finals, but our league form just continued to stutter.

Our League Cup run gave us some respite from the league and a chance of silverware once again. We claimed a 1-1 draw down at Plymouth in the first leg of our semi-final. The return game went as anyone would expect, a 2-0 home win put us into a Wembley final once again. Colin Bell got our second to wrap it up with a neat lob but, for me, it was a good start to the game but not a brilliant ending. I put us ahead in the tenth minute with a right-foot drive. But

I ended it with ligament damage to my left knee after a bad tackle by Colin Sullivan, who was booked. I said at the time that I'd have been okay … had Sullivan played the ball!

I missed a goalless draw at home to Spurs, a 1-0 home win against Derby and then a good 2-0 away win at Southampton … leaving just a week to go before the League Cup Final at Wembley. Would I make it? Few expected me to, especially after Ron Saunders complained that I was lucky not to have had my leg broken by that Sullivan tackle. But I did make it to Wembley.

I put my ability to shake off injuries to my family genes. I seemed to be naturally resilient. You're either resilient to physical breakdown or you're not – and we all know plenty of players who are weak in that respect. Maybe it comes from my grandfather on my mum's side, Henry Tonge – he was a wrestler, and he was pretty tough. Perhaps I've got him to thank for both my middle name and my resilience.

I could be kicked in the back of the leg and I wouldn't have a bruise for four or five days. Some players get a whack on the ankle, and it's like a balloon straight away and they bleed easily internally. I was lucky in that I've really only had three significant injuries – all were to my knee medial ligaments, such as this one before Wembley 1974. They're not the most catastrophic knee injuries, and all were caused by bad tackles, not something that I could have avoided.

They were impact injuries rather than strains or pulls; in fact, I never once pulled a muscle.

So it was I lined up in this side to face Wolves at Wembley:

> **Manchester City:** MacRae, Pardoe, Doyle, Booth, Donachie, Summerbee, Bell, Towers, Lee, Law, Marsh. Sub: Carrodus.

There wasn't much in the first half, although Alan Sunderland smacked a shot off a post for Wolves. And they nicked the lead just before the break when Kenny Hibbitt's mishit shot looped over Keith MacRae. We had much more possession and got back on terms when Rodney found Colin Bell with a lovely cross and Belly had more time than Big Ben to stroke in the equaliser. We had numerous chances after that – young keeper Gary Pierce had a fine game for Wolves. Belly saw one shot come crashing down off the bar – before a deflected cross from Sunderland fell kindly to John Richards, who knocked in their 85th-minute winner.

Defeat hurt. It hurt me, because I'm a winner; it hurt Rodney Marsh, who was criticised for walking off the pitch and to the dressing rooms ahead of the trophy presentation to Wolves; and it hurt Colin Bell, who years later disclosed the discontent in our camp under Saunders:

> Despite all the changes that had been made off the field, we expected to beat Wolves. Ron Saunders' approach to the big game was very different than it had been under Joe and Malcolm. Ron was much stricter in his approach, and we weren't allowed to drink alcohol during the build-up to the game, not even a glass of wine with our meals. It wasn't as much fun as it had been under Malcolm. It was the only time in my career that I wasn't happy as a player at City.

I'd say amen to that.

Well, we might not have been celebrating after the game, and Saunders may have clamped down on us having a snifter in the days before it, but I didn't see any reason why the Wolves boys should be denied. We'd won their respect, it turned out, for lining up on the Wembley pitch and applauding captain Mike Bailey and his side as they picked up the trophy. After all that, I decided to nip round to deliver some champagne to the celebratory party they had organised at a London club.

Their winger Dave Wagstaffe – a former City player – seemed to appreciate those gestures. He said later:

> That [City's applause pitch-side] was great. Wonderful. If you looked at our team, none

> of us had ever won anything. Even Derek Dougan! I think City were saying 'well done'. We really appreciated that. It meant a lot and said something about City.
>
> That night we celebrated at a club after the formal dinner and Franny Lee walked in with bottles of champagne. He gave them to us and said well done. It was a great gesture and said a lot about him and City at that time.

I like to think it did say a lot. Just as Belly's remarks and Rodney's actions said much about our own disappointment and dissatisfaction with both the result and life under Ron Saunders. It was not to last much longer.

Before we'd even got to Wembley, our league roller coaster was mirrored in the FA Cup. We'd beaten Oxford in the third round, only to exit the competition – in the club's inaugural Sunday fixture at the City Ground – with our collars being felt in a 4-1 thumping by Second Division Nottingham Forest. Serious questions were being asked about all of us, and our new manager, after that one.

That was all before the League Cup Final. After Wolves' win, we followed that with a 1-0 defeat at Leeds. Things were not looking good at all, so Ron rolled the dice with a deal worth £200,000 as he signed two of Sunderland's 1973 FA Cup winners, winger Dennis Tueart and midfielder

Micky Horswill, with Tony Towers the part-exchange makeweight.

There was no immediate uplift. Even a derby – which I missed – with United at Maine Road reflected the dour mood, a 0-0 draw with Mike Doyle sent off. A 2-0 defeat at Arsenal, with me back in the side, came next. That was a night when keeper Bob Wilson stopped everything we threw at him … and a bit more besides! We managed to average a point a game against Newcastle, Wolves and Everton before two awful results led to the inevitable. We lost to Ipswich at Maine Road, 3-1, and I was missing again, before we went down 3-0 at QPR. I was back in the side at Loftus Road … and probably wished that I wasn't.

Peter Swales had to admit his own mistake. Ron had only started work in December and now, before the season was over, Swales took the decision to fire him. The fans didn't like him much, nor did we, the players. Mike Doyle later recalled Saunders's instruction: 'Listen, I don't want my back four to play football. If you get the ball, just lump it forward and we'll go from there!'

Right-o, Ron! From the progressive coaching of Malcolm Allison under Joe Mercer – and then Malcolm on his own – we were being told to 'lump it forward'! Swales explained his huge cock-up this way: 'Ron may be the victim of a bad decision I have made. He came here to do a job and we changed our minds about the course he should take. He tried to do a particular type of job which has not gone down well with the players.'

Player power? Of course it was. Swales knew how we felt. But would Saunders have been sacked had his methods worked? As ever, managers live or die by results and his results were awful – as was his style of man-management. Saunders bemoaned a lack of support from the man who'd appointed him. He left feeling let down by Swales and walked away 'amazed, shocked, humiliated and very disillusioned'. Pretty much the full house there, Ron.

For Swales, it was back to square one with the man he first turned to when Johnny Hart fell ill – Tony Book. He was made manager permanently this time, and Swales was no doubt more confident he could control affairs with Tony in the manager's office.

The press noted the return of our swagger post-Saunders as we drew 1-1 at home with championship-chasing Liverpool. I'd bagged our equaliser, reacting smartly to Keith MacRae's long clearance. The return at Anfield was not so clever, City going down 4-0, all their goals coming in a blitzkrieg opening 35 minutes. We bounced back, though, to end our Maine Road campaign with a 2-1 win over West Ham. That just left a final game for us at Old Trafford. It was another derby with United now struggling and, incredibly, staring relegation in the face.

This was to be one of the most memorable derbies of this era because of the ramifications. United were in a mess. Post-Sir Matt Busby, post-Wilf McGuinness, post-Frank O'Farrell and now post-George Best. The odds of them beating the drop were stacked against them: they had to beat us and hope either Birmingham or West Ham would lose their final game. The fact that we ended up winning – and that Denis Law, of all people, got our winner with a cheeky backheel – was immaterial, as both United's rivals won their games. The derby was actually abandoned after Denis's 82nd-minute goal sparked a nasty crowd invasion. Belly had run forward from halfway and fed me on the edge of the box; I ran from left to right and then turned to hit the ball across the six-yard line, where the Lawman became the villain of the Old Trafford peace with a typical bit of opportunism.

On came the angry United fans, but if they thought they'd get the game replayed, they could forget it. The result stood and United were relegated. Denis was distraught afterwards. He said it was the worst result for him since England won the World Cup! But United's demise was not his doing. Even so, he cut a miserable figure in our dressing room afterwards.

So, the season ended with us in a disappointing 14th place; I top-scored again with 18 goals from 44 games across all competitions. Not bad but, as I was soon to discover, not good enough for the new chairman, Swales, and his new manager, Book. My playing days at City were already numbered.

Swales decided he wanted to go on our end-of-season trip in 1974. I'm sure he thought it was a nice way to mark his first season as chairman. Tony Book was there, of course, as our new manager. Tony had been at the helm for just a couple of weeks, from 12 April until the league season ended against United on 27 April. Tony told us we had three friendly games – go out and win them and we could have some fun. Well, we did win all three – including one against Greece's top club side, Panathinaikos, who'd got to the European Cup Final in 1971, with the Hungarian legend Ferenc Puskás as their manager.

We beat them easily – it was 5-0 if memory serves, and we went for a night out with Puskás ... 'Buzzer', me and Marshy. There was a banquet after the game and then we went out with the great man, he was everyone's hero. This was the guy who'd been part of Hungary's 'Magnificent Magyars' who humbled England both home (6-3) and away (7-1) back in 1953. He was also an integral part of Real Madrid's great 1950s side that dominated the early years of the European Cup.

Puskás said to us, 'I can't stand these fucking Greek players! They can't play football and they can't fucking drink either ... and while we're on the subject, I think you've cost me my job. I reckon I'm going to be sacked!'

Swales came over while there was a row going on in the room next to us. There were chalets in the grounds and Swales was going mad. He was upset about not having had a special car sent for him to the airport and all this nonsense. Anyway, we went out for a good night and rolled up back at the hotel at five or six o'clock in the morning. We went to our rooms, got out of our gear and had a swim and a lounge about. The next day was the last day of the trip, so we decided to have a players' dinner. We told Booky he could come along, and we extended the offer to Ken Barnes, who was the assistant manager, and to the physio. Swales said he would come along with another director, too. Sure enough, we were at our boisterous best!

We were taking wine and it was a real boozy do. I think someone was taking notes, certainly mental notes. And I'm sure that after that dinner Swales said to Book that he had to 'get rid of Lee and Summerbee', because we apparently had too much influence on the players. I'm pretty sure that's what happened. We'd gone from a talented but indulgent coach in Malcolm Allison to a season of confused leadership. First Johnny Hart, followed by Booky in caretaker charge and then the disciplined clampdown of Ron Saunders, before the return of Book in the final days of the campaign. Is it any wonder we wanted to let our hair down when the shackles of the league season were off and we were on a summer tour?

We then went into the close season, and one day Booky rang me. I knew something was up. I'd been tipped off that Manchester United, desperate to get back into the top flight, wanted to buy me. I was coming out of contract, and I'd just turned 30 a couple of days after the United derby game. By now my business was doing well again, and I thought, *If I'm going to play on for another two seasons, I want a good contract.* I told Booky that if he wanted me to sign, I'd have to have a rise. I was in a good place. My company had recovered, and I knew I was still pretty much on top of my game and that I had admirers at other clubs. But Book turned around and told me there was no one interested in me. Shades of Bolton?

'Don't give me that,' I told him. I also let him know that I knew Manchester United wanted to buy me and he asked how I could possibly know that. I told him I'd been around to the home of a big, influential United fan, Paddy McGrath, three weeks earlier. With the blessing of the United directors, we sorted out what I was going to get paid and everything else in the proposed offer. Book said he had no knowledge of anything like that, so I told him that the board may not have disclosed it to him yet. Then he hit me with it. He told me City had received an offer from Derby County to sign me.

'Oh, I'm not interested,' I said. 'It's too far to travel for my business.' This was Tony Book, my old team-mate, who I'd lived and played with for six years. I'd have stayed if City had looked after me with a good new contract. I reckoned someone else was pulling the strings and I told him straight: 'Anyway, I don't believe you want to sell me – it's the chairman, isn't it?'

Book simply replied, 'I didn't say that.'

Then he said that he'd given Dave Mackay, the Derby manager, permission to speak to me. So, I did speak to him. And I told Dave the same thing … I didn't want to travel that far, and he said that if I signed, he believed Derby County could win the league. He'd only recently taken over from Brian Clough, who'd built a terrific, championship-winning team there.

The other thing key to my departure was that City were trying to sign Asa Hartford, and they just didn't have the money.

Worse, when it was obvious I was to leave, City made me train with the kids at a school sports ground – they didn't have their own training ground then – and the trainer, Dave Ewing, said to me, 'Well done, son, you've done all right for us since you've been here.'

I couldn't believe what I'd just heard. 'Done all right?' I demanded. 'Done all right? We've won the league championship, won the FA Cup, won the League Cup and the Cup Winners' Cup … and we've done all right? Fuck me, hang on.'

I'd had some great years at City, the best of my career. But when they want you to go, you go. Yes, I was more than a bit sad but that was offset by my determination to look forward to a fresh challenge at Derby. I wanted to do well for them. Then the rest of the players trooped in, and I told them I was off to Derby County. They all wished me well; I was mates with them and pretty popular. But I made sure that I left them with something to think about.

'Before I go, just one thing …' I told them. 'Why, having won the league title in my first season six years ago, and all those other trophies we've won, are we still training on a school playing field? After the success we've had, we should have a purpose-built facility with big letters etched in gold … Manchester City Training Ground. Do you know why we haven't got that? Because this club has been run badly all the time we've been here – and it will be run badly going forward. This club will never go anywhere.'

Those were my parting words to them. And apart from the 1976 League Cup Final win a couple of years later, those words were the truth. City was a badly run club and the glory days were over. They did absolutely nothing – for many decades!

Chapter Eleven

Derby Success – and It's Looking Good on Paper!

BACK IN those simpler, pre-Premier League days of the 1970s, there wasn't the same clamour to amass suitcases of mighty dollars by playing in pre-season Stateside tours or Asian Cups against multiple teams. Instead, there was modest stuff like the Anglo-Italian Cup to get our rested limbs toned and ready for the proper action to come. Before I waved goodbye to Manchester City, I actually started the 1974/75 campaign in City's blue shirt for the mighty Texaco Cup, a pot put up by the petrol company for a slice of curtain-raising action.

We had three games, two away at Blackpool and Sheffield United, and one at home to Oldham. We drew the first, 1-1, and I played in that one with Dennis Tueart scoring; the Sheffield United game was lost 4-2 and I sat that one out with the Derby move imminent. That left Oldham at Maine Road, on Saturday, 10 August 1974.

It's worth noting that Oldham game, as I scored in a 2-1 win – Dennis Tueart getting the other – that this proved to be my last game in a City shirt. The rain lashed down before the game and there were only 13,880 present. Oldham had just been promoted as Third Division champions and they gave us quite a game, taking the lead through Alan Groves early on. We got it back to 1-1 when Dennis poked in a Rodney Marsh cross, but it was nip and tuck after that. Still, I made my mark ... even if my goal came in the last minute!

I'm not sure how many of that small band of City faithful stayed to the end to see it. I burst through the middle and fired in a crisp, low shot. That was it, my Manchester City career was over. It also turned out to be Denis Law's last game, too. He'd been substituted in the second half after another knock. His heart wasn't in it any longer and he announced his retirement shortly afterwards.

Exactly a week later I'd be in a Derby County shirt at Goodison Park, making my debut for them against Everton as the league season got underway. Guess what happened first? Yes, City got their man and signed Asa Hartford for more than £200,000 from West Brom. It was an open secret that Tony Book wanted him. Asa had multiple medical checks before the deal went through, just days after that Oldham game. That's because he'd had a 1971 transfer called off by Leeds when it was discovered he had a hole-in-the-heart condition. In fairness, it never seemed to affect Asa's playing career. Tests completed, Asa signed even though City couldn't afford him!

How could they do that? Easy, flog me to Derby for £110,000 and then winger Frank Carrodus was shipped out to Aston Villa for £95,000 – job done, books balanced. Frank had been in and around the team for about four years and, when I'd recovered in time to play in the 1974 League Cup Final a few months earlier, Frank was the unlucky guy to miss out. He linked up again with Ron Saunders at Villa.

Rodney Marsh, for one, wasn't impressed by my departure. In his book, *Priceless*, Rodney claimed that my sale was one of many Tony Book 'cock-ups' and he added: 'Book didn't just shoot himself in the foot, he almost blew City's legs off.' If Swales hadn't told Booky to sell me and Summerbee – because Buzzer would follow me out of the door less than a year later – I'm sure City would have won the league title in that 1974/75 season. Instead, Derby – with me in their team – won it instead!

City clearly wanted Hartford, and Booky obviously wanted a midfielder, above all else, at that time. But just a few months later they also went and bought Joe Royle from Everton. Now, as I've said, I like playing off a big centre-forward and I both knew and liked Joe. We had been squad-mates with England in Mexico in 1970. I'm sure that had I played with Joe, for City, I could have done really well with him. He'd have been great to play off.

That was all hypothetical now; I was at the Baseball Ground. Yet before the transfer was sealed, it seemed as though Nottingham Forest were coming in with a late bid. It was academic in the end, as Forest wouldn't have been so amenable to my continuing to live in the North West and, anyway, I quite fancied County's chances. Derby had finished third the previous season, even if they were a distant third behind champions Leeds and runners-up Liverpool. Dave reckoned they needed to improve their ratio of away wins. If they could do that, he told me, the league title would be within Derby's grasp.

I made my Derby County debut on 17 August against Everton, and Roger Davies, Derby's tall striker, was playing centre-forward. He started dribbling about and rolling the ball under his foot. I said to him, 'Roger, if you're going to dribble it, and lose it, do it in their fucking penalty area and not down here in our half.' I liked to put a marker down.

We drew 0-0 at Goodison and Dave said to me on the Monday, 'What d'you think?' I said that I knew why they didn't win away from home. I told him they weren't playing the ball into feet when someone was marked. I also told him that if they played me at centre-forward, marked or unmarked, I'd get the ball and set it up from there – without losing possession. So, Dave changed it there and then. I was moved to centre-forward and played there all season, much as I'd done at City, and I had a really good season for them, scoring 16 goals, 12 of them in the league.

But don't get me wrong, Roger was a very good player on his day, and he could do amazing things. He scored as many league goals as me – including all five in our 5-0 home win over Luton, in March. Yet I recall an incident early in the season when the ball was played across the box and it should have resulted in us scoring. I was running away from goal and backheeled the ball across the area. The ball flashed between the goalkeeper and Roger – he didn't get a touch and it ran out of play to groans from the crowd. At half-time he said, 'For Christ sake, don't make a **** out of me – the fans had a go all last season!' We weren't always on the same wavelength.

We were, though, a very good team and I fitted in straight away, just as I had at City after leaving Bolton. I slotted seamlessly into the Derby team. It was the same with my England career, where you have limited time to impress. So, you have to take your chance after a transfer … and fit in. And I did just that at the Baseball Ground. Derby shared the goals around. Kevin Hector up top got 13, too, in the league. Plenty came from midfield, where Bruce Rioch weighed in with an impressive 15. By the time the league season finished, we ran out as the First Division's most attack-minded side – and that was where our strength lay. It was a bit like City at their best when I was there. We were confident we could outscore anyone we faced.

Truth is, though, we hardly looked like champions material when the season got underway. That first game at Everton was a goalless shut-out and we followed that with another point – and I got off the mark – in a 1-1 draw at home to Coventry, my first goal at the Baseball Ground. In our first seven league games, we'd chalked up only one win, a 2-0 home victory over Sheffield United. It was not *yet* the stuff of champions.

But then we managed a 3-2 win at home to Burnley and we settled down. Three more wins in a run of five games unbeaten saw us roll into some real form. The last of that five saw me hit both goals in a 2-0 win at Sheffield United. Even so, the form was decent but inconsistent, and by the time we lost 1-0 at Luton on 21 December, we were tenth in the table. Whatever Dave Mackay said, or maybe it was having a nice Christmas Day celebration, we emerged from the holiday with two handy 2-1 victories, the first at home to Birmingham on Boxing Day, before I made the emotional trip to my old stamping ground – Maine Road – two days later.

I'd been looking forward to this Yuletide treat and, had I consulted old Will Shakespeare through a seance, it couldn't have been better scripted. City had plenty of the ball, more than us, but we got our noses in front midway through the first half when Henry Newton's volley hit the target. City had league aspirations of their own and they put us under pressure, finally getting an equaliser on 62 minutes when Asa Hartford and Rodney Marsh combined to set up Colin Bell to hammer the ball in.

Cue delight at Maine Road and they revelled in it for all of 90 seconds. And then I had my say! I reacted first to a ball played forward by David Nish and I cut in from the left wing, beat two or three blue shirts and then let fly from more than 20 yards. It screamed beyond Joe Corrigan and inside his left-hand post, just under the bar. Fantastic!

BBC's *Match of the Day* Barry Davies's commentary still gets a run-out on YouTube today. As I turned, 30 yards out, to run towards the area, Barry said: 'Interesting …' and then, as the ball left my right boot, '… very interesting!' Barry paused and picked up the mic again as I wheeled away beaming with a huge grin: 'Oh! Look at his face, just *look* at his face!' The City fans *were* looking and, bless them, I know that they joined in my celebrations. It was a cracking goal, one of my career highlights, and my smile just betrayed my love for the game at that very moment.

City were beaten and, after the game, the press pack wanted to talk to the prodigal son, back to haunt his old employers. Of course they did. I was chatting to the press boys when Tony Book's new assistant manager, Ian

MacFarlane, showed his face. I couldn't resist asking a question to which I already knew the answer: 'Will it be all right if I come in tomorrow for some treatment on my knee, Ian?' Ian, who could curdle milk if he wanted to, was nice as pie: 'Certainly, Franny. I'll fix that for you.'

No fixing required, actually. Part of the terms of my move to Derby was an understanding that I could go into City for treatment. I was also able to train there for part of the week. This was all thrashed out when I was telling both Tony Book and Dave Mackay that I didn't want to travel to the East Midlands because of my business commitments in the Lancashire area. That was a clause that would have an interesting postscript.

Sure enough, I went into City on the Sunday morning, after helping my Derby team to beat them. I'd got a kick on my left knee, but I really went in to have a bit of a laugh with the lads. The physio, Freddie Griffiths, who could be a bit of a so and so, said, 'You've got a bit of a nerve coming in here after yesterday.' I told him it was all part of my agreement – and that he should grow up! It was finished, the game was over. Get over it. But perhaps they didn't or couldn't get over it. Because I was told a short while later – and it came from Swales – that I wasn't to go there for treatment again. I had to go to nearby Bury's Gigg Lane instead! That was the story's postscript, with a sting in it.

That was typical of how City was run. If the club had been run right, with United having just been relegated, the world would have been City's oyster that season. United's and City's gates were very similar at that time, and it could have been a very different story for City had they been able to kick on.

As it happened, my new team were far superior. We won the Football League title with 53 points, two clear of Liverpool, with Bobby Robson's Ipswich third. It was City holding Ipswich to a draw on the penultimate Saturday that helped tie things up – we drew with Leicester on the same day. City? They were down in eighth place, seven points adrift.

In the FA and League Cups, we never really got out of second gear (crashing out to Southampton in the League Cup third round and later going out in the FA Cup fifth round against Leeds) but we enjoyed better luck in the UEFA Cup with a couple of decent wins against Servette and Atlético Madrid before we went out to Velež Mostar.

It didn't really matter, I was a Football League champion again – this time with Dave Mackay's very good Derby side, and I was in a very good place.

Certainly, my business was on the up. After the earlier horrors of my partner, Peter James's treachery, I was optimistic again. The lorries belonging to my new company, F.H. Lee, in their City-inspired blue-and-white livery, were a constant reminder to everyone that I'd moved on beyond James. It had been tough, but I'd succeeded in not allowing that devious man to bring me down. The recovery had started as soon as I could find a way forward. I'd discovered the full severity of my situation from our company accountant, Alf Gill, after that awful showdown. And I had to act.

I needed an immediate buffer, a breathing space. I went to see my bank manager, Tom Barker, and asked for a £10,000 overdraft. I told him I didn't want to take anything out of the business for myself and I explained we had a few problems – but that we could get through it. He listened, he understood and, thankfully, he agreed to do it. But he warned me that he'd never have done it had I still been involved with my old partner.

What I needed to tie down now was a market for F. H. Lee's products. When I targeted VG (remember the old VG food stores?), Hallmark, Makro and the big cash and carry operators, I went in for high-quality recycled Scandinavian paper. I'd started making brand-leader-quality products for private labels – the store's in-house own-brands, if you like.

Everybody could supply the own-brand private-label products in those days. You had the top-drawer products, such as Andrex and Kleenex at the top of the range, and then the private-label alternatives, which were very much bottom of the range, poor standard and off-colour – not nice, inferior-quality stuff. There was a big gap between these two types of products. I could spot a gap in the market, and I intended to fill it.

The big producers, such as Bowater-Scott and Kimberley-Clark, didn't want own-brand stuff to catch on in the shops, but I could see that gap. I could fill that gap with my low overheads, offering high-quality, own-brand products. That's what I did … I provided good-quality, own-brands for the supermarkets, and the retailers loved them. The supermarkets could bang the brand leaders on their heads with their own range, a quality range at that.

My overheads were low. We didn't need a managing director, because I did that; nor did we need a sales director, because I did all my own big deals. And I ploughed the money back into the business, so we had the best equipment, the best converting machinery producing the finest finished product.

I've always had that desire to be very successful. Two things inspired me. Firstly, my school principal, Mr L.G. King, saying, 'I think you are a complete fool,' when I told him I saw a future for myself in football; and secondly, my Bolton boss, Bill Ridding, who said, 'When all comes to all, you are just a bloody road digger.' He liked to put me down when I stood my corner on pay, his inference being that if I didn't have football, I'd just be an unskilled navvy. I was determined to prove them wrong. I *did* prove them wrong.

We invested in new plant and then I moved into a new factory, in Parrott Street, Bolton. When my brother, Arthur, first saw it, he nearly fell over. He couldn't believe it. 'Too fucking big,' he said. I told him, if we kept expanding, we'd soon fill it, but he said it was four times the size we needed.

'I want nothing to do with it,' said Arthur.

'Too late for that, I've just bought it,' I replied.

Arthur thought for a moment, then said, 'Oh, right, we'd better make a go of it then!'

Sainsbury's was my next target. I started making their private labels. They'd been hamstrung by the big-name firms, who refused to make them a decent private-label product. Mine were high-quality … and profits took off.

I then had some problems meeting the demand, partly owing to the success of my strategy, because I was snowed under with supermarkets wanting me to make their private labels. Safeway wanted in, a big deal with Sainsbury's, a bit for Tesco – only because they wanted to take my stuff to their supplier and demand the same quality. But the brand leaders were quite smart, they knew I didn't have the capacity to do everything that was being demanded. I was allowed to grow, and my profits rocketed.

From 1972 when I was virtually bankrupt and on skid row, up to 1980 the business was turning over something in the order of £20 million and making £2.5 million profit. And we were cash-rich all the time because we turned over the product so quickly and all our machinery was paid for. We paid for the machinery in cash and got big discounts, and the gear was never mortgaged. We also got good discounts on the paper we used because we were good payers.

By 1985, newly divorced from my first wife, Jean, and with my two children, Gary and Charlotte to take care of, I needed to raise money to help pay for that divorce. But nothing is straightforward – especially in the world of business.

I was doing great business with Sainsbury's at this time. I was making them a product that was worth 18,000 cases a week at £5 a case, or £90,000 weekly – £360,000 a month on one product! It was very high-quality recycled paper. At this time, I was negotiating to sell the business to Hazlewoods Foods to help pay for my divorce and, in the middle of this, Tim Sainsbury, who had just become an MP, told the Conservative Party that he'd do his best to solve some of the problems in Northern Ireland by getting some of Sainsbury's company business into the province … and there was a paper mill in Larne. They took my £360,000 a month business with them – nearly £5 million a year – and gave it to Larne Paper Mill. Christ!

I was blissfully unaware of all that politicking when Sainsbury's called me to see them. I thought I was going to get a pat on the back; this was going to mean still more business for F.H. Lee. We were doing facial tissues for them, cling film and other products. I was struggling to imagine what else they possibly had in mind for us.

So, I got into the meeting with them. We were told, 'We brought you here today to tell you that we won't be needing your own-label economy lines, your toilet tissue and kitchen towels.'

'What?' I demanded.

All I got back was, 'It's a corporate management decision.'

I asked if it was a question of quality. Was it price? I knew it couldn't be price. Was it service? No, none of those … all were top class. So, what was it? 'I can't tell you, it is a corporate management decision' came the by now stock reply.

I walked out of Sainsbury's London offices with my sales director, Vic Gaunt, and continued over a bridge with the river Thames beneath my feet. Vic was a few years older than me, but he was thunderstruck too. I turned to him – and he knew nothing about my proposed deal with Hazlewoods – and I told him that I felt like diving over the wall and into the river. He said I'd get over it, but Vic knew nothing about the upcoming sale of my company. I did tell him that losing Sainsbury's business could mean us making 35 staff redundant unless we could replace the business. But I really did – for a moment – feel like ending it all. Sometimes, however, the darkest storm clouds can have a silver lining. So it proved.

Just a week later I was flying down to London on the Manchester shuttle, and I found myself sitting next to a guy who asked me how I was. He was a City fan, and he told me how much he'd enjoyed watching me play. We got on to talking business and I told him what I was up to. He turned and said, 'One of my pals is on the board at Safeway, why don't you see him. He'd be worth seeing.'

He gave me his card with an intro to his friend and I later made the call. He invited me to see him after I'd told him about the better-quality, private-label work we did. Safeway were supplied by Kimberley-Clark from their plant at Larkfield in Kent. Off I went. We discussed what he wanted; the quantities, whether or not we could do six-packs, and the upshot was very good indeed. I got *all* of Safeway's own-label business.

I was also the first to do printed kitchen towels. They'd never been done before with printed patterns on the towels, because union rules then meant you couldn't have printers in a paper mill ... the unions SOGAT and NATSOPA would never have agreed to that. But my place was non-union, and I could do it. I was the best printer of kitchen towels and we did very, very well with them.

But then I got a call from Peter Barr, the chairman of Hazlewoods, who could be very stern, and he wanted to see me. It was about the upcoming deal. I went to see him at their HQ in Derby and when we met, he said, 'You didn't tell me about this Sainsbury business.'

He knew all about how we'd lost £390,000 a month of their business. Why had I not declared it? I told him I had a surprise for him, and then revealed that I had the Safeway business. It was worth more, and at a better margin, than the Sainsbury's deal. I also told him that I felt the Sainsbury's business might end up returning to us down the line.

And so it was that I sold my business to Hazlewoods Food in 1985. They gave me £8.5 million for the business, and they gave me an earn-out agreement … for every £1 I earned over the next three years, they'd give me £3 back. What then followed were three very successful years so that, in the end, I probably got between £12 million and £14 million for the company. I'd also taken a third of my money in Hazlewood shares and became, along with the chairman, the biggest private individual shareholder in the Hazlewood business. When we eventually sold Hazlewoods in 2000, it was a £1 billion-turnover company with 40 companies and 10,000 employees. We sold it to an Irish company, Greencore.

I like to think I looked after the people who worked for me. Former Conservative leader Iain Duncan Smith, a few years back, insisted that employers must give everyone a pension fund. I was doing this four decades ago. When an employee had completed 12 months with us, the company gave them seven per cent of their wages, tax-free, to put into a pension fund – the employee could put in what they wanted.

People like my old mate Freddie Hill, who worked for us for about 15 years – well, he came into the building, I'm not sure how much he worked! He got his state pension of £120 a week and something from the ex-players' provident fund. But the F.H. Lee pension fund, where he worked for those 14 or 15 years, paid about £225 a week. And he was delighted with it. We ran a good scheme.

I also had my mate and all-round legend Denis Law work for us for a while. He was in 'sales' – well, if a bloke with the aura of Denis couldn't work a bit of magic or open a few doors, who could? Another ex-player who was on our books for a while was my old Derby County and horse-racing pal Rod Thomas.

I even had thoughts of building company houses, delusions of grandeur perhaps, and I then went off the idea. But we treated our people very well. Despite that, I had my battles with the unions, especially SOGAT, the Society of Graphical and Allied Trades. We worked a 37-hour week against the union agreement of 42. And we paid a higher basic rate than the union's pay agreement. All our conditions were better than those the union had struck.

So, it was ludicrous that they tried to black us, just because we were a non-union workplace. They tried to stop our suppliers, because we had no union membership. We opened the canteen to the unions once every 18 months and they could petition the employees to join the union, but our workers just walked out. The union thought it was a conspiracy with us threatening our people that they'd be out if they joined the union – but it wasn't, so that was completely wrong.

I travelled down to London to meet Bill Keys, general secretary of SOGAT, a couple of times. I went into this room in a hotel they used near Russell Square and there were five guys sitting there around this table, all of them smoking and looking pleased with themselves. They quizzed me about our hours, our hourly pay rate and our overtime rates. I told them the facts.

'How many? How much? What rate?'... they wanted to know. Then they asked if I could prove my figures! I had the documents to prove my case – complete with National Insurance numbers – and Bill Keys took it all in. Meanwhile all his lieutenants, with florid faces, sat back and looked like they were waistcoated parasites, waiting for lunchtime to get stuck into the booze. Keys said, 'Right, I've got the story. This is all genuine is it, son?' I told him it certainly was and that I wanted to pacify him – not anger him! He got on the phone to the SOGAT Bury chapel (the print trade's name for a branch) and discussed my case, and how my production was threatened by the blacking of supplies to my company.

Keys ended it by thundering into the receiver, 'Have you gone fucking mad? This guy is doing exactly what we're aiming for – in fact, he is at a level that we'll never get to in the next ten years and it's twats like you wasting your time by blacking him and fucking him about. Why don't you get your job done properly – otherwise you'll be out of a job!'

Then Keys turned to me and said, 'There you are, is that all right for you, son?' I said it most certainly was and he promised me the ban would be lifted in five minutes. By the time I found a phone to call my office, the ban had indeed been lifted. I was impressed by Keys, a Second World War veteran who stood no nonsense. He dealt with it brilliantly, but I wouldn't have liked to have been against him with a poorer hand.

So, this was all in the background of my football life … my business recovering, from being on the floor to prospering and then its eventual sale making me millions. That dividend was long in the future. I was a champion with Derby County in 1975 and still had a football career to conclude!

We were in the European Cup, as league champions, and we had that First Division title to defend. We gave it a go but weren't quite able to reach the consistency of 1974/75. It began well enough with two away draws at Sheffield United and Coventry but then the wheels came off in our first home game, thrashed 5-1 by QPR, who were a very good side in the mid-70s. We then came from behind to beat Newcastle 3-2 before losing at Everton. We had a run of just one defeat, at Stoke, in 14 games before we lost again at Birmingham in early December.

Our results were mixed going into Christmas and the New Year but, when we should have been kicking on, we stalled with four 1-1 draws in a run of six games between February and March. I finished the campaign quite strongly, scoring both of our goals in a 2-2 draw with Midlands neighbours Leicester, and another brace in our fine 6-2 last-game-of-the-season victory at Ipswich.

We'd not been able to repeat our title win of 12 months earlier, but a fourth-placed finish behind champions Liverpool wasn't a bad way for me to bow out. Yet all of this seasonal assessment is to ignore something that's remembered above all else in my final season – a certain coming together with Leeds United's Norman Hunter. It came in our home game against Jimmy Armfield's side on 1 November and, if the kids in the crowd didn't already have their Guy Fawkes rockets and bangers, there were plenty of fireworks on show on the pitch that day.

The bald match details are these: Derby won the game 3-2. Leeds took the lead from a left-wing corner when we made it too easy for Trevor Cherry to head in; it was 1-1 when Archie Gemmill slid in to put away a Charlie George shot that David Harvey could only parry; then Charlie put us ahead from the penalty spot before half-time. The next goal went to Leeds, making it 2-2 in the second half, when a Frankie Gray mishit was poked in by Duncan McKenzie. And then big Roger Davies, on for the injured Bruce Rioch, won it late for us with a cracking shot after a jink into the box.

Those facts serve to disguise the big talking point at 2-1, in the second half, when Hunter and I were sent off after a scrap that had been brewing ever since the incident that led to our first-half penalty. Hunter didn't like the fact that I'd won the penalty – and that he'd given it away – leading to Charlie despatching the spot kick. I'd picked the ball up ten yards inside the Leeds half and I ran directly at Hunter, feinting left then taking him on the outside. I ran into the area, he caught my left leg, and he had a hand in the small of my back. I went down and referee Derek Nippard called it immediately: penalty!

Leeds liked to referee their own games. I remember Sunderland's Bob Stokoe warning the FA Cup Final ref not to let Leeds 'referee' the 1973 final. So, they didn't like decisions going against them. After Charlie George put the penalty away, the Leeds players were full of moans. And on and on it went, before and after the interval. Then I picked the ball up and ran at their defence again, and I managed to get a snapshot away. As it was cleared, Hunter clattered into me, and all hell broke out. He'd tapped me on the shoulder, hit me with a haymaker right hand and split my lip with a gold ring.

This was not play-acting! I wasn't having that, so I had a right go back. All the lads then stepped in and the referee sent us off. Hunter was still chipping away as the ref spoke to him and, as we walked to the tunnel, it broke out again when we still had 20 yards to reach the touchline. This time, I got in first and went for him with a couple of right hooks and two straight lefts. He went flying. Gordon Guthrie, our physio, came on and pulled me away, and Dave Mackay was in there, too. Dave had deputed centre-half Roy McFarland – who was injured and watching from the stand – to be my minder as I was led away. Roy had his work cut out as I got my lip stitched under the stand.

It's a good job I didn't get in their dressing room afterwards, as I might have just been coming out on parole now! I'm not proud of the episode but the red mist had descended. 'Let me get at that bastard Hunter!' I apparently shouted at big Roy, as the medic tried to stitch my wound. I was fuming.

Did I dive? Not that day. There was a lot of controversy throughout my career about diving to win penalties. I won't say that I always stayed on my feet unless I was absolutely knocked down. There was, though, some shocking treatment handed out by defenders in that era.

The upshot was I got a four-match suspension and a £250 fine … and, by default, I was destined to be a 21st-century YouTube sensation, alongside Norman, decades later when social media rediscovered the grainy *Match of the Day* footage.

I did score a lot of penalties – 15 in all – in my goal-laden 1971/72 season. That's because they'd changed the law to give forwards more protection and we were flat out for the title – putting sides under immense pressure, and defenders reacted. But *I* was fouled only five times out of the 13 league penalties we got.

And I admit that when we attacked, I'd play the odds. If a defender confronted me, I'd carry on, or I'd run towards him. Chances are one of three things will happen: he pulls me down; he wins the ball off me – fair play to him; or I get my shot in with a high chance of scoring. So, the odds were 2-1 in my favour, and you have to roll the dice.

In the 1972/73 season, I think we only got one penalty. And when I moved to Derby, they already had a penalty taker, so that was it. I'd say that for every dubious penalty that was awarded there were another 20 that we should have had.

In the domestic cups, we went out early at Middlesbrough in the League Cup, but we had a good – and demanding – FA Cup run, beating Everton, Liverpool and Newcastle on our way to the semi-finals. There we met Manchester United, now back in the top flight, and we lost it 2-0 at Hillsborough in a feisty old clash. I came on from the bench for Kevin Hector in the second half, but it wasn't our day.

We could have won the European Cup in that second season I spent with Derby. First, we saw off Slovan Bratislava and then we were paired with European aristocrats Real Madrid. We won the first leg at the Baseball Ground 4-1, but I missed the return because I'd been sent off in the Hunter incident against Leeds. The second leg finished 4-1 to Real and we went out 5-1, after extra time. That was tough to take.

And that sending-off affair actually led to a rule change by UEFA. It was considered unfair to automatically ban a player from a European game after a domestic match when the player had yet to be proved to be guilty or not guilty. Mind you, there wasn't much chance of me being 'not guilty' – the footage was there for everyone to see!

So, there was no final season Wembley farewell in the FA Cup, no European Cup win, but how could I complain? What a great time I'd enjoyed as a footballer! I'd only signed for Derby County for a year but agreed to stay on for that extra season. Now Dave Mackay asked me to carry on again, but my mind was made up. I did say to Dave that, if I changed my mind, I'd not play for anyone but Derby. That, however, wasn't going to happen.

I was only just 32 and I could have carried on playing … I could have gone on for another two years, no doubt about that, but, if I had done, I'd have started to pick up injuries. I managed to finish without any serious injuries. I was quite lucky because I was naturally fit and resilient. So, I could have played on, had I nothing else to do in my life. But going to Derby in the first place was dictated, to a large degree, by their willingness to let me commute from home in Lancashire, where I was restoring my business to health and profitability.

And I'd loved it at Derby. I had another title winner's medal to show for it and made a host of new friends, including Thommo – Wales international Rod Thomas – who was a good defender. He also loved a bet and was really into his horse racing. His love for the turf was something he passed on to me, too.

So my life was full with my business growing and new interests. These were the reasons why I wasn't going to carry on playing until my body gave out. I had about 110 people working for me at the time and my business was demanding a lot of my time. I was travelling all over the country for my company, and I was trying to fit the football training in as well.

I'd had a fantastic career. Time to move on.

* * *

Derby Postscript:

Around this time, when I was playing for Derby, I hired a chauffeur to ease my commuting; I'd be driving to play for County, driving for my business in Bolton and at Hazlewood Foods. The chap who got the job wasn't a stranger, it was Don Dootson, who also lived in Westhoughton, and he was to become my trusted driver and ally for more than 20 years. Here are his reminiscences …

> I was Franny Lee's chauffeur for 22 years, all the way back to the days he was playing for Derby County, and he was running his paper business from his mill in Parrott Street, Bolton. We went back a long way because I was from Westhoughton, like Franny, and he was friends with my wife's father.
>
> He was an absolutely fantastic boss, the best. He didn't treat me as a worker, but more like a friend. I wasn't just his driver; I was a jack-of-all-trades. He trusted me to do the right thing. For example, when he was negotiating to go back to Manchester City as chairman in the 1990s, he was waiting to emerge from the offices, but the place was surrounded by newspapermen, anxious to get the latest on the unfolding story. At the right moment I flashed the lights on his Bentley and Franny was able to dive out and into the sanctuary of the car.

It's funny, I've never drank, or smoked a cigarette in my life, but Franny liked a drink and he smoked some of the biggest cigars I've ever seen. There was one race meeting we were at when Franny ran into his old boss, Malcolm Allison. And wasn't Big Mal delighted to be presented with half a dozen big Havanas from his old player!

I can't tell you the number of football grounds I drove Franny to – and I never went into any of them. I might have gone in for a quick look but then it was back to the car.

I had a few cars in my years with Francis; the Bentley, of course, was special and he also had a magnificent 6.5-litre turbo-charged Mercedes for some time. That was a flying machine. He had the Merc decked out in his horse-racing colours: white, red and Manchester City blue.

To illustrate what a good boss he was, let me take you back to a holiday I had in Majorca. I fell ill and they thought I'd had a heart attack. I was taken into hospital and Franny, through his business colleague Peter Barr, of Hazlewood Foods, laid on a private jet to take me back to England. It was at my disposal but wasn't needed in the end – even though I spent four days on holiday and ten days in a hospital out there.

It shows how much he was prepared to do for me.

At Westhoughton, where he was born and brought up, he went on to live with his first wife, Jean, in the oldest house in the village. It was a lovely old place with stone walls, white with black beams and a thatched roof … magnificent fireplaces.

I remember taking him to play squash with his brother, Trevor, and his dentist, who came from a small town west of Bury. Franny used to call him the Tottington Tooth Tugger! I once got a job done – gold inlays and porcelain on my front teeth. I was charged just £30. Franny had said, 'Put his bill on mine.' Goodness knows what that really cost – but that was Franny.

He was obviously a great footballer; he was a very decent cricketer, a good golfer, a pretty good snooker player and he certainly proved himself in the world of racing. It seemed, when it came to sport, there wasn't much he couldn't turn his hand to.

In Barbados, where he liked to spend some of his time off in the Sandy Lane area, he'd meet up with racing chums after the flat season ended. They would, of course, end up playing golf and they'd all throw a few quid into the pot. Guess what? Franny would invariably win the pot – he was a good golfer.

He was also very, very good at supporting charities, especially the Bolton Lads and Girls Club. He did so much for them down the years.

What a man – that was Francis Lee.

Chapter Twelve

I'm Easy-Going – but Not in Troubled Waters!

AFTER THE many highs and occasional lows of football, and the roller-coaster peaks and troughs of business, I can now reflect on some of the big-dipper incidents that affected me as a young man and helped me appreciate what life can throw at all of us. I was always determined to make a success of my dual careers, always mindful of my father's advice and equally determined never to take anything for granted. I suppose that's why I always stood my ground at Bolton, in those early days, and it's probably the reason why I was labelled a troublemaker. I never was, though; I just refused to be subservient in an era when footballers were only just emerging from the serfdom days of the maximum wage.

Joe Mercer told me I was the easiest of players to get along with. That's because Joe and Malcolm Allison treated their players as adults. And to illustrate just how amenable I could be, let me take you on a 12,000-mile round trip from

Manchester to Cape Town and back. Because it shows how easy I was to deal with when I could have cashed in on a big mistake City had made.

This dates back to the early 70s when it became fashionable for top players to go over to South Africa during the summer and play a few games as a guest – and I did this with Cape Town City. It suited me and it was a good way to keep fit … I might not have been driving my own lorries at this point, but I didn't like lazing around. And, as I pointed out earlier, I found the extra cash came in handy because my then business partner, Peter James, was spending money for fun.

The first time I did this, at the end of my spell down there, the Cape Town officials asked me what I wanted to do with my registration. City had mistakenly given it to the Cape club instead of retaining it. 'Give it to me and I'll sort it out with City,' I said. I knew City had made a huge error. Here I was, with my own registration – at the time I was worth maybe £350,000. So, I was actually a free agent for about three weeks!

I could have cashed in, but I simply went back to City for pre-season training and, sure enough, one day I was summoned after training to see chairman Eric Alexander, and John Humphreys, who was chairman of Umbro. They looked very serious! We spoke in the boardroom, and they asked me if I knew why they'd called me in.

'It's not something to do with my registration, is it?' I asked. They went very quiet. 'You know we've made a mistake?' Alexander asked. I said that I certainly did, and I had no wish to string them along. I could have done. They told me they would give me a signing-on fee for 're-signing' with City, but I said that wouldn't be necessary … just give me a small pay rise!

So, yes, I was easy to get along with. Can you imagine modern-day players having such a conscience? Carlos Tevez's advisors spring to mind. There was a lot of controversy over his registration status and third-party ownership during his early days in England. He was at neighbours United before he became one of City's most significant signings of the early post-Maine Road era, back in 2009. I can't imagine Carlos's people being so 'easy' if the player's registration had suddenly been found!

South Africa was an eye-opener. I stayed at a nice, small place on the seafront – the Elizabeth Hotel, in Cape Town. I'd trained for a couple of nights and then two guys came to see me on the Tuesday. They were good-looking fellas, and this was in the middle of apartheid, but I never gave their racial background a second thought. I suppose they looked Mediterranean, but they were very personable, and they asked if I'd do some coaching with their kids team.

'They're all mad on English football,' they told me. So, I agreed and went up next day to a place called Paarl, a township outside Cape Town. I met the kids and did a bit of coaching and some five-a-sides. We had a few photos taken for the local Paarl newspaper and it all went very well. I then went into the club for training on the Thursday and, when I got back to the Elizabeth, the barman pointed out two chaps who were waiting to talk to me. I thought they looked like hard nuts, and I was worried they might be gangsters, but instead, when I went over, they threw a newspaper on the table with pictures of me coaching.

'Can you tell us what this is about?' one said. I told them I was a professional footballer and had gone there to do some coaching – that the kids had enjoyed it and they loved English football and we'd all had some fun.

'You don't go up there,' I was told very firmly. 'It's out of bounds, and next time you go there, you are in big trouble.' I asked politely why that was the case. I was told the 'rules' and I replied that I was a footballer, not a politician.

'Don't care what you are,' they warned me. 'You don't go up there.'

So, the two good-looking chaps from Paarl came back to me and asked if I'd do more coaching and I had to tell them I couldn't – and why. Bless them, when I returned home by ocean liner – to have a bit of a rest, rather than fly – they'd bought me a pair of smoked kingfish to have on the way home!

It was a different age. This was the apartheid era in South Africa where the whites-only government kept the races apart. It was years before Nelson Mandela was even known about by most Britons, never mind freed from jail. Cape Town City got quite good crowds, but one side of the ground would be whites-only and the three other sides would be for the black South Africans.

Geoff Hurst had a spell, like mine, out there, and Southampton winger Terry Paine, who'd been in Sir Alf Ramsey's 1966 squad, went out and ended up retiring there and working as a TV commentator. Many other players did the same thing. Anyway, the whole Cape Town episode just showed how wrong Bolton were – and how right Joe Mercer had been – about the pros and cons of me being difficult to manage.

Back in England, once I'd walked away from Derby County in 1976, the worries of football commuting were over and, with my business doing well, I could walk across bridges without a passing thought about throwing myself into the river below. The only thoughts I had about rivers involved a pastime I became passionate about: angling.

Football has had its fair share of fishermen. Jack Charlton, bless him, springs to mind. He loved going fly fishing anywhere, but especially the riverbanks on Ireland's west coast; famously, his fellow Geordie Paul Gascoigne was partial to casting his line – he even tried to talk wanted criminal Raoul Moat into a bread-and-chicken picnic and a spot of angling as Britain's police were desperate to catch the fugitive back in 2010!

Well, I got into fishing too, but it very nearly cost me my life, not too long after my playing days had finished. I was having a brilliant break in Scotland back in July 1977, but it all ended scarily – with me literally seconds from death.

I was with a few pals – Bill Openshaw and his girlfriend, Ian Shaw, a market trader from Westhoughton – and we were fishing on Dalguise Beach on the river Tay, near Pitlochry. It's a great spot for salmon and I've since been told that it was one of Beatrix Potter's favourite beauty spots. It's truly stunning but what happened to me at Dalguise was no fairy tale.

I was fishing there, and Callum Gillies was the ghillie guiding me. He's a legendary expert on this famous fishing spot. When the water was shallow, the ghillie would wade out and fish from the boat and then guide you down on a rope with every cast ... and that way you could cover the breadth of the river. As it happened, I felt – and saw – this fish take the fly and it came straight out of the water.

Callum, who'd been a ghillie on the river for something like 45 years, said, 'Mr Lee, that is the biggest fish I've ever seen on the Tay!'

He may have been flattering me, but I turned and said, 'You'd better get used to it, 'cos it's on the end of my line!'

The first feeling I had was that I'd do very, very well to land this fish. Callum let me down on the rope gently and I was playing the fish ... down about a mile to where a fishing hut stood on this large pool with a great big eddy. I had it on the line for about an hour and half! On occasions, if you've had a fish on for that long, you get a bit fed up, but Callum, by this time, was in the boat and had rowed it to get us into the slow water and we were getting the fish out of the deep stuff. *We've got it now*, I thought to myself.

Just as we started to draw it to the surface, the line went slack. I couldn't believe it. The hook was an Esmond Drury black treble, a black-coated fly hook with three barbs – black, so that it would not shine in the water. It turned out that I only had it hooked on *one* of the trebles. If I'd had it hooked on two or three of the trebles, I'd have got it. But when Callum got the line back in, because of the fight we'd had and the time the fish had been on the line, the hook was bright silver! The black coating had gone and one of the barbs had disappeared – with the fish!

In the hut at Dalguise, there's a little note on the wall with my Esmond Drury pinned to it. It says: 'This hook caught the biggest fish ever seen on the river Tay!'

Was I unlucky? Some might say. There was to be another roll of the dice, however.

By late afternoon, we'd drowned our sorrows with a few drams. Old Callum liked whisky, but he wasn't a great drinker – he'd get a wobble on. Then we heard his wife shout down to the river, 'Where are you?' We dropped him off in the Range Rover and went back to our hotel.

The next morning was a Sunday, and you couldn't fish for salmon on the day of rest in Scotland. It was a boiling-hot day – yes, in Scotland! We went down to the river to the same pool. There was Bill and his girlfriend, Ian and me. We took a picnic and started taking the sun, in our shorts. It was so hot I thought I'd have a swim. I knew the pool because I'd fished it so often. Half of it is quite rapid but it eddies round into a flat, deep, still area. I thought I could dive into that spot and swim over to the embankment, get out there and then come back over the railway bridge over the Tay.

I started swimming towards the bridge, but it soon dawned on me that it was getting further away from me. *That's funny*, I thought to myself. I'm not a good swimmer, so I decided to tread water while I worked out what I should do next. I put my feet down to do just that but suddenly – in a flash – I was sucked straight down; right down to the bottom of the river. It was as though I was in a washing-machine advert, swirling around. Suddenly, I was choking and panicking because I knew I wasn't the strongest in the water. 'Get me out, get me out,' I started shouting to my mates. At first they thought I was joking, but they couldn't get me out. There was no way they could get me out. I was in a whirlpool. And I thought I was going to die. No, I *knew* I was going to die.

In the end the world seemed to go quiet – serene, even. Some say that drowning is the best way to go and now I can understand why they say that. At the same time I was giving myself a bollocking for being such a fool. Talk about your life flashing before your eyes! I was seeing business competitors, delighting at my being dead. All the while, my pals couldn't dive in, because they weren't great swimmers themselves. They were helpless, watching me drown, right there in front of them. I was exhausted – done in.

Just put your head under the water now, Franny, just take a mouthful of water and it'll all be over …

And then, out of nowhere, Bill Openshaw and Callum Ghillies appeared. Callum just popped up on the bank at that moment because he wanted to lock the boat we'd used for our fishing episode with the big fish the day before. His wife suddenly calling him away meant he'd forgotten to lock the boat.

Bill shouted to him to unlock the boat because I was in trouble, but Callum shouted back, 'It's not locked!' My friends had been standing next to the boat all the while, and it wasn't locked! Anyway, they got the boat and rowed over and I just managed to hang on to it. I reckon I was ten seconds away from drowning.

I clung on, made it to the riverbank and just lay there for about 20 minutes. I just couldn't move. I was so completely knackered. At the end, I hadn't even been swimming, just wriggling to stay alive. Eventually, they got me into the boat and they rowed me back to the hut and I was coughing and spluttering water for about another 15 minutes. I was exhausted and I said that I'd better go to hospital. They took me to the hospital in Pitlochry, where my heartbeat was racing and they told me I'd had a real fright. They also said I probably had water in my lungs.

Callum leaving that boat unlocked saved my life. No doubt. Otherwise, he'd have never come down to the river the day after my fight with the salmon. I was unlucky with the big fish … but far, far luckier that next day. It was also a good job that we'd given him so much whisky on the Saturday … otherwise Callum would have surely remembered to lock the boat!

I eventually went back to the hotel and drank about five pints of water and lemonade as I'd been so dehydrated by fear. And I took a Valium – I always kept one with me after my problems with my partner, Peter James, in case I ever felt panicky. I crashed out about 7pm or 8pm. When I woke up, everything in the world looked bright and sharp and I packed my bags into the car, said cheerio to the lads and headed for home. I couldn't stand to be there a moment longer.

I drove all the way home, more than four hours on the road and, when I got back, my wife, Jean, asked what I was doing home. I explained what had happened and she told me to go to bed, but I couldn't. I was so lit-up, fired-up, illuminated by the experience. Instead, I sat up until four or five in the morning. Boy, was I glad to have survived!

It all had a profound effect on me. After that I wouldn't go into any water where I couldn't put my feet on the bottom. Even now, in a pool, I just swim straight for the wall and get my hands on it. No way will I turn and mess about. I'm just so panicky in water.

I'd had a lucky escape – and was so relieved to come out of it alive.

Chapter Thirteen

A Racing Certainty

FRANCIS HENRY Lee, racehorse trainer. It has a nice ring about it, doesn't it? And once I'd sold my company it also helped open the way forward for the rest of my life after my playing days ended. Selling the company helped fund my divorce from Jean and I now needed a new reason to get up in the morning. And that was horse racing.

Like a lot of guys in football, I loved racing both as a sport and for the buzz it can give you. It's a great social sport, but I thought it would be good to see if I could get involved in the sport myself.

I'd already dabbled, by owning a few horses. My first horse was called Clydebank and I had it stabled up in Yorkshire. Others followed and I had them stabled with trainers such as Michael Jarvis, at Newmarket, and that got me really intrigued. Rod Thomas, my great pal at Derby County, had got me interested in the racing game and I did a bit of research, reading up on the training side of racing. It certainly planted a seed. After a while, I thought I could probably train horses myself. Why not give it a go?

I'm not the first footballer to fall in love with the world of the turf. Think Mick Channon, the former Southampton and England forward, who started as an assistant trainer about the same time as I got my stable going. He then went on his own in 1990 and ended up with more than 200 horses. Sir Alex Ferguson is a well-known owner and enthusiast and now has interests in more than 30 horses. Add to that Michael Owen, who owns horses and has his own yard near me in Cheshire, and the likes of Wayne Rooney, Ian Wright and Joey Barton, who all love racehorses and the racing game.

I'd always loved a day out at Haydock, which is on my doorstep, and a trip to the wonderful Cheltenham Festival. But I saw a whole new world of possibilities when I spotted Little Stanneylands Stud Farm, in Wilmslow, back in the late 1970s. I bought it, and it was to become my home and my business. I enjoyed the space and the land, and I officially began my training career in 1984.

I was still deeply involved in my paper business at this point, and I split my time, mixing my two businesses. I'd be up early to look in on the horses and the lads in the stables and then I'd give them a wink and tell them I was off to earn some 'proper money' at my mill in Bolton's

Parrott Street. Other days, I'd be driving to a track with my chauffeur, Don Dootson, and perhaps with my apprentice jockey, Rodney Lappin, in the back seat. There was one day when young Rodders – actually, I nicknamed him 'Slappin' – found himself in the hottest of hot seats when he heard me putting a big-ish treble bet on as we drove to a meeting at Haydock, one of my favourite tracks.

Slappin was in the back of the car as we motored north of Warrington to Newton-le-Willows and on to Haydock Park for a big evening of racing in August 1991. Don was driving as I put together a £500 treble, all of it on my own horses in the meeting. The first was Charly Pharly, with jockey Darren Biggs in the saddle; next up was Killy, with Ray Cochrane riding; and the final leg was the horse that Slappin was riding – Sir Arthur Hobbs.

Slappin didn't seem that nervous at first about all this … largely because, as he told me later, he thought Killy was useless and had no chance. We'd soon find out, because we got underway and Charly Pharly galloped home for the first leg of the bet, winning at 9/4 favourite. Next up was the 'useless' Killy. Ray, a very good Irish jockey, did everything right and it won at an impressive 12/1, edging the favourite on the line.

So, my £500 treble was looking pretty good, but it was now all down to young Slappin! I'll let him take up the tale …

So, the treble was all resting on me. Franny came to see me and I knew a lot was riding on it for my boss. I don't know how many thousands of pounds altogether, but it must have been an awful lot! He just said, 'Slappin … you know what you've got to do – just go and fucking win it.'

That was brilliant. He didn't try and give me detailed instructions. He knew that I knew the horse inside-out and how to ride it. He didn't try to overcomplicate things. I brought Sir Arthur home and Franny had his treble!

I was delighted to have been the jockey to complete the big bet but it wasn't without its drama. The horse I'd beaten into second was Granitton Bay, ridden by my good friend, Tony Culhane. I led in the final furlong but strayed a bit left and there was a stewards' enquiry. When I was in with the stewards, I could hear Richard Whitaker, the other trainer, and Franny going hell for leather outside. They were having a scrap … but Franny came away smiling!

I'm pretty sure that was the day we got back to his car in the car park and Franny was approached by a little Scouser with a bucket, sponge and dusters. He asked, 'Hey, Fran! Can I clean your car? Go on, let me clean your car!' Well, Franny didn't care for Liverpudlians too much. He winked at me as

> we walked on towards a fine-looking limousine. Franny stopped, and the man with the bucket and sponge got to work – wheel arches, headlight surrounds, mirrors, the lot. 'How's that, Fran?' he asked. 'It's very good – very good indeed,' Franny said, 'but it's not my car!' And Franny promptly walked away, leaving yer man open-mouthed. Francis then turned around and gave him a fiver … he'd had his fun and he'd had a very good day indeed. The champagne flowed that night … as it always did, with Franny.

Good lad is Slappin! Training horses, I was to discover, is like training footballers. Find out what they like and give them plenty of it … and feed them well, too! Again, it applies in both cases, football and racing. That's how I treated the feeding of horses in my care … lots of small meals, five times a day rather than three, so they didn't have bulk in their system.

Again, with a nod back to my football training, I'd apply a similar approach to my horses. Some might think I was hard, but I often got results. I'd do a lot of interval training with the horses, just as I did when I first joined Manchester City! I'd run them over different distance intervals, especially the sprint horses. I wasn't averse to using what I'd learned as an athlete myself to train the horses.

I started out in 1984 as a National Hunt Permit Trainer to begin with, before stepping up to a full National Hunt Licence and then on to a Dual Licence for flat and jumps. I liked whenever possible to take away any risk with the training at my stable. I always liked to do my best for them. One thing I'd do was take almost every horse's blood for testing. Not many other stables did this, certainly not at that time. I'd do it, say weekly, and kept their records in the files. I had chiropractors for them; we had the horses on regular intravenous drips after exertions, again something rarely done then – it was glucose to replenish what they'd sweated out. I invested fair bit of time and money looking after them.

Some trainers might cut a few more corners, but I liked to be fastidious with the horses. I also liked to get to the point where I owned at least a half stake in nearly every horse in the yard because, that way, if I was also training it, I could have final say on how they were looked after. There may have been the odd horse that was owned outright by someone else, but I had a sizeable stake in the majority of those in the yard.

We had 40 horses in the yard at one time – that was every box filled. We occasionally had a few more with another stable run by Mick Molyneux. So, there may have been a few more than 40 at one point.

We had one horse that was head-shy; we couldn't put a bridge on it, and it would rear up into the air. When I made my enquiries, the yard it had come from told us it was a 'nutter'; it was frightened of its bridle and all this and that. We were certainly worried it would hurt itself in the stables. So we put a 'twitch' on its nose … a piece of rope on a stick to control it and then we cut the cups out of a pair of blinkers. We led it out into the paddock for two or three hours and it was fine. And then I started putting the bridle on over the blinkers and he accepted it, no problem. We eventually took the blinkers off, and he was fine with the bridle alone – all psychology. I tried to put myself inside the horse's head and figure out how I'd react to any particular problem.

I could detail all the big wins that gave me great pleasure in a 13-year career in racing but sometimes the little wins – or near misses – could give me such a thrill. So, let me tell you how I reacted to a particular problem with another horse; one that looked like a hopeless case.

The horse in question gave me a real burst of excitement at Sandown Park. He was up against the Queen Mother's fine horse Insular, which had won a string of races in succession over the previous three years. My horse was called Peter Martin and he'd previously been trained by Paul Kellaway, a vastly experienced ex-jockey and trainer. Then we got it and found it was a big coward, a chicken-hearted thing, frightened of its own shadow. After we bought it and settled it down, we thought we'd try it over some hurdles. So, we took it up to a little hurdle 40 yards away, and it reared up and pissed off! It wouldn't go *near* a hurdle.

I figured that Paul Kellaway, who'd been a jump jockey, might have been quite stern with Peter Martin, and it was having nothing to do with it. I racked my brains for a solution. Then I had the idea of putting him in between our paddocks, which are about six yards wide and there are two five-bar gates. We put him into the gap between the paddocks and shut the gate to try to cure his claustrophobia. We did this regularly to try to get him accustomed. Then we walked him into the gap again and shut the gate, but we left the other five-bar gate open with some very small hurdles in front of it. The horse looked at this arrangement and started shuffling about. We gave him a handful of nuts and the horse jumped out. We did it again and it kept jumping over the hurdles. It took to it and, because it was a coward, it became a very good jumper because it never touched any of the hurdles! It didn't want to get hurt! Peter Martin had suddenly become a very good hurdler indeed.

I often wondered what Paul Kellaway must have thought when he saw the horse in action … how the hell did *they* get that horse to jump like that?

And so to Sandown, in March 1986. There's a handicap hurdle over two miles – the William Hill Imperial Cup – at that lovely track in Esher. The Queen Mother had

Insular running in it. It turned out to be a very good jumps horse indeed. Insular was hot and had won something like eight races on the bounce. It was trained by that wonderful trainer, Ian Balding, father of broadcaster Clare Balding. I told Kevin Mooney, who was on my horse, not to go near the front and to hold his ground. That was because Peter Martin just loved passing beaten horses.

Anyway, we turned into the straight rather further back than I'd hoped! The race had been strung out and Insular had tracked the early pacesetter and then hit the front. Peter Martin was almost two hurdles behind and looking like he might be tailed off when, suddenly, he picked up. He finished like a train, cut down the field and reached Insular on the line.

I was celebrating for a moment, but we were just beaten. The photofinish placed Peter Martin third behind Insular and Hypnosis by a short head. And if Peter Martin had been within ten lengths of the final hurdle, where I expected him to be, we'd have won it easily. I was just watching my horse and I didn't then realise the winner was the Queen Mother's – or anyone else's – horse. I thought we'd won it! But, in the unsaddling enclosure, it was announced we were third. Well, I was disappointed, and I was just about to go and say something to the winning trainer, along the lines of, 'Well done, but if my jockey had given it any sort of ride, he'd have fucking beaten yours,' before I realised the crowd was about ten deep around the winner. I wondered, *What's going on there?* I thought the horse might have collapsed. Then someone told me it was the Queen Mother's horse. 'Oh, is it?' I spluttered. 'Well done!' But I actually thought, *You lucky so and so, Your Majesty! Peter Martin should have won it by a street!*

Another trick I had was how I handled horses after they'd raced. We'd bring them back to Little Stanneylands and let them have 45 minutes in the paddock, picking at the grass and having a roll about before we put them in the stable. There was a big sandpit there to let them give themselves a rub down. Rest, relax and enjoy – that was my prescription for them after a race. By doing that, they'd go straight into their food. Often, after racing and being in a horsebox, they're off their food and won't eat. Our routine meant they were always ready to eat.

I married my wonderful second wife, Gill, in October 1987, in Macclesfield Register Office. It was a major new chapter for me and that was perfect for my fresh life at Little Stanneylands. I still had major interests in my businesses, but I had the most enormous fun in 13 years of racing, using my home base to run an operation that was both my home and my business. I saddled 181 winners in Britain and Ireland during that stretch and I suppose my biggest win was the 1990 Cartier Premier Challenge Race, at Dublin's Phoenix Park, with Sir Harry Hardman.

Sir Harry was 7/4 favourite, and the jockey was a young Dean McKeown. He romped home at the head of a field of 12 in this race over the classic sprint distance of six furlongs. Dublin's famous old racecourse closed after 88 years of racing just after this meeting, so I was glad to have had that experience there.

Going back to Slappin, who'd started as an apprentice with me, he and I loved our trips to Ayr, where one of our very decent horses, Aahsaylad, had a very good time of it. His name – Aahsaylad – was a nod to his owner, a farmer from Skipton, in North Yorkshire, called Malcolm Stapleton. Because 'aahsaylad' was exactly how Malcolm greeted you! What a horse. You'd think it had no chance at all, that you might finish last, but then he'd just run better and better and he'd finish like a tank. He was so good.

Aahsaylad loved the left-handed oval of the track at Ayr, with a long, wide, half-mile run-in to finish with its gentle undulations. It obviously suited Slappin, too, because he was on the horse at Ayr for successive victories in the Bogside Cup in July 1990, and exactly a year later, in 1991. He won the first one at 11/4 and 12 months later he carried the favourite's tag home – and a fair bit more weight – to win at 13/8. My best season for winners came in the same year as that second Bogside success – 1991 – when I had 31 wins.

My most notable UK success came three years later when Encore M'Lady – a 20/1 shot – won the 1994 £40,000

William Hill Trophy, at York. She had surged clear with a furlong to go, and jockey Nick Carlisle eased her in after that. She won by a head, but Nick never resorted to the whip and the horse won it well. That success was a great one for me, and the BBC made it part of the running order for that night's *Nine O'Clock News*. By that time, in the mid-90s, I was starting to cut down my stable as I needed more time to devote to football once again, so that York win was very special. The same horse, Encore M'Lady, also gave me my final win as a trainer, at Musselburgh in 1996.

I loved to celebrate a good win, but whether the prize money was big or small, we'd raise a glass of bubbly. That was particularly true of those Ayr wins with Aahsaylad. Don't get me wrong, they weren't in the class of Sir Harry Hardman's 1990 Cartier Premier Challenge win at Phoenix Park, but they were still good, quality race wins. The champagne flowed and Slappin reckoned it needed two guys to carry me to my car after one of those Ayr wins – in fact, it might have been both!

Rodney went on to ride for Mick Channon, among others, but he recalled his time with me fondly:

> In a nutshell, working with Francis Lee was the best job I had in racing. He just gave me so much confidence – he was a man with an aura, and I loved working for him and being in his company.

> Walking into a room with him was like walking in with Elvis Presley. Franny just had a presence and a big personality. But he always had my back.
>
> I remember another run-in with the stewards when they were looking at my alleged excessive use of the whip. Franny came in with me and he told them, 'Jesus Christ, he couldn't hit the horse with both hands, never mind one!' That got the stewards laughing – and I was off the hook. The man was different class.

There was a certain jockey at the other end of the pedigree scale who I must mention. I was proud – honoured in fact – to have given the legendary American jockey Bill Shoemaker his final win on British soil. He didn't come to Britain too often, but he was here in the summer of 1989, and he was on one of my horses, On My Merit, in the evening meeting at Warwick. The date, fittingly enough, was 4 July, Independence Day for our US cousins.

It's hard to underplay the legend that was Shoemaker. Think of Lester Piggott but add to that a layer of Stateside glamour and glitz. I had a special regard for someone who was regarded as probably the finest horseman in the history of American racing: Bill 'The Shoe' Shoemaker, as he was known.

His total of career wins – 8,833 reached in 1990 after a career spanning 41 years – was testimony to his brilliance. I had the distinction of training the horse that gave him that final UK win of his career. His victory came courtesy of On My Merit in a one-mile handicap. At the off, the favourite was Hackforth, ridden by a British great, Willie Carson, who started at 5/4. But the mighty Bill made all the running and he was clear in the final furlong. He romped in for me at 7/1, and Bill was so impressed, I think he wanted to buy the horse. Well, I was the horse's trainer, but I also owned it! There was no deal.

That was quite something to put on my racing CV, given that, at that point in racing history, Shoemaker had more race wins than any American jockey – ever. Bill rode only occasionally on our shores, but he won the Kentucky Derby four times and the Bellmont Stakes five times. You can add to that 11 Santa Anita Handicaps and eight Hollywood Gold Cups. In England he was close to a Derby win on Hawaiian Sound, finishing second to Shirley Heights in 1978. Six years later he won the Britannia Handicap at Royal Ascot on Sikorski.

Back home in the States, he'd won pretty much everything there was for an American jockey to win, including, as I said, those four Kentucky Derbys. The fourth and final one came in 1986 when he was 54 – and 21 years after his previous Derby triumph. He was incredible.

Being in racing brought me into contact with all the social classes, from the regular guy at the bookies who likes a punt to the highest strata of British society. Consider my experience with Charles Spencer-Churchill, who was related to Sir Winston, of course, all the Dukes of Marlborough, and also the late Diana, Princess of Wales. He was very well connected and a serious champion of the family seat, Blenheim Palace. Charles was also very much a fan of horse racing.

I was at the Two-Year-Olds in Training Sale in Florida with my wife, Gill. I was also with Michael Jarvis, the well-known Newmarket trainer, Major Johnnie Lewis from the British Bloodstock Association (BBA), and Josh Collins, a bloodstock agent. This guy, Charles Spencer-Churchill, was known to one of the BBA guys and he got invited into our company. One of the trainers knew him, and Charles was there while we were there for a week, looking at the horses and going to the auction in the evening. Charles, I think, was on holiday and he had family connections in the States, too, because he was related to the seriously wealthy Vanderbilt clan. He became part of our group, drinking with us – yet he never once bought a round! He probably thought that he didn't have to. Maybe, a bit like the Queen, he never carried cash?

I set him up one day when we were going to the races at Gulfstream Park. He'd asked the night before, at dinner, if he could 'tag along' to the races. The way it worked in the restaurant was that they asked for your room key as a warranty. Normally, whoever put their key down ended up paying. So, usually, a couple of us would put keys down and so split the bill that way. That night about eight of us were having dinner – nine with Charles – and when we were in the bar, we organised it so that there was a bell boy calling out a phone call for Mr Jarvis, a message for Mr Lee and so on, until only Charles was left sitting there when the head waiter arrived, asking for a key! He very reluctantly put his key on the table, and he had to pay. Nobody bailed him out … but we had to do that, to force him to pay on at least one occasion! Think about it, a Churchill related to the Vanderbilts with short arms and long pockets.

We then went to the evening race meeting and Charles had to leave early to catch his plane back to England. He was with us, enjoying our hospitality again, when he asked me for a couple of hundred dollars, so that he could have a bet. He told me he only had sterling currency on him. Gill asked me what he'd asked for and I told her. 'You stupid man!' she scolded me.

I said, 'Look, Gill, when my grandchildren are sat on my knee, later in life, I want them to know that if they ever bump into him, they can say to Charles Spencer-Churchill, "You owe my grandad $200!"'

He was tighter than a submarine's door. Yet, I'm told he could be generous to his ex-wives, and he was brought up in Blenheim's great wealth and style. His money must have gone somewhere, because, when he died in 2016, he left a net estate of just £37,128. Mind you, it's still enough to pay back my $200!

That episode raised a smile and, above all, racing for me was fun. And it was, I'm sure, fun for my family and for those working for me at Little Stanneylands. All my kids loved our days out racing and our life there in general. Fun was such a key ingredient, and I had my ways of bringing a smile to work …

I remember Peter Moore, my loyal assistant trainer, got caught out when I set him up just after he first started with me. I gave him a bit of a test … well, you might as well start as you mean to go on. I had another property away from Stanneylands that I had in mind for him to live in – but it had a sitting tenant still living in it. Never mind, I told him to go and take a look to see what he thought of the place.

Later, Peter recalled:

> So Francis sent me up there and it looked a bit derelict, to be honest. Suddenly, a guy emerged from the house with a shotgun, and he chased me off the land! When I got back to the yard, Francis was waiting, and he said, 'Was he there?' I said he was. He said, 'Did he have his gun?' I said he did. He was laughing his head off and he'd stitched me up. He was a hoot! You never knew when Francis was being serious or taking the mickey!

But Peter got his own back many years later when he thought I was piss-taking again. This time, I wasn't! It was years after I'd finished the racing business and, indeed, I'd moved out of Little Stanneylands altogether – but Peter was still there, looking after the gardens for the new owners. I'd often call round to see him with a weekly delivery of fish.

On this occasion, I'd phoned ahead to tell him I was on my way with his fish. I could hear he was mowing the lawns as I walked around the house when, suddenly, I lost my footing over a ridge and clattered into the side of the house. I'd cracked my ribs on the wall and ended in a heap on the ground with my fish delivery cast akimbo to one side. 'Peter! Peter!' I shouted. I was in agony.

He dashed around and saw me – then roared with laughter! 'What is it?' he blurted. I could tell he thought I was pranking him.

'I've bust my ribs!' I screamed in pain. He was still laughing, and how could I blame him? 'Just make sure you pick up your salmon!' I insisted, through my tears … he finally realised that, for once, I wasn't taking the mickey.

No wonder he laughed. He wasn't the only one – my chauffeur Don Dootson, was also part of the Little Stanneylands team as part of his jack-of-all-trades work with me. He recalled:

> I also worked at the stables as an assistant trainer, if he needed me to be, mending fences and rails and looking after the gallops. I could also drive a horsebox, which not everybody there could do. Apart from driving Francis to all the football grounds in the early days, I took him to all the race tracks, of course.
>
> While I was with him, he made that move to Cheshire and he went from one lovely black-and-white thatched-roof house in Westhoughton to another – only much bigger!
>
> Little Stanneylands is a fabulous place, and I'm sure the similarity with Westhoughton would have appealed to him. What made it very different was the land and open spaces – 48 acres' worth – so he had plenty of room for horses when he decided to make a business out of racing.
>
> I remember once on the Little Stanneylands gallops, a horse emerged without its jockey. Off went Franny after it, shouting, 'It's not much of a racehorse if I can keep up with it in my wellies!'

I roped in both Peter and Don at times to do my bidding – literally – at charity auctions. Once, I was on a top table and I had Peter placed in the room for the auction. I wanted one of the items but didn't want to be seen to be bidding from the top table. The item in question was a pair of boots worn by the legendary Pelé in the wartime film caper *Escape to Victory* – Pelé was in the movie alongside the likes of Michael Caine, Sylvester Stallone, Bobby Moore and my great pal, Mike Summerbee. I wanted the boots to present as a surprise to 'Buzzer'. I gave the nod to Peter and watched him sweating as he carried on bidding until the boots were mine.

On another occasion, Don was in the audience at a function where I'd put one of my England shirts up for auction to raise funds for charity. The only problem was I didn't want to lose my England shirt – it was precious to me! So, Don got to do my dirty work – he kept on bidding for me, anonymously, until the shirt was 'his'. Result? I got my shirt back; the charity got a fat donation at my expense and everyone was happy!

We had to laugh. So, having fun was a key part of my life at the stables – indeed, in my life, full stop. But I didn't like people acting out of order. It happened in technicolour one day at Stanneylands and, although it might have seemed funny in retrospect, it could so easily have been more than a little bit naughty.

We had a Scouse lad who came to work for us – and I don't mind admitting that Scousers had to win me round. So, perhaps this lad was on the back foot to start with. I got him to drive the tractor and we had sand gallops – in the shape of a letter 'P'. So, you'd go up the straight and round at the top, around the circle. The tractor would follow the horses to level the sand for their next run.

On this occasion, the horses went past me, and I was watching the horses intently while this guy on the tractor came up behind me. Because I was concentrating on the horses, I didn't hear it coming until, at the very last moment, I looked around and it was right on top of me! I was startled and I dived for my life under the white-painted rails. It was a last-ditch leap to get out of the way.

Well, this Scouse lad switched off the engine, jumped off the tractor and whistled at me! He then stood over me and shouted 'penalty', just like a referee! It was a clear mickey-take, aimed at my reputation for diving to win penalties in my football days.

I like a laugh but, for once, I was *not* amused. Two days later, I called him into the office and said, 'I don't think this is working,' and he was let go. I didn't like that.

But life was invariably good at Little Stanneylands, and my racing set-up there was immortalised on celluloid when the *Coronation Street* cast and crew rocked up in the early autumn of 1986. This was *Corrie* in the days of famous characters such as Ken and Deirdre Barlow, Jack and Vera Duckworth and Rita Tanner. They needed a racing stables location to fit their current storyline – Jack Duckworth had put money on a horse called Betty's Hotshot – it reminded him of the Rovers Return dish Betty's hotpot – and Jack and his pals had won a small fortune. They decided to buy the horse with their winnings and have it stabled … and Little Stanneylands was its fictitious home.

So, in they all came … Gill and I welcomed the Granada TV hordes; an all-day job filming one of the episodes. They had a big marquee on the lawn, and they had some of the stars in the scenes – Bill Tarmey played Jack Duckworth, and, in the story, he asked to ride his horse. Well, of course, it bolted. Then a stunt rider took over and he fell off the horse and was 'knocked out'! Bill Tarmey took over again and was seen flat out in a wagon, and an ambulance then came to the rescue.

It was a good day! Barbara Knox was there as Rita, and Gill remembers how Barbara refused to use the toilets provided by Granada TV and insisted on using the facilities in our cottage!

See what I mean about fun? Peter Moore, my assistant trainer, was one of a few of our staff who got a £50 extras fee and I'm sure they deserved their reward. They say life can be stranger than fiction, but that was one day when the two worlds collided. The episode was in the can and broadcast a couple of months later in November 1986.

I'll give the final words on my approach to racing to Slappin, who served me well and learned a lot in the back of my car – I think!

I never took him for granted. He could be demanding and tough. He wanted his jockeys to be as fit as his horses. I once took a Pot Noodle out in the kitchen at Little Stanneylands to try it – I never ate them, but I fancied trying one – and he grabbed it off me and threw it away. 'I want you to be the fittest jockey around,' he said. 'You're not eating that rubbish.'

Another time, I'd walked out in a strop and went home to Yorkshire because I wasn't happy with the rides I was getting. Some time went by, and I decided to ring him to see if I could go back. 'Yes,' he told me, 'you can come back here.' I was relieved, and when I returned, he said nothing. It was as though nothing had happened. But then three, four weeks and more went by – and I'd received no pay! I felt intimidated at the thought of going to ask him why … so I waited and waited. Eventually, after about seven weeks, skint and living off beans on toast, I went to see him and asked why I'd not been paid. 'Remind me,' he said, 'you asked me if you could come back, didn't you? I didn't ask you to return?' I told him he was right. I also told him I was very sorry for walking away and it wouldn't happen again. 'Dead right,' he told me. 'Never do that again.'

And with that I was back on the payroll – and he even paid me an extra week's wages. He was right. And he was a special, special guy.

- Stables as trainer: Little Stanneylands Stud Farm, Wilmslow, Cheshire 1984–97.
- First winner trained: Miramac, novices' hurdle, Ludlow, 6 February 6 1985.
- First flat winner: Foilinski, Beverley, 11 August 11 1987.
- Biggest winner: Sir Harry Hardman (1990 Cartier Premier Challenge Race, Phoenix Park, Dublin) ridden by Dean McKeown.
- Biggest winner in Britain: Encore M'Lady (1994 William Hill Trophy Handicap, York) ridden by Nick Carlisle.
- Other good winners: String Player (Five handicap hurdles 1986–87); Aahsaylad (1990 Bogside Cup); Beau Venture (1990 Potter Nursery, Newmarket); Don't Worry Me (1994 Horn Blower Stakes, Ripon).
- Pattern-race runner-up: Sir Harry Hardman (1991 Palace House Stakes).
- Last winner: Encore M'Lady, Musselburgh, 22 July 1996. Ridden by Joe Fanning.
- Most wins in a season: 30 in 1991 (flat).
- Total wins: 181 (including one in Ireland); 149 flat, 32 jumps.

Chapter Fourteen

Maine Man – Forward with Franny

I'D LEFT my favourite football home, Maine Road, in 1974, and in the years that followed the successful conclusion of my playing days at Derby and the development of both my business and racing interests meant there wasn't too much time for looking back. Indeed, I'm not the kind of bloke who cares to look back, I'd rather press on and look ahead. So, I took no satisfaction from that farewell prediction I'd delivered to my team-mates as I left City for Derby … that a badly run club had years of struggle to come. I was right and wish I hadn't been. Struggle did duly follow, and not even the return of Malcolm Allison, later in the 1970s, could prevent that.

They shuffled the pack of managers like a cabaret magician flipping cards, and City were twice relegated from the top flight in the 1980s – seven managers came and went in that decade alone – but they were back in the top flight in time to become founder members of the new Premier League in 1992. Nevertheless, it was a rocky road.

Peter Reid had inherited the manager's hot seat as player-boss when Howard Kendall departed for another date with his beloved Everton in 1990. Peter started well with two fifth-place finishes, followed by ninth in the first Premiership campaign. Steady enough, but a poor start to 1993/94 saw Peter Swales (yes, he was still in charge) pull the trigger. He'd just taken a small but significant step back from front-line duties by appointing ex-*Sunday People* newspaperman John Maddock as general manager. That hadn't stopped 'Swales Out' chants from the Kippax as the side struggled. Instead of Swales out, it was Reid who was out on his ear after just four games. There had been an anti-board demonstration outside Maine Road after a 2-0 home defeat to Blackburn, and the fans wanted change ... but not the one they got, as Oxford United manager Brian Horton was appointed. It was the chairman, not the manager, the fans wanted to see move out.

I wasn't actively pursuing a return to City, or even football in general. I was successful outside of the game, and I was certainly happy. But I'd first been sounded out some time before these events unfolded, and I was interested to hear what was going on. Alec Johnson, a veteran football writer for the *Daily Mirror*, had approached me and said a lot of people wanted to see changes at the club. City's turnover was very low at that time, and Alec said he was representing a bunch of the supporters who were disaffected. This was the group that would soon be known as 'Forward with Franny'.

I was full-on running my racing business at this time, and I was on my way to the races at Doncaster when Alec put this to me. I told him to come to the races with me. He did just that and later it got to the stage where two or three of the City directors were the instigators. I met them, but it was two or three months before my return to the club *really* got underway. I met shareholders, too, and they were unhappy with the club accounts and with what they were being told.

Yet there was no way that Peter Swales wanted to walk away after two decades as chairman, even though his opponents thought the club was in jeopardy. And they were right, it was. The club was in deep doo-doo.

It never got to the point where I sat around – or across – the same table as Swales. I didn't want to speak to him or meet him. His right-hand man was vice-chairman Freddie Pye, a former chairman of Stockport County who had made his money in scrap metal, and the moment it looked like a takeover was going to happen, Swales told Pye that he would be out, too.

Pye immediately came to me and said he needed to be on the board because he had shares in the company –

and he was eventually co-opted on to the board. It was chaotic. Twice it looked like the deal was off because of misinformation, and I wondered on more than one occasion why I was bothering. At times, I still wished I hadn't!

Swales was the man – and I knew this – who had engineered my sale all those years earlier at City. But it wasn't about that, it was about turning this fine old club around. He'd issued a statement saying neither he nor fellow director Stephen Boler would be selling any of their shares. The same applied to Greenalls, the brewers, Swales said – and that was 80 per cent of the club's stock. Then Boler changed his mind and said he would talk … if Swales was amenable.

We made an initial bid to buy 29.9 per cent of the club but that was flatly rejected by Swales. Then two defeats in early November, one away at West Ham (3-1) and at home to Manchester United (3-2), darkened the mood. A couple of drawn games followed but after losing at home 3-1 to Sheffield Wednesday, Swales resigned. The catalyst seemed to be a shocking report alleging some City fans had attempted to enter the chairman's elderly mother's nursing home. No one can do anything but condemn something like that.

The deal was done and sealed on 4 February 1994, after City lost to Cardiff in the FA Cup, leaving me nothing but a relegation battle to look forward to on the pitch, and all sorts of horrors off it. Part of the takeover provided for £5m to be made available immediately for team reinforcements. Even though the crowd rose to hail my arrival, and the team gave me a winning start with a 2-1 home win over Ipswich, that cash would certainly be needed.

There were creditors who'd been owed money for six months, others 12 months and some were waiting as long as 18 months. One guy had lent £250,000 to pay the wages. He was on a promise that he was to go on the City board, and the first thing I did as chairman when I took over was to return his £250,000. We had to appoint new auditors, KPMG, to do the due diligence. The club's bankers, RBS, weren't happy with how the club had been run and didn't want to extend the overdraft. Another bank, the Co-operative, was interested and pitched for the business, and they got it once we took over the club at the start of February.

When I got the keys to the office, so to speak, there was lots more mess to find – and clean up. For example, I couldn't understand how the visiting teams and the referees had stood for having to take cold showers – although the ref, in fairness, was afforded the luxury of three buckets of hot water taken into his room. How he got that, I don't know. Maybe from one of the houses across the road! But the boiler did look just like the one Humphrey Bogart had on the *African Queen*. It had patches on it and steam coming out of all sorts of places. It was the very same boiler as the one they had when I joined the club back in 1967.

Peter Swales would have board meetings maybe every six months. I immediately set about holding monthly meetings, with all the directors having input. We did that with everyone having a fair chance to put their views. It was done on a very democratic basis.

But it was a voyage of discovery. And I didn't always like what I discovered. There was one player in the accounts who had been 'sold' at £1.5m. Sold? As far as I was aware, he'd never been sold. Something didn't look right in the accounts to me. I asked Bernard Halford, City's loyal and long-serving secretary, but he said he knew nothing about that. I suggested to him that he knew nothing about it because he got his accounts together and passed them on to one of City's leading shareholders, who then got an accountant, who was Peter Swales's man, on to them. My opinion was that, although the accounts appeared to declare a small profit each year, there was no profit at all.

Bernard was a good man and he looked stunned when I spoke to him. I was also intrigued by what to me were some strange-looking transfers. When I mentioned these to Bernard, he asked, 'In what way?' I suggested that the agent got a cut, but that other key people seemed to be getting a cut out of these transfers too. I suggested that the club didn't want the outside world to know about this and asked Bernard what he thought of my views? 'Oh aye,' he said.

My vision was for everyone to pull in the same direction, and it began that way. Chartered accountant and City fan David Bernstein came on board after I'd met him at the Mottram Hall Hotel. He expressed his interest and said he wanted to buy some shares after we'd created a new holding company with new shares – Manchester City Football Club plc – and we got quite a few people to invest in the club. The principal investors in that new company were the guys who ended up on the board, new directors such as Colin Barlow, John Dunkerley, David Holt and Ashley Lewis.

I put John Dunkerley in charge of rebuilding the training ground at Platt Lane, because it was in a dreadful state – dilapidated, poor changing rooms and pitches – sending out all the wrong messages to young players interested in joining the club. It was a disgrace. John was a good entrepreneur, and he did a very good job. When we opened the dome, the last phase of Platt Lane, and my successor David Bernstein's name went on the plaque, well, it should have been John Dunkerley's name up there, no question.

Colin Barlow was a good friend. He'd played for City long before I arrived at Maine Road in 1967, and he also joined us as chief executive – City's first – and also as a board member. Colin had been a fine, goalscoring winger and only lost his place in the side after the emergence of

Neil Young. He later set up his own successful import-export business and he was a good man to have on board. In fact, both Colin Barlow and John Dunkerley were absolutely key allies in helping me navigate the early, choppy waters of the takeover. They stood four-square with me as we worked to get the deal done and then began with the task ahead.

The biggest immediate headache, off the pitch, was having to build a new stand on the famous Kippax terrace. This was both necessary and unavoidable, as the Taylor Report into the Hillsborough disaster of 1989 signalled the end for standing-only terraces at major club grounds. The Kippax, no matter how beloved by City's faithful, had to go. It was unusual, anyway, in being a standing-only terrace running the length of the pitch. We ended up paying £16 million, more than some clubs paid for entirely new grounds, to create its towering replacement. Clearing waste from under the old terrace should have cost £80,000 but ended up being an eye-watering £1.8 million. That was before a brick was laid! More than once I reckoned my good luck, because I've earned my good fortune, had run out!

At that stage, early 1994, the team was bottom of the Premier League and without a striker. Niall Quinn was crucial to the side, but he was missing with a cruciate ligament injury. We bought four forwards that season. Paul Walsh was one of the first and Eric 'Monster Monster' Hall was his agent, and wanted more money than we were prepared to pay. Eric, a one-time record plugger in the music business, used that word 'monster' all the time and he wanted monster money! In the end we signed Walsh from Portsmouth for £750,000.

Then Jerome Anderson, the well-known players' agent, phoned to tell us about a striker he had in Germany who had been injured. He thought we might like him. He was East Germany international Uwe Rösler, and we took him on a month's trial. We played him in a reserve match against Burnley at Maine Road, and he had a good game. At half-time our manager, Brian Horton, asked me what I thought about him. I said, 'He's had the ball 22 times this half and given it away only twice – and he has scored a goal. That's better than what you have in the first team. For the asking price, £350,000, I think we should take him and put him in the team.'

We signed him on that initial loan and played him at QPR on Saturday, 5 March. He wasn't match fit because of his recent injury – an ankle knock – but he played well and we got a result there, drawing 1-1. The place started to buzz a bit and we began to play well. We nearly signed Anders Limpar from Arsenal, but I thought he was talking to us simply to up the money that he was on at Arsenal. I was pleased those talks broke down because I didn't like his demeanour. Instead, he went to Everton and, when he did that, we signed Peter Beagrie from Goodison. He made his debut for us in a goalless draw at Oldham on 26 March.

The old Kippax was due for demolition at this point, and there would be nothing there for a while, awaiting the completion of the new grandstand. We always said Beagrie never played well on that side of the pitch, he only played well in front of a crowd. At times he could be really devastating. We were starting to gel and went on a seven-game unbeaten run, only ended by a 2-0 derby reverse at Old Trafford. That was offset by a 2-2 draw with Chelsea at Maine Road, the final home game of the season and the very last sight of the old Kippax – cue a sea of celebratory balloons – before its demolition.

Another draw, 1-1 at Sheffield Wednesday, saw us finish in 16th place. It sounds comfortable, doesn't it? It wasn't, but we got out of trouble in the end.

I got a buzz, no pun intended 'Buzzer', when a famous name returned to City that summer. Yes, Summerbee was back. Not Mike, but his son, Nick, a £1.5m signing from Swindon. We also made Rösler's three-month loan deal permanent, at what was a bargain price. The season started in a predictably *unpredictable* fashion, with good home results contrasting poor away form. But the goals were flying in when Spurs were beaten 5-2 at Maine Road, followed by a 4-3 success at QPR in the League Cup. No time for complacency, as our neighbours, leading the table, hammered us 5-0 at Old Trafford. And after losing the experienced Steve McMahon, who left to become player-boss at Swindon, we sanctioned Brian Horton's loan signing of German schemer Maurizio Gaudino on loan. At the season's midway point, we were mid-table on 28 points.

Our promising League Cup run ended in the fifth round with a chastening 4-0 exit at Crystal Palace, not long before a Rösler hat-trick helped us ease past FA Cup third-round opponents Notts County, in a Maine Road replay. Our interest ended after beating Villa in the next round, when we were on the wrong end of a 3-1 result at Newcastle. That wasn't great, but our league form was the real concern in the spring. We went ten games without a win, finally ending the barren run by beating Ipswich 2-0 at home, and bagged another home point in a 0-0 shut-out against Leeds United.

We were just about treading water above the relegation zone as the vital Easter programme loomed, and we first faced a daunting home match with Liverpool. What a response from the players, though, as two of our relative new boys, Summerbee and Gaudino, got the goals either side of a Steve McManaman equaliser, to bag us all three points and make it a very Good Friday indeed. We weren't out of the woods, though, and faced an Easter Monday trip to high-flying Blackburn Rovers.

Rovers, inspired by owner Jack Walker's incredible chairmanship and led by Kenny Dalglish, were on their way to win the title that year, whereas we'd struggled. We'd settled to around third-bottom with a run-in of five games to go. I asked Brian Horton if he'd mind us all getting together for a bit of a pep talk. He said he didn't mind at all, so I spoke to the squad – it consisted of about 15 or 16 players then. I said to them, 'We have five games to go and if we win two or three of them, we will definitely stay up and progress. Is there anyone in this room who thinks we can't do it? If so, stick your hand up now.' No one raised a hand, so I told them that was fine – let's all get on with it.

So, off we went to Ewood Park and, with the Premiership trophy beckoning, it looked like a home banker. Jack Walker said to me before kick-off, 'I see you've bought a few players … do you want a bet on the match?'

I agreed that we'd signed a few, but I declined the bet, saying, 'You're top of the league and we're nearly bottom, do you think I'm stupid?' But maybe I *was* stupid not to take it … because we won 3-2! Uwe Rösler got a good goal that night to get us back to 2-2 in the second half. Alan Shearer had put them one up early on before a Keith Curle penalty got us back on terms, only for Colin Hendry to make it 2-1 before the break. Then came Rösler's goal, before his strike partner, Paul Walsh, got us the winner 20 minutes from time. What a win that was!

It was a terrific result for us, and everyone was buzzing. We ended the campaign a few weeks later four points and two places above the relegation spots, so the players had dug in and done what was asked. It's on public record now that the team coach left Ewood that night and the players ended up at a pub near Haydock Park for a pit stop on the way back. The players may have thought it was to celebrate a good win but, instead, they were locked into a side room and Brian Horton told them he was leaving at the end of the season. There's quite a story behind that!

Horton remained very much in charge as we drew the next game at home to Newcastle and, in fact, was boss for the remaining three games, in which only one point was picked up from a 1-1 draw at Aston Villa. The last game ended in a 3-2 win for QPR at Maine Road and, two days later, we announced that Horton would indeed be leaving. It's a story that provides the unbelievable key to the mystery of how my old England mate Alan Ball became City's next manager – and a very unpopular one, at that.

Horton was on a two-year rolling contract, along with David Moss, his assistant. Horton had been to a managers' meeting at the Lilleshall coaching centre, in Shropshire, and Malcolm Allison had been to a dinner, 'An Evening with The Blues', in Manchester. Malcolm sold a story to *The Sun* along the lines that Horton was to be sacked. Brian rang me up, furious about this story and I told him I knew nothing about it. I told him the truth, that there would be a review-of-the-season meeting of the board a fortnight after the end of the campaign. Nothing was happening before that.

Brian, however, wasn't happy. He came to see me at my home in Wilmslow and I told him that I'd phoned the other City directors and their opinion was clear: if that was his attitude, he could go. I told him to see his solicitor because I'd had nothing to do with the drawing up of his contract – I'd inherited him as manager from Peter Swales.

We decided we'd better get ourselves a new manager so I got Colin Barlow to take the project on for me. Colin was a devout Roman Catholic and went to the same church as Brian Kidd, Alex Ferguson's number two at Manchester United. Brian was a United legend – scoring in their 1968 European Cup Final triumph – but he'd also enjoyed a good spell as a player at City in the late 1970s. Colin and I both reckoned he was well worth sounding out.

Kidd said to Colin, 'Yes, I'll do your job. I'll be the manager.' Now, as Fergie's right-hand man, this could be quite an appointment and represent a real coup for us. We met him and went right through the job. He would do this, he told us. He would do that. He'd be in charge of the players' diets, training and so on. This went on for a couple of weeks and I think he was on £70,000 or £80,000 a year at Manchester United at that time as their number two. We offered him a £300,000 basic wage to make the switch and make the step up as our manager. Nobody knew of our interest, let alone the size of our offer. It was all agreed and we shook hands on the deal. Brian Kidd was in the bag as the new manager of Manchester City!

This was a guy who seemed a proper football man. He had a profile as a major figure in United's dugout next to Fergie; he'd been a star at both Manchester clubs and had played for England, too. We'd bagged a good 'un. I was absolutely delighted.

I told Brian that, as it was the end of the season, he'd better go and tell the United chairman Martin Edwards – or Fergie – that he was leaving. 'Leave it to me,' he replied. So I did, but then it all went strangely quiet until, in early June, he sent me a fax – remember them? – saying he would *not* be taking the job. I'd actually asked Colin Barlow to get in touch with Kidd, to find out what was going on ... but Kidd's sledgehammer fax arrived first.

I was stunned, dumbfounded, and, of course, I rang Brian Kidd. 'What do you mean, you're not taking the job?' I asked. 'We've shaken hands on the deal! The wages are on the table!'

When he eventually spoke, he explained that when he went to see Martin Edwards, he couldn't bring himself to tell him that he wanted to leave. 'It's such a big wrench to leave Old Trafford,' he said, as he gave me a load of crap by way of an excuse. I was not impressed.

'You didn't tell him that you were going to be paid four or five times more money?' I asked, suspecting he'd used us as a lever to better himself at United. 'So, he's given you some more money and you're going to stay there, is that it?' I drove home my point. And I told him that if he couldn't make a decision with the courage of his convictions, he'd never make a manager.

Christ, we'd even discussed our first signing! We'd agreed to go for Gareth Southgate, then a bright young defender at Crystal Palace. Kidd wanted him and I think he'd been impressed with Southgate when United played at Selhurst the previous January … the same night Eric Cantona decided to take a diversion into the crowd by aiming a kung-fu kick at a fan! Palace wanted about £4m, maybe £5m for him at the time. I said that was fine – we were prepared to give him an initial budget of £10m, a lot of money back then. Southgate was to be just the first. That's how far we'd gone down the line for Brian Kidd. It was cut and dried, signed and sealed – and *then* it wasn't.

I was absolutely furious – and completely banjaxed. And so, the search for a new manager began again. We spoke to two or three managers. I interviewed Dave 'Harry' Bassett, who was at Sheffield United, in the Derbyshire home of my business colleague Peter Barr, the chief executive of Hazlewood Foods. Bassett had done a good job at Bramall

Lane, winning two promotions, and getting that club into the fledgling Premiership.

'Yes, yes,' he kept saying, everything was okay.

'Right,' I said to him, 'have a think about the job and give me a shout.'

All seemed well and he called back to fix a meeting – and our rendezvous was at Colin Barlow's house. He was all for it at our first meeting, but at the second meeting we had, he was less certain. 'What's your problem?' I asked him. I had to understand, he confided to me, that he'd been a non-league performer as a player. How could he take the City manager's job with a guy like me, a former England international, as chairman?

'You understand the game at the very highest level, but I've had to work my way up from non-league,' he said.

'But you'll be the manager, you're not bloody playing,' I told him. I hoped my words had the desired effect as he left Colin's house. I certainly didn't want to be left in the brown stuff again, but I did tell Colin that I was now having my doubts.

The next morning, at about 7.30am, he phoned. I was still in bed and 'Harry' told me he'd decided not to take the job. By now I was getting bloody concerned. We'd tried for Kidd and Bassett and had 11th-hour knock-backs from both – and it was now mid-June. I was only too well aware that the press was slagging me off for apparently not

SPORT | SOCCER EXTRA

I'd heal City wounds says £30m Franny

By JOHN BEAN

FRANCIS LEE put himself forward last night as the people's choice to heal Manchester City's wounds.

The guy who ran through brick walls for Joe Mercer and Malcolm Allison has a fortune of around £30 million—and the character—to do it.

I have known Franny Lee since the days he did a weekly national newspaper article with me in the late Sixties.

He was never short of ideas and as a player Lee, now 51, was a 5ft 7in powerhouse with a total disregard for anything in his path.

He was the most chirpy member of the Bell-Lee-Summerbee triumvirate that helped fill City's trophy cabinet in the late Sixties and early Seventies.

Lee was the brightest and busiest member of that squad and proved it by building business interests that have made him one of England's richest ex-footballers.

His wastepaper collection business grew into a paper conversion company which he sold for £8m, while remaining a director. When he was through playing centre-forward for City, Derby and [illegible]

Faces of Franny: Left, the Seventies soccer star. Right, the racehorse trainer, with jockey Steve Perks. Above, yesterday at Wilmslow with son Gary, ex-City team-mate Mike Summerbee and legal advisor Nathan Marks (right)

Herbert . . . big plans

Herbert aims for one over the eight

From MARTIN HARDY in ROUDNICE

TINY cox Garry Herbert is looking for bigger things in the rowing world.

Double gold medallist Herbert, a coxed pairs champion with the Searle brothers at last summer's Olympics and the World Championships here, wants to move into the blue riband event of regattas.

Herbert is keen to make himself one over the eight . . . and steer the long boat to Olympic glory.

He wants to take his two golden oarsmen with him and form an eight on their powerful shoulders. "I'm sure Jonny and Greg could give us the basis for a magnificent eight," he said.

The search for a new event has been prompted by the coxed pairs being dropped from the next Olympics to bring in lightweights for the first time.

Reeve is hit for six

By COLIN BATEMAN

DERMOT REEVE, hero of Warwickshire's dramatic last ball win in a [illegible]

Franny, pictured by the Daily Express *ahead of his 1994 takeover, with son Gary, left, legal adviser Nathan Marks, far right, and close pal Mike Summerbee.*

having someone ready to take Horton's job. 'You'd think,' the whispers went, 'that someone of his experience would have had a successor before mid-summer.' If only they knew about Kidd!

That's when I decided to ring my old England mate, Alan Ball, who'd just had a good season with Southampton, finishing tenth in the Premiership. When I reached him, he was at Royal Ascot. He was knocked out by the prospect and came up for a chat, and we went through it. By this point we'd actually appointed Asa Hartford as Brian Kidd's assistant, and he was at the club. It wasn't Asa's fault that Kidd had turned turtle on us. I asked Bally if he minded having Asa, but Bally didn't have a problem, reasoning that he was an England international, I was an England international and Asa had caps for Scotland, so the more knowledge, the better. So it was that Alan Ball eventually took the job.

It was the start of a shocking period when my worries about Lady Luck running out proved to be spot on. Picking a manager proved not to be my strongest suit and, off the pitch, the club still had a way to go.

Final England cap: It's Franny's 29th birthday, April 1972, and it's those West Germans again! He waits for a chance as keeper Sepp Maier defends.

Final England goal: Lee pounces to score, but the West Germans were worthy winners.

Sheepskin coat, new Jaguar XJ6: Francis Lee, outside his Bolton premises, is a businessman on the up in this 1969 press shot.

Francis Lee and pal Mike Summerbee enjoy a City spa day at Blackpool's Derby Baths, January 1973.

Jokers wild: Our dynamic duo are at it again – sharing an aero-bath at the same spa day.

It's January 1975 – and Francis is on his way to another league title, this time with Derby County.

Derby's Roy McFarland and Francis Lee parade the Football League championship trophy to the Baseball Ground's fans, May 1975.

Leeds' Norman Hunter (No 6) and a bloodied Francis Lee are sent off after their infamous bust-up. Franny, however, was just getting started! 1 November 1975.

Francis Lee and Real Madrid's Jose Antonio Camacho; European Cup second round, first leg, 22 October 1975.

Company man: Francis at the helm of F.H. Lee.

On the up: Marking an F.H. Lee company milestone with brother Arthur, right, and Davyhulme MP, Winston Spencer Churchill.

Franny with his Uncle Fred.

Home sweet home: the Lee family home at the Little Stanneylands Stud Farm estate.

The picturesque stables at Little Stanneylands.

The thatched office at the stables.

Talk to the animals. Franny talks tactics with one of his horses.

Rod Lappin on the Francis Lee-trained Beau Venture wins the 1994 Coral Handicap, 6 August, at Haydock. Photo courtesy of Daniel Abraham.

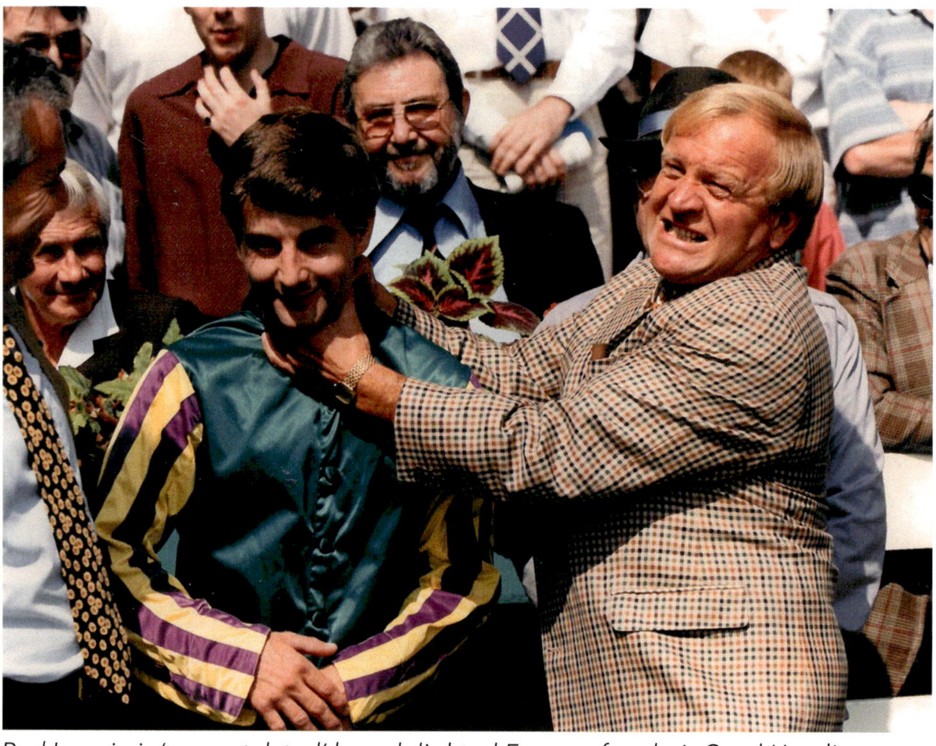

Rod Lappin is 'congratulated' by a delighted Franny after their Coral Handicap success. Photo courtesy of Daniel Abraham.

This Is Your Life: *Francis and Gill with, from left, Charlotte and Nik with Jonny, far right, after their TV show surprise.*

Mr Chairman: Francis Lee takes his seat in the directors' box for City's match with Nottingham Forest, 8 October 1994.

In the saddle: Franny shows once again that he was accomplished in many sports.

Can you play up front, Rod? Francis chats to Rod Stewart ahead of the star's Maine Road gig, 22 July 1995.

Welcome Steve – and goodbye! Francis unveils Steve Coppell as City boss. Too soon he'd be gone, 7 October 1996.

Francis and Gill display his CBE, flanked by sons Jonny, right, and Nik, after his investiture at Buckingham Palace.

Francis and Gill relax in Portugal.

On the Etihad turf: Francis Lee is greeted by the crowd ahead of City v Huddersfield, 6 May 2018. They were presented with the Premier League trophy after the match.

Francis, son Jonny, and grandson Freddie.

Good times: Franny and Nik in Quinta.

Gill and Franny in their 'happy place'.

Freddie with 'Dodo' – grandad Francis – in Portugal.

Lee and Sons – Franny flanked by Jonny (left) and Nik.

This will be competitive: Franny (right) about to tee off with Nik, left, and Jonny.

Franny remembered: At the first home game after Francis's death – against Brighton – fans unfurled this banner in tribute. 21 October 2023.

Immortal: A tremendous trio immortalised forever in bronze – Bell, Lee (centre) and Summerbee grace the Etihad's grounds.

Chapter Fifteen

Back to the Future

THERE WAS so much challenging work ahead of me, but I never lost sight of my desire to make Manchester City the very best club it could be. To that end, a conversation with another high-profile club chairman proved pivotal for me – and for City. Before Alan Ball's appointment, I'd gone to a Premiership meeting during the previous season and Newcastle United chairman Sir John Hall said to me, 'You've landed lucky, haven't you?' 'Why was that?' I asked. 'Because Manchester has got the 2002 Commonwealth Games … and there will be a fabulous new stadium funded by Sport England and your city council,' he replied. 'It must be good for you, because Manchester United are not based in the city – they're in Salford.'

He was right. I got on to it right away. For all the work we'd done at Maine Road, updating the old ground and improving turnover, facilities and the like, this was a chance to be seized. I did the initial negotiations with Howard

Bernstein, the chief executive of Manchester City Council, and Graham Stringer, the MP for Blackley in Manchester. We discussed whether we'd trade Maine Road for the City of Manchester Stadium at Eastlands, and I said 'yes' – so long as I could get the fans on board.

There was a civic backstory to all this. Manchester had made bids to host both the 1996 and 2000 Summer Olympics, the bids headed by Bob Scott, the noted theatrical and cultural impresario. Much groundwork was done but both failed, with first Atlanta and then Sydney winning, respectively. But Howard, who'd been made deputy chief executive of Manchester City Council in 1990, and Graham, the former council leader who went on to Westminster, were dogged in their pursuit and they'd then pressed on with a bid to host the Commonwealth Games in 2002. In November 1995, with City showing signs of improvement on the pitch after a dreadful start – Bally even won the Bell's Manager of the Month award – it was announced that Manchester had won the Commonwealth Games bid.

Howard and Graham were great, and interesting, allies. Howard was a City fan, while Graham was a red, but they were united in helping me with the first steps towards securing the stadium for City. The initial idea behind the Olympic bid was the legacy of an 80,000-capacity national stadium to take the mantle from the then ageing Wembley

Stadium. Both Manchester clubs had been approached but United, firmly embedded at Old Trafford, weren't interested, and their chairman, Sir Roland Smith, swiftly said 'no'. I could only see advantages for City and pressed on, though we couldn't, at that stage, agree to an 80,000-seater. I knew we had a chance because everyone behind the Commonwealth Games bid couldn't countenance the legacy of a post-Games white elephant stadium on their hands.

Fortunately for us, Wembley was in no mood to relinquish its hold on hosting FA events, and their plans for a rebuilt 21st-century stadium went ahead. So, ultimately, Manchester was not going to have a national stadium. But I was fighting hard for City to have a shot at taking on the Commonwealth Games stadium!

I knew we had to woo the supporters over, and our secretary, Bernard Halford, was initially completely against it. For good reason. Bernard must have taken a first look at the idea and thought of the upheaval and the end of his own 'island' at Maine Road, with everything in order and just so. This opportunity was seismic but would change all that. And the fans, or many of them, might baulk at the idea of all the City history linked to Maine Road coming to an end. I knew their feelings more than most – and shared them – this was my football home. But times change, this was the Premier League, we had to make this move. Just *had* to.

So, I began a campaign to sell this idea to the supporters. I went to several fans' meetings and explained what a fantastic stadium would be coming on stream for the Commonwealth Games and then, with the end of the event, the athletics running track could be removed and the stadium transformed into a very, very fine football ground.

I asked them one key question: Would any of you rather see Manchester City playing in a better, newer, more modern stadium than Manchester United? I asked for a show of hands, and everyone stuck their hands up. Thank you very much, I said. A big relief … but who wouldn't vote for that? We did a poll in the match programme and Colin Bell told me quite a few had voted against moving. I told him I hadn't seen those! This was the chance of a lifetime and no one was going to mess this up.

I was given the task of speaking to the Rugby Football League to ask if they would play their semi-finals and finals at the new stadium; pop and rock concerts had to be considered (we'd already done quite a few at Maine Road) because part of the contract, so to speak, of turning the Games venue into a football stadium was the understanding that it would be used for far more than just football.

Graham Stringer recalled later that he has a clear memory of talking to me and Colin Barlow about City moving forward with this plan and that we 'snatched their hands off' – he's absolutely right!

We then got multi-events lined up so that Sport England could be satisfied that it wasn't merely to be the fiefdom of the football club. Manchester City Council were absolutely top class, notably Howard and his team. So ended, pretty smartly, the development of Maine Road's new Kippax stand because we'd planned to extend it and attach it to the North Stand. We put in temporary seating instead, in the corners – not 100 per cent successful, as it was nicknamed the Gene Kelly Stand after *Singing in the Rain*! That increased our capacity back up to about 36,000, which got the income up nicely.

On the pitch there were clearly quite a few problems, but off the pitch we were still a million miles off the pace at Maine Road. We had this huge stand that was doing sweet FA for us, in terms of generating cash for the club. I formed the 'Boardroom Suite' for people wanting to invest in the club. They paid £50,000 for a table of four and in exchange got convertible loan stock with interest on the money – one per cent above bank rate – and they also enjoyed a top-class restaurant and entertainment. They paid more on top and got their football too, of course, and this sort of elite season-ticket option for wealthy fans is something that has been widely developed in the English game in the years since.

We had to raise £1.5 million to do the conversion in the stand for this and, to make way for that, I cleared all the club offices out and relocated the staff (making myself quite unpopular along the way) and upgraded all the bars. We tried to make everything a selling point for the club.

I was later to find out that for every home match, a bloke came up to Manchester from Bournemouth to oversee and handle the match programme sales. He was paid £1,500 each game for his services. Nobody knew about this. But, subsequently, Mike Turner, the chief executive we'd appointed in 1997 to replace Colin Barlow, told me about this trick and how it had gone on for years. It was astonishing – that was very quickly stopped.

The Kippax stand redevelopment was intended to raise money for the club with great hospitality and catering facilities. We'd appointed a top caterer, Gordon Beech, who was first class. Behind one of the goals, at the Umbro Stand end, the catering was let out to Letheby & Christopher, who'd fitted out all the hospitality boxes. This company has a reputation as the UK's leading caterer at leisure venues and sports and racing stadia, but the kitchen units that they had put in and the club had paid for were re-leased back to them. I couldn't believe that because I'd turned my attention to the area beneath that Umbro Stand. I wanted to do something with it and there was plenty of room for bars and lounges there.

That was my plan, but I found I couldn't do anything because Letheby & Christopher had the contract for all the catering in that stand. It was unbelievable. We were stuck. Letheby & Christopher had a small restaurant under the main stand, the Executive Suite, which wasn't in the same ballpark as the work we were doing on the same floor nearby. And what we had in the Umbro Stand was nothing like the quality of what we were doing in the new Kippax.

It seemed only right and normal for us to upgrade everywhere, but we couldn't. In fact, Delia Smith, the Norwich City director and famous TV cook, came to our club and said, 'I have to tell you, Francis, you have got the best stadia catering in Europe.' I knew Delia through my contacts in the grocery trade, but I'm sure she was right and not merely being polite.

We also had, on the final Thursday of every month, the Luncheon Club with a top meal and guest speaker. It was always packed out and it all generated money for the club. All of this was designed to build up a new team spirit in the club, not just on the pitch but for everyone working around the club, and the fans who wanted to be part of it. There were three gyms under the stands, where I remember playing head tennis as a player, and I altered all that and transformed one gym into a very good players' lounge. The others were turned into restaurants and corporate facilities.

The turnover jumped as a result, but we couldn't do our own kit sales because that had been leased out to a guy for £60,000! He paid the club that amount for the privilege of selling *all* our replica shirts and other kit. That was some deal – for him! Not for Manchester City! That had to stop.

Brewery company Greenalls were shareholders in the club and owned the social club. The club had been mortgaged and remortgaged and they owed the brewery quite a lot of money on it. I pestered and pestered Greenalls to turn the social club into a big, big superstore, and in the last year I was at the club that became a reality.

Our turnover was going up all around the club. From an £8 million turnover when I took over in 1994, it was up to something like £15 million at the time I left, four years later. All done at the same old ground! JD Sports expressed an interest in running that City superstore – they were very good sports retailers and very, very professional. They did a good job and bit by bit we were starting to look like a proper Premier League club. All this and my early work with the various authorities to make the move from Maine Road to Eastlands gave me great confidence that the future was bright.

That was the catalyst, I'm sure, for the interest in City from David Makin and John Wardle, who were building up their fast-growing sports retail firm, JD Sports – JD represented their initials – at that time. They were also building their shareholding in the club. At the same time, Bernstein, who I'd brought into Manchester City, appeared to me to be becoming quite close with them. I wondered whether he was thinking that he should align himself with them, rather than me, given the poor results on the park. And that, indeed, is precisely what he did. When Makin and Wardle then invested quite a lot into the club, the duo put my old team-mate Dennis Tueart on to the board as their representative.

That seemed all good and sound, but what our faithful fans were seeing on the pitch most certainly was not. Bally had his season – in 1995/96 – and it couldn't have been worse for Alan, the club or for me. That November recovery proved a false dawn and we got relegated and were *out* of the Premier League. A disaster, plain and simple. I'd heralded Bally's arrival in July by exclaiming that this was the job he'd been waiting for – and that he was willing to die for the club. In the end, sad to say, it was a slow crucifixion.

Alan had problems with some of the players and he didn't get off on the right foot when, very early in the season, he traded Paul Walsh back to Portsmouth in exchange for Gerry Creaney. That put Walshy's strike partner Uwe Rösler's nose out of joint; he was *not* impressed.

Alan also seemed to be at odds with some of the higher earners in the dressing room. He fell out with Rösler and Niall Quinn, while Keith Curle didn't really want to play for him. He sold them on. There was also discontent among some of the players about Alan's wife being spotted around the training ground, showing off her man's World Cup medal. I don't know what that was all about.

There were a few bright spots. I'd told Alan that I'd bought him a really good player – and I still think he was – Georgi Kinkladze, the Georgian forward from Dinamo Tbilisi, who was magnificent that season. In fact, he was the club player of the year for two successive seasons. I signed him in the close season after Brian Horton had left.

We were still to win after nine Premier League games and sat firmly at the bottom of the league. The tenth brought another defeat, 1-0 in the Old Trafford derby, followed by a goalless draw against Leeds at Maine Road. It was poor, let's pull no punches, and the fans were now taking aim at me, not just at Bally. A poll in the *Manchester Evening News* resulted in 83 per cent of those responding wanting me to stand down as chairman.

I responded with this: 'I have made a commitment, and I am prepared to see it through, I will stick it out as long as the genuine fans want me to stay.' Not many fans would have been brave enough to say so after two quick-fire visits to Anfield. The first, a 4-0 exit in the third round of the League Cup, was followed by a 6-0 mauling in the league just days later. We finally got our first Premiership win of the season at the 12th attempt, shading it 1-0 against Bolton. Two further 1-0 wins lifted the mood as we beat

Wimbledon and then Villa – the latter featuring a wonderful show from Kinkladze.

This November awakening won Bally that Manager of the Month gong, but December yielded just a single point from a 1-1 home draw with Nottingham Forest. Then a decent five-match unbeaten run in the league ended with a 2-0 defeat at Everton, and that result put us back in the relegation zone. Our FA Cup interest ended at Old Trafford in the fifth round. And we remained in the bottom three.

Another derby, this one in the league on 6 April, was costly. United came to Maine Road and beat us 3-2, and then a 3-0 loss at Wimbledon made relegation a distinct possibility. But there was still hope with two slender 1-0 wins – one at home to Sheffield Wednesday and then away at Villa. We needed to get a result in the final game of the season against Liverpool at Maine Road, and a 2-2 draw gave us hope. But the two sides immediately above City, Coventry and Southampton, both got positive results for a three-way tie on 38 points – but their better goal differences confirmed the worst: City were down and out of the top flight after seven years. Just another point or a goal here or there would have kept us safe, but I've never really been one for what-ifs. We just hadn't been good enough.

That was bad enough, for certain, but it got worse. We started the following season poorly in the second tier and Bally was getting stick from the crowd. We'd started the league campaign with a 1-0 home win against Ipswich but then lost at Bolton. We managed to get Arsenal's busy little striker, Paul Dickov, in for £1m and he made his debut in the next game at Stoke. But we lost that game 2-1, and Bally got fearful flak from both City supporters and his old Stoke fans.

This was a really tough call, but the other directors agreed with me that it was time for change. I had to speak to Bally, to end the agony. My old mate had to go, and I sorted his contract out for him. He was gone on the Monday after the game. It was a difficult decision and a tough conversation for me but, in fairness, Alan knew it was coming.

Chapter Sixteen

Can You Manage? And the Enemies Within

I COULD certainly play the game; I didn't need to look at the record books or my medals and caps to convince myself of that. I reckoned I could run the business side of the club, and the work I'd done since becoming chairman in February 1994 was testament to that. But what about running the team? Could I pick – and work with – a successful manager? My experience with Alan Ball had been a bruising one for both of us. He was my friend and a good man.

What happened next was the wonderful experience – and yes, I'm being sarcastic – of City being managed by Steve Coppell. Steve had been the most wonderful player and a deep thinker about the game. He was a big name in Manchester, and indeed the country, after a great career at Manchester United and 42 England caps. He had two spells in charge at Crystal Palace and I thought he had the right qualities to succeed at Manchester City.

He came in on the back of an interim spell in charge for our coach – and former player – Asa Hartford. Asa stepped up on 26 August and was in charge throughout September while we looked for our preferred appointment. And that appointment was Steve Coppell.

Coppell's City stats tell the stark story in retrospect … a mere six games and just 33 days in charge, the shortest spell in charge for any City manager. The story behind the bare stats is even starker.

Keith Pinner, a big bear of a businessman and a huge Manchester City fan, knew Steve and he told me that he might be interested in the job. At the time, Steve was in his second spell at Palace, and he was regarded as a really bright managerial prospect. He was experienced for such a young man as he'd started early, his fine playing career curtailed at just 28 by injury. He was thoughtful, intelligent – he had an economics degree from Liverpool University – and clearly presented as a very good football man.

David Bernstein and I interviewed Steve in London. After that he came north to see me and he asked if he could have Phil Neal, the respected ex-Liverpool and England captain, as his assistant. We agreed to that and changed everything around in the coaching set-up so that Steve came into the job on his terms.

We all thought Steve would do a good job. He'd already been reasonably successful, and he was still young, at 41.

But right from the start, after he walked into Maine Road, I was concerned. He hardly ever seemed to be at the club. He'd come in on matchdays, but there appeared to be a lack of leadership about the place. Within those very few – 33 – days he'd packed in and left us! It turned out he'd been seeing the club chaplain, Tony Porter, from day one, asking for help. He was apparently feeling suicidal and would curl up into a ball. What was he doing? And what had we done? What had I done?

We went to the press conference when he announced his resignation. We just had to wish Steve Coppell all the best and that was it. It's difficult to delve too deeply into it because he was so rarely seen about the place. Only Steve knew what was going on in his head. Afterwards, he explained it like this:

> I'm not ashamed to admit that I have suffered for some time from huge pressure I have imposed upon myself, and since my appointment this has completely overwhelmed me to such an extent that I cannot function in the job the way I would like to. As this situation is affecting my well-being, I have asked Francis Lee to relieve me of my obligation to manage the club on medical advice.
>
> I am therefore resigning for personal reasons. I'm extremely embarrassed by the situation and I would

> like to apologise first and foremost to Francis Lee, and his board, who have done everything in their power to help me.

I felt for him, but as I said at the time, there's pressure with all big jobs. Yet that sort of overwhelming pressure doesn't come along in the space of three or four weeks!

We then put Phil Neal, Steve's pick as his number two, in caretaker charge. Phil had been a wonderful player, but I soon formed the opinion that he couldn't manage a piss-up in a brewery. Before one game when he was in charge, he was playing music from a ghetto blaster. I thought to myself that I wouldn't even ask him what that was for! Wimbledon, with their Crazy Gang reputation, were doing stuff like that at the time, but for a guy with such an outstanding pedigree at Liverpool, he was a big disappointment to me. I thought with his Anfield grounding he'd want to get hold of the ball and pass it and play. But no, it was all route-one stuff.

Neal made it abundantly clear that he wanted to stay and make his pitch for taking on the job full-time. That wasn't going to happen, given how his audition went. He was in place for ten league games. We won only two (West Bromwich Albion and Bradford City, both 3-2). His last game at Barnsley ended in a 2-0 defeat. I was away in Barbados for that one – but I didn't need to be at Oakwell to know it was time to look for an experienced manager.

So I turned to Frank Clark, a man who'd learned from one of the very best managers – Brian Clough – at Nottingham Forest. Frank had played for Clough during four glorious years in the late 70s before starting his own managerial career, first as assistant boss at Sunderland and then as manager in his own right, at Orient. When Brian retired in 1993, sadly coinciding with Forest's relegation from the Premiership, Clark was the man chosen to replace him. Not only that, despite losing star players Roy Keane and Nigel Clough, Clark got Forest straight back up at the first time of asking, in 1994. As winter loomed in 1996, Forest were struggling at the foot of the Premiership and the club was mired in takeover talk. At that time, Frank publicly expressed his concern at the boardroom distractions, and I decided to make our move.

I went with David Bernstein to meet Frank at London's Heathrow Airport. Frank wanted to know how much of a free rein he'd have with his staff. Or, more pertinently, who could be let go if he brought his own staff.

Bernstein told him, 'There are no sacred cows here!' The man in Frank Clark's sights was clearly Tony Book; like Frank, a veteran full-back-turned-manager. Booky was, by now, a City institution. But now I'd just made Clark our new manager.

This shadowboxing at Frank's Heathrow interview led to the dismissal of Tony Book. It should never have happened the way it did. I told David Bernstein to do nothing about Tony until I returned from a trip, so that I could explain the position to him. Booky always seemed to have in the back of his mind that his dismissal was an act of revenge on my part, a payback for him having sold me to Derby back in 1974. That was completely wrong.

When Frank arrived at City with his assistant Alan Hill, on his first morning he met the staff and his first words were: 'Where's Tony?' But Frank had himself said at the hotel, just a few weeks before, 'When I get to the club, I don't want Tony Book anywhere near the place!' So, for him to ask about Tony's whereabouts was, at best, odd. Frank was told that Tony had been asked not to come to the meeting of staff and that his job had been terminated.

Alan Hill duly began work as Frank's number two and he also came with good experience. He'd worked with Brian Clough at Forest, before his time there with Frank. Now Frank was installed and he could get on with the job in hand at Maine Road.

But Frank Clark spent very little time talking to me – we rarely spoke. He only lived 400 yards away from me in Wilmslow, but he seemed a little intimidated. I'd invite him to have dinner with me, but he'd never come down. He apparently liked to stay in his apartment and play his guitar!

He did come to one of my birthday parties – with his guitar – and at one point piped up, 'Here's a song for the chairman!' He proceeded to sing me Woody Guthrie's song 'Worried Man Blues', which has the famous line, 'It takes a worried man to sing a worried song.' Most amusing – not! He also came to us for a garden barbeque that my wife Gill and I put on. He had another sing-song then, too.

At the restaurant at Platt Lane, the old former City players – the 60 to 80-year-olds – used to get together every Tuesday for a bit of lunch and a natter. Frank said to me, 'We don't like them here.' I asked, 'Why ever not?' 'They are talking about us behind our backs,' he said. I told him they were all stalwarts of the club, who wanted to see City do well. What was his problem? Did he want me to turn them out into Moss Side to go to the local Labour Club when we had a nice facility for them?

Another of Frank's backroom team always seemed to be at the ground if I ever called in late in the afternoon. I don't think he was on football business and something didn't seem right. I told him, 'Look, you'll get caught. One of the papers will have a photographer here. I don't know who it is you're seeing, but you're risking it. Don't bring any controversy on to the club.' I like to think he heeded my advice.

One of the few times Frank asked for advice came when he approached me about a problem he was wrestling with over one of the first-team players.

'Look,' said Frank, 'we're having a problem with Kinkladze.' I asked Frank what this problem was. 'Well, what do you think is his best position?' he asked.

I said, 'What? His best position? Well, you've got 11 players, one of them plays in goal, four at the back, three in midfield and three up front. Whether you play him in midfield or up front, just let him go where he wants because he's such a good player, he makes things happen. You can't tell him where to go, because he's a flair player with loads of natural talent. You can't systemise him.'

He looked at me as though I'd dropped in from Mars. There was certainly space between us! In fairness, Frank steadied us after his December appointment, as it looked like a second successive relegation battle was in store. In the end he guided the side to a steady but unspectacular 14th in the First Division.

Along the way, my big ally Colin Barlow, who'd been so key in our takeover of City, stepped down in January from his chief executive role. I was to lose his boardroom support the following December when he resigned as a director to concentrate on his businesses. That was a shame because we were great pals. Mike Turner took over as chief executive.

The next season was a knife edge from start to finish. We'd kept Gio Kinkladze and brought in £3m striker Lee Bradbury from Portsmouth – I wish I'd seen Lee play before

Frank Clark signed him! When I did see him play in our shirt, I knew it was a mistake. Our start to the season was, shall we say, inauspicious, quickly bundled out of the League Cup by Blackpool and then a 2-1 defeat in the league at Charlton at the end of August, which meant City were without a win, and bottom of the table. When we lost 2-1 at home to Norwich on 20 September, the City fans turned on Frank and things didn't look good.

It was a struggle for him all winter, and when we played our first derby with Stockport County for the best part of nine decades, the result was an embarrassment – losing 3-1. Three successive January draws were followed by a 1-0 defeat against Bury. And that sort of form was the backdrop to yet another managerial firing … and I wasn't sure I was in control at this point.

The serious struggle on the pitch was one thing but, in the boardroom, forces seemed to be lining up against me, and I no longer had Colin Barlow around. My difficulty, it's true, was due in no short measure to the demise of a couple of the managers we'd appointed. This led to a split and the eventual reason I left the club.

Frank was going to watch a match at Sunderland when Peter Reid was manager there. Dennis Tueart told me they – the boardroom faction of Makin, Wardle and Bernstein – should approach Joe Royle to be our manager. What? What had I just heard? I told him they couldn't do that because we already had a manager – Frank Clark. I'd have to first tell Frank that he was no longer the manager.

Dennis said they were meeting Joe Royle at Sunderland that same night because Joe was the guest of Peter Reid for their match that evening. I warned Dennis that it would be very interesting, because I'd heard Frank was going up to the same match! They'd probably all be in the same room at the new Stadium of Light. I rang Alan Hill to check if Frank *was* going up to the game. Alan said yes, he was, and I immediately advised him to get Frank to pull out of that trip. I told Alan it would be very embarrassing for Frank. Alan asked if it was because Frank was going to be axed. I told him honestly that I didn't know. By now I'd had enough, and I reckoned that if they wanted to appoint a manager that way, it was time I wasn't here.

Frank, who previously had clearly not liked social calls at my place, came to see me at my house at nine o'clock the next morning. He walked on to my drive. 'What's all this about, chairman?' he asked, and then went on and on about the situation. I thought to myself, he's said more to me in the last few minutes than all the time he's been at the club!

I told Frank that what was happening hadn't come from me, and I had no idea what was being done – or why. I admitted that his contract would be terminated, but that I wouldn't be the one to do it. 'I'm like you, Frank – I've had enough,' I told him. Frank was dismissed on 4 February after little more than a year in charge and with City third from bottom.

The timing of all this couldn't have been worse for me. At the time, my mother, Millie, was very ill and had suffered a stroke. She was very poorly and within days of the Frank Clark/Joe Royle episode – Joe was officially appointed on 18 February – she died in hospital after they turned off her life-support machine.

David Bernstein came to the funeral, along with an awful lot of people from the club, and they attended the wake at the Brothers Restaurant. The very next day, Bernstein came to see me with Ashley Lewis, who represented leading City shareholder Stephen Boler's interests on the board. Stephen had a large shareholding and had made his fortune from selling everything from car exhausts to kitchens. I was still very upset about my mum. Bernstein and Lewis had offered their condolences at her funeral 24 hours earlier but now had other things on their mind.

I'd let it be known just how unhappy I was with how the whole Joe Royle approach had been handled. Bernstein and Lewis told me they'd spoken to the major shareholders and they thought I should resign. That was interesting … because I *was* a major shareholder! But I was so brassed off at the time, especially having just lost my mother, that I said I'd go.

I'd had enough, that's for certain. But, looking back, what I should have done was clear my shareholding out and got one of the others to buy my shares. However, after I walked away, I kept my shares. That didn't count for much as I was treated pretty much as a leper. Nobody would have anything to do with me, and all the publicity – notably in the *Manchester Evening News* – was anti-Lee. Many people queued up to have a pop, especially Dennis Tueart. This was their plan: to portray me as the man who'd caused all the club's problems while they were the ones riding to the rescue to put things right. I'd have been better off severing my ties with the club.

Yet they weren't shy about ringing me for help with their problems after I'd gone. Bernstein would call and ask about contractual obligations with players and similar stuff. I'd tell him to check the contracts ... I didn't want to be involved. Then he'd write letters telling me that as a shareholder I had an obligation to the club. I had an obligation to do nothing of the sort! To my mind, I'd been shafted, deceived and tricked while I was down, miserable and grieving for my mother. Why do I think this? Let me explain.

After I'd resigned, Stephen Boler rang me, and he said, 'What the fuck is all this about? You're resigning?' I asked what he meant, and he replied, 'Well, I thought that you'd have told me if you were thinking of quitting. I was backing you all the way – just like I backed Swales.'

I was dumbfounded. I said, 'But Stephen, you asked me to resign!'

I told Stephen that Bernstein and Lewis – his man – had come to see me with a mandate from the major shareholders to request that I step down.

'Well, that did not bloody well come from me,' Boler told me. The truth dawned on me. I reckoned that the 'major shareholders' calling for me to go were Makin and Wardle. I wondered whether Bernstein was orchestrating it all. They fooled me into thinking it was a united front, with Lewis there representing Boler, but according to Boler that wasn't the case. He hadn't wanted it to happen.

They knew I was down, flat, mourning, and they picked that day – the perfect day – to do it.

City then got relegated, despite the Joe Royle appointment. When I left, we were about sixth from bottom, but the results didn't pick up. The last game before I resigned was away at Port Vale, horrible weather, awful result, with Joe Royle apparently seething with Kinkladze that day. Vale had put a man-marker on him, and he certainly didn't have one of his better games.

I later wrote to Bernstein, before the last two games of the season, because Kinkladze had been to see me about not being picked. Joe Royle, apparently, thought he was a circus act – or worse. I said in my letter that the boy wanted to play and do his bit to help keep City in the division. By the time they brought him on at Stoke, as substitute for the last 20 minutes or so, City were as good as relegated. We won the match 5-2 – and Stoke went down to the third tier of English football along with City. A sad, bleak day indeed.

My departure happened in March, so they still had time to get clear of relegation trouble when I went. Of course, I'm portrayed as the chairman who led us to the brink of the third tier, but that's not strictly true. I can easily recall it being March, because I went to Cheltenham for the festival to get out of the way of everything in Manchester once I'd resigned. I checked the files as I wrote this and, sure enough, I quit City on 16 March 1998. I telephoned Thommo – my old Derby County racing pal Rod Thomas – and stayed at a pub near his house, and just went racing. The famous festival was on that very week.

I told the press as I quit:

> There are, behind the scenes at Maine Road, some very insincere people who have tried to blacken my name. There are enemies within and without. The quality of my life began to suffer as did my family's. I have had four years of unfair pressures and I have even been blamed for performances on the pitch, why, I do not know.

That bit about being blamed for performances on the pitch may be a bit naive, but I stand by the rest of those sentiments. Even so, I had to explain my dissatisfaction with what had gone so badly wrong on the pitch:

> However many improvements are made off the field, it is the improvements on it for which the chairman is judged. I leave with my integrity and character intact … we have not bought quality and organised them right. It has not worked for us on the pitch.

I'd been cut down by some of my fellow directors convincing me that the rest of the major shareholders wanted me gone. And I'd since discovered this was not true.

I departed leaving my deputy, David Bernstein, as the new chairman, and me feeling totally misled. Others who'd manoeuvred against me now stepped into the light. Dennis Tueart became director of football, and John Wardle, whose stake in the club had been represented on the board by Dennis, became a board member. Then Chris Bird's time came. He'd been Dennis Tueart's pal and the club PR expert. He rose to be managing director and chief operations officer the year after I left. As a PR man, he knew the editor of the *Manchester Evening News*, and the campaign against me really got going. It was unforgiving.

I was at Maine Road about two years later for a match and I was sat behind the editor of the *Manchester Evening*

News, and he was talking about the team. 'I can't tell the difference between Paulo Wanchope and Shaun Goater,' he said. I couldn't help but say to him, 'They have different numbers and names on their shirts, have you not noticed?'

I got hassle, I got stick. It was uncomfortable for me at the time. They had the grace to invite me to the opening of the new Platt Lane training facility. Only one man should have got the credit for that: John Dunkerley. He'd put so much work into it after I charged him with the task of transforming the place. His name wasn't on the plaque.

David Bernstein, to be fair, came over and thanked me. 'Without your input,' he said, 'none of this would have happened.' They asked me to put a signed programme into a time capsule to be placed in the wall of the new place. Let's just say that when they open that time capsule, whenever they choose to do that, there will be some very revealing facts in it!

I had no axe to grind with Joe Royle. None whatsoever. We'd been team-mates for England in Mexico and I got on fine with him – I still get on fine with him. Anyway, before my resignation, I went out for lunch with him at the Four Seasons Hotel in Hale. He asked me about our players and what have you. That's when he told me Kinkladze was a circus act. I told Joe that he was looking at a different game to the one that I saw. I stressed to Joe that you always had a chance if you had skilful players who could hold the ball, do something with it and pass and move. Joe's response was to say that I had a clouded vision and the game had changed. Now, he said, it was about six foot two players going box to box; big players who could win the ball in the air, win it on the ground and show real power.

'That's your view, Joe,' I told him, 'but give me ten players of five foot ten or less who can actually play the game and they'll always beat your clodhoppers, don't worry.'

And I reminded him of that when I bumped into him at a match in the winter of 2012/13 … we were discussing Barcelona's wonderful team of players who were largely short in stature but with bundles of class! He laughed and claimed he hadn't actually said that. But he had!

Once I was out of the club, I stayed away from the game for a good while. I just didn't go. There was an atmosphere and there was no way that they'd have welcomed me at Maine Road – I'd probably have ended up with a brolly in the 'Gene Kelly' Stand! But I did go to the game marking the closure of the old Maine Road ground, on 11 May 2003, when Southampton arrived and were party-poopers, winning 1-0.

The club was now ready to move into Eastlands, and I was pleased the club asked me to attend this Maine Road curtain call. Denis Law, Mike Summerbee and I were there, and we were introduced from the pitch. It was great, enjoyable and – as players – we'd all done our bit for the club. It was an emotional day.

I'd been back a few times before that final game. Only occasionally, though, when invited as a guest. All the anti-Lee publicity was responsible for a rift between some of the fans and me. Some were abusive when I did go to a game, but the supporters can't always see when someone is winding them up. They perhaps didn't appreciate some of the work I did under the radar as chairman, building up the club academy and links with the community. I'd started Soccer in the Community with eight satellite training grounds, and I'd helped get the Co-op Bank's support. We had professional coaches coaching the kids at these satellite venues – and the kids were only charged £1.

That was recognised by Kevin Keegan one day, after he'd succeeded Joe Royle as City manager, long after I'd left. I was attending a luncheon at Platt Lane when Kevin and I had a chat. He thanked me and said it was good for me to be there because, without me, the Platt Lane development would never have happened.

All this behind-the-scenes work created a lot of new supporters for the club; they felt part of what City were about. I used to go down myself on Tuesdays or Thursdays and do some coaching and join in the five-a-sides. That gave me a lot of pleasure.

For the first time in my life – perhaps Peter James aside – I'd been unlucky; unlucky with the managers I'd chosen, unlucky with how the team performed on the pitch under those managers and unlucky with those I chose to work alongside me as directors. As City chairman, I rolled the dice. Frank was dismissed on 4 February after little more than a year in charge and with City third from bottom.

Lady Luck just didn't smile. The biggest blow – the biggest mistake – was the Brian Kidd debacle. I'm sure, looking back, it was the biggest single blow to my time as chairman. It was my first big appointment as I'd inherited Brian Horton as manager. When Horton went, Kidd was the man we wanted. We thought he'd be great for us. He ticked the boxes, he'd done his apprenticeship under Fergie and was well liked as a top player, not only for United, but for City, too. But he didn't succeed as a manager after all. What was to follow when he managed Blackburn was maybe foretold in how he treated our offer. He left United in December 1998 to take over from Roy Hodgson at Blackburn. He spent £20m on new players but Rovers were relegated at the end of that season – only four years after being Premiership champions. Rovers sacked him later that same year.

Or maybe we should have looked further back ourselves. Kidd had managed Preston North End briefly, in 1986, his first managerial job in the Football League after winding up his playing career in the United States. He first landed at Deepdale as assistant to his old City team-mate Tommy Booth, and when Booth quit he was given the chance to manage. Or rather, he didn't manage. The stats show he was boss for four games between late January and 1 March: played 4, won 0, drawn 1, lost 3. After that he wound up back at United to start working under Fergie, initially with the youth team. On reflection, in my opinion, Brian Kidd simply was *not* a manager.

At the time, we set out our stall for Brian. We'd been backed into a corner with Horton's departure, but Colin Barlow had got the clearest signals from Kidd that he wanted our job. Who knows, maybe I'm being harsh. Perhaps – just perhaps – had Brian taken the job when he agreed to our offer, we might just have been the right club for him. The fans could well have taken to him, and it might have stabilised us just when we needed precisely that: stability.

It's ironic now, two decades later, that he did return to City and enjoyed some of their success under Roberto Mancini. He stayed on to work under both Manuel Pellegrini and Pep Guardiola before leaving in 2021. To me that indicates that perhaps he was simply a good number two or three, and nothing more. But there's no doubt that 1995 was his big chance. And he walked away from it. Perhaps it's something he regrets to this day.

Chapter Seventeen

Minding My Own Business

SO, I was out of Manchester City. There was no racing business to keep me occupied, either. I'd decided to taper down Little Stanneylands racing operation in the mid-1990s because returning to City as chairman more than kept me busy. I'd continued to keep some horses in training, and I enjoyed some great days, even with a smaller string, but I finally wound it up in 1997, the year before I was forced out at City.

It was now time to take stock and reflect on a few things. I had a lot of life to live and wanted to give as much of myself as I could to Gill and to look after my four children – younger sons, Nik and Jonny, plus Gary and Charlotte from my first marriage to Jean. It wasn't long before I rationalised my business life.

I kept my interests with Hazlewood Foods and my own company F.H. Lee until 2000 and the bright new millennium.

Then we sold Hazlewood Foods for about £290 million to Greencore, an Irish company. F.H. Lee was sold to Kruger, a big, big French-Canadian company in the tissue industry, based in Quebec. They wanted me to work with them, but I found them very difficult people to get on with. They offered me a post, which was effectively a PR role, and I've never been a PR man in my life. I'm a doer, so I let that go.

I look back with a lot of pride on what I've achieved in business – and I'm sure my dad would look down with an approving gleam in his eye. The highlight has to be selling my own company for a lot of money to Hazlewood Foods as we moved into the 1980s. I sold my business initially to a Scandinavian paper mill for about £750,000 – I sold them 40 per cent and they had an option to buy 60 per cent. They later tried to put the squeeze on me by charging me more and more for my raw materials when paper was scarce, so, in the end, what we thought was good business was turning unprofitable and it led to a row – they offered me the company back at asset value. And that wasn't a lot in those days. They'd paid me half a million for the 40 per cent, and the asset value was just £200,000, so I gave them that. It more than paid off in the long run.

We had great fun with the business, from me getting rid of my partner in 1972 for the next 30 years. Even so, the ultimate decisions to sell up my business interests in the years immediately after leaving City could have signalled the end of my business life, but that's not me. Instead, I moved on to new businesses, into property, where there's more to do but much less aggravation! That gave me time to look back on issues that have given me both pleasure and pain – and that includes football, of course.

One of the issues that certainly caused problems and pain was my run-in with my great City team-mate Colin Bell, who's sadly no longer with us. As I detailed in Chapter Seven, Colin and I were brilliant team-mates on the pitch, but weren't always so close off it. Certainly, my relationship with Colin wasn't as close as the one I've enjoyed with Mike Summerbee, for example. We were buddies both on and off the park.

But none of that was relevant to the breakdown in the relationship with Belly that occurred after I returned to City as chairman. I got so much stick over that. Colin was fired as a youth coach after the appointment of Frank Clark as manager. What was it that Frank asked at his interview to be told by Bernstein there were no sacred cows?

I was lambasted at the club's AGM over Colin's dismissal, and sometimes you need people to stand up and be counted, to spread the load, if you will. I'd certainly been set up to be given a bad time over Colin Bell's departure. There had been problems with the youth set-up. The youth coach, Neil McNab, could be a bit abrasive and neither

Colin nor Terry Farrell, both youth development coaches under McNab, got on well with him. Frank Clark decided the solution to end the friction was to fire them all and start afresh. A board meeting confirmed that decision and so that's what Frank did – and he saw Terry and Colin, one after the other, at Platt Lane in May, just as the 1996/97 season finished. McNab was also fired.

Frank Clark had wanted his own staff, and I said to him, when the questions at the AGM came in, 'Answer them, tell them the truth. Just stand up and tell them.' He was sat on the stage alongside me at the Bridgewater Hall in Manchester ... and he never said a word. I'd been away from Manchester in Jersey when Frank fired Colin. So, the very least I expected when the questions came in was for Frank to have an input. What he should have said was: 'It was unanimously agreed at the board meeting that all the coaches involved with the youth set-up should be fired. And so, I – and my assistant Alan Hill – did this while the chairman was away.' That's what I wanted him to say. Frank Clark, however, kept his mouth firmly shut.

It was as though I was put on a pedestal, with potshots coming my way, with no one else to share responsibility. Don't get me wrong, I'm a big boy and I did stand up – and I was counted! But everyone at one time or another needs help. The lucky thing from my point of view was what happened next. Suddenly, a fire alarm went off – and the AGM was cancelled! There was a suspected bomb or something serious that triggered the alarm and I, for one, suspected a bomb was going off under me.

Sure, I take responsibility as chairman for a controversial decision. Firing Colin was definitely in that category, and I was certainly party to that board decision. And, though I knew it was coming, I was on the English Channel at the time of the sacking.

Colin Bell and Terry Farrell took the club to an industrial tribunal for unfair dismissal. It was supposed to last three days, but halfway through the hearing, the two sides reached an out-of-court settlement. The club admitted unfair dismissal and the lads were paid undisclosed compensation. Colin was understandably unhappy. He'd been back at City and coaching for four years before I took over as chairman. He'd tried so hard to overcome a crippling injury to his right knee, back in 1975, not long after I'd moved on to Derby. It was a bad one and he didn't attempt a comeback for two years. His knee was not up to it, though, and his magnificent City career ebbed away in 1979 after starting fewer than 30 games after his return to action. He concluded his playing days with a few games for San Jose Earthquakes in 1980.

I knew he enjoyed working with our kids. But once the decision was taken to let him go from the youth set-up, we both dug in. We were both proud blokes and neither of us gave an inch in the years that followed. He vowed never to attend a City function if I was present, even after I resigned as chairman. That was sad and perhaps understandable, but it was certainly his prerogative.

I could also reflect on some of the better outcomes under my chairmanship. One involved Peter Coates, whose family has put so much financial clout behind Stoke City in recent years. Everyone knows Peter as the man behind Bet365, the sports betting platform, but when I first ran into him after I took the helm at City, he was running Lindley Catering, their speciality being catering at football grounds. Lindley Catering had the concessions at Maine Road for kiosks and Peter came to see me in the close season. He said he was pleased to meet me, and I told him of our plans for the new Kippax stand. Peter said he was going to forfeit two or three of the kiosks down the Kippax side. He said they could put a couple somewhere else – and he asked if we could come to the same agreement he'd had with Peter Swales.

'What's that?' I asked. Peter told me I'd get 20 per cent of the profit and he'd get 20 per cent of the profit and the rest of the profit would go to Manchester City! I said, 'No, it's the club's property, the club's ground, the club's business and the profit goes to the club. I know *you* will make a profit out of, it but I don't want anything.' Astonishing! That got nipped in the bud, but it underlined what I'd inherited.

Another little operation featured at the club shop. It was run by a guy called Eddie Phillips and he'd pay the club £60,000 a year to sell all the replica shirts and the other memorabilia. Sixty grand gave Eddie the right to sell all the City merchandise – the lot. It was certainly a good deal for Eddie, and he wasn't in the wrong. But Swales gave him that, carte blanche. How much did Peter get out of that deal? I did wonder. It was *not* a good deal for City. There was a lot for me to clean up.

In the space of three years after I took over, we'd taken the sales figures to £5 million. When I went to City the turnover was flatlining and when I left, it was more than £15 million. I'd increased it massively. If I could do that in three years, then someone should have been doing it before me.

With that quality we all love – hindsight – I'd do some of the things I executed as chairman differently. We spent too much money on the infrastructure of the club, £16 million alone on the Kippax redevelopment when, prior to that getting underway, the club had been turning over only £4 million a year. I was really backing myself, and my colleagues, to generate enough cash to pay for it.

We needed to act fast to comply with the Taylor Report and Swales had used all his allowance from the Football Trust to build the Umbro Stand at one end of the ground. His idea for the Kippax was to keep it pretty much as it was – there would be two tiers, and a different roof over it. Incredibly, there was no corporate provision at all. The toilets alone were a disgrace, a throwback to the 1920s. It was a non-starter.

What we tried to do was make City look like a successful Premier League club and, to an extent, we achieved that by getting the turnover up to the levels that we did. We weren't to know when we pledged that Maine Road redevelopment money that a brand-new stadium would be on the horizon, courtesy of the Commonwealth Games, only a few years down the line.

When we opened the new Kippax, the tallest stand in England, we had about 40 hospitality boxes to fill. I gave this demanding job to our commercial manager, Geoff Durbin, who went on later to be commercial director at Lancashire Cricket Club. His brief was to sell the boxes by the time the stand was ready for the start of the season – and Geoff was very, very good. I told him he could use Mike Summerbee to help sell them, and I sold the first one for him – to Gordon Taylor, my old Bolton team-mate, at the PFA. But Geoff and Mike sold all the rest.

I felt confident, because of the work that I'd done in securing the City of Manchester Stadium, that I'd be invited to open it when Eastlands, as it was then known, was officially opened in 2003. I was very disappointed not to be. In the end, Prime Minister Tony Blair opened it but I was glad to be there to see it.

That hurt, of course it did. Because when I go to the Etihad Stadium, as it now is, I do feel that I'm walking into an edifice that I've helped create. I'm glad that I had the chance to be involved in moving City on to where they are now – and I'm proud of it, too. I'm even more delighted that they've had such success on the pitch, something I couldn't bring when I was chairman. It's great to go there and see the quality of the players they have at City now, especially under Pep Guardiola in recent times.

When you look at our neighbours United over the years since I started playing, the number of truly outstanding players they've had is probably somewhere between 20 and 30. By comparison, the number of truly outstanding City players was far fewer for such a long time. That was until the turn of the 2010s, and then it started to change. Now it's like night and day, compared with the pre-Etihad days. The stadium's name officially changed in 2011 to the Etihad and the playing fortunes have changed with it – and it's truly great to see!

Chapter Eighteen

Now and Then

OLD FOOTBALLERS can be terrible sentimentalists, steeped in nostalgia and a yearning for the so-called good old days. I like to think I'm not one of them. Sure, I do miss some things about the way the game was played in my time as a player. But I'm not an 'in my day' individual. For example, I love my cricket, and Freddie Trueman was one of the all-time great pace bowlers, but he loved to hark back to his playing era. That approach is not for me … there's plenty to laud and applaud in the current game.

One of the key catalysts for the major changes in the football we see today was the creation of the Premier League. When it began, it brought with it – slowly, but then surely – the proper footballer. Route one had had its day. Leeds won the last First Division title. Their manager, Howard Wilkinson, admired Charles Hughes, the infamous FA coaching guru who espoused route one and the POMO, the position of maximum opportunity. Remember Wimbledon in their pomp? They were mostly all beasts, big lads … knock it long, get into them and fuck them up. That was the mantra. Yet those days, the days of Hughes and coaches of his ilk, were numbered. It was horrible to watch and I, for one, was absolutely delighted.

It's not just at the top professional level where proper coaching is critical. It starts at grass roots level. I recall going to see my youngest son, Nik, play when he was young. The coach had them playing the route-one stuff. All the young lads were following the ball. I was encouraging Nik to pull away, to find space up front. Nobody would pass the ball to him, they just kept humping it. The coach said to me, 'Why does your son not do as he is told?' I asked him what he meant by that, and I told him he was trying to find space and, when a player does that, he can do some damage when he gets the ball. He said, 'Oh no, we don't play like that.' I asked him where he'd got his coaching badge from, and he said it had come from the Manchester FA. I wasn't going to tell him how to coach his players, but I did tell him I didn't care for the fact that so many parents were on the line screaming and shouting at their kids. That was dreadful, and I told him that would ruin the kids. It certainly wasn't coaching!

That's the way it was when Hughes and his route-one disciples were in vogue. And that's when we lost the plot and lost a lot of natural players. It was worse in Scotland. In the post-war years up to, say, 1990, if anyone wanted a skilful player they could do worse than pop up to Scotland. They were good ball players; most could dribble and beat a man.

Brilliant winger Jimmy Johnstone, of Celtic's European Cup winners, would dribble a tennis ball around milk bottles outside the Glasgow tenements. That 1967 Parkhead side he was part of – Britain's first European champions, remember – were all born within 12 miles of the club. Jimmy and co. were wonderful players. Nobody coached them, although I'm sure Jock Stein was a great, great manager.

The Scots were great competitors, too, but where are they now? Gone, to be honest. There are none of real quality. They've partly been killed off by poor coaching, although cheap imports, especially from Scandinavia initially, did not help the Scottish game.

For 25 years people like myself were bemoaning a lack of quality players. That's because we were inundated with coaches such as Charles Hughes and the tactics he dictated. Now, with the Premiership, the clodhoppers couldn't get anywhere near the better players who came into the league, which was now being won by the likes of Arsenal and Manchester United.

This was progress but it created a problem as many of those new players weren't English. Money from the new league's TV deals meant the top foreign stars could be tempted to ply their trade on our shores, which was great.

At the same time, the penny suddenly dropped that we were going down a path that would slowly strangle the development of top English talent for the national team. That's a route that has intensified and we've been following it for some time.

When I was playing, England could have picked three different teams that would have given most international sides a damned good game. There was strength in depth, real strength. The squad I was part of in Mexico was undoubtedly world class – but there was another team of 11 that could have represented us really well, waiting in the wings. And arguably another 11 under that.

But away from the impact imported talent has had on the national team's fortunes, the domestic club game in England is now fantastic. The Premier League today is much more of a spectacle and more exciting than the top flight was in my playing days. That's because of the rule changes, rule interpretations and the state of pitches. Back in the day, with the marking systems and the tackling that was then permitted, it was far more ruthless and ferocious ... but much less of a spectacle.

Yet I really enjoyed my football because it was the best way (if not the only way!) for me to earn a living. I had no worries about playing because I knew I was good at it – I knew I could play. The very top players never had any worries about performing. My only concern was whether

I'd have a good game, a very good game or a blinder. They were my options.

It's not a black-and-white comparison, though. It's not a case of old days equals bad and modern day equals good. I do think a lot of aspects of the modern game could be improved by taking a look back at how we played it. Positional play at throw-ins being a case in point. Today it's abysmal, whereas we were always taught to keep away from the point of the throw and arrive late to provide an option. Today you see six or eight people all in a bunch around the thrower.

With free kicks, today they don't seem to rehearse the passing free kick, bypassing the wall. Same with our old routines with short corners – that seems to have gone. Some of the defending at corners is atrocious, with the pulling and tugging. Why don't the attackers stand on the edge of the area and come and attack the ball, instead of being static and waiting for the corner? If you make your run from 18 or 20 yards and someone pulls your shirt, you have every chance of a penalty – that's not the case when everyone is pushing, shoving and pulling in a bunch eight yards out.

I remember in the 2012/13 Champions League when City conceded goals by failing to have defenders guarding both the near post and far post from set pieces. How can that be, especially in the Champions League, where you don't get many bites of the cherry? It's beyond belief not to have defenders on the posts. Bring everyone back to defend the set piece and just leave one little fella 40 yards from goal, in case there's a clearance.

You have to have variations – and the more variations you have, the better chance you'll have. The game today is superb, though, and football has always been a joy. The equipment doesn't cost much, and training is enjoyable – although I didn't enjoy the running much, especially long runs! I always thought it was a fabulously enjoyable game, even if it wasn't quite so nice having lumps kicked off you on a shit-tip of a pitch!

Who's impressed me in the years following my era as a player? You wouldn't have the Premier League as we know it today without those overseas stars who have brought all their qualities into it. But let's not kid ourselves, they come here for one thing only: the money. The clubs are prepared to pay the big money and it has made it a fantastic league, the best in the world. The Premier League has to be up at the top alongside Spain's La Liga – but our league is the better spectacle.

I think of Dennis Bergkamp, Thierry Henry, Patrick Vieira – funny they all played for the same team! No wonder Arsène Wenger's Arsenal was a good side, these players were wonderful additions to English football. Bergkamp was a lovely player with a great touch for a big man, and he could look after himself, too. Henry was devastatingly quick and a fabulous finisher. Vieira? What a midfielder; you'd want him to have your back.

Players such as those elevated the Premier League, as did Gianfranco Zola, Eric Cantona and Didier Drogba. Peter Schmeichel was a great, great goalkeeper and I liked watching him for both United and City.

More recently, at City, I've absolutely loved going to matches regularly again and seeing such wonderful players: Yaya Touré, Sergio Agüero, Vincent Kompany and the superb David Silva lit up the 2010s. Even more up to date, how can you not purr with appreciation when you're entertained by the performers in Pep Guardiola's side, such as Rodri, Bernado Silva, the wonderful Kevin De Bruyne and, up front, Erling Haaland looks such an exciting talent.

In the Maine Road days, we had an honours board with the names of all City players who'd been capped for England, Scotland, Wales and Northern Ireland. It did have the odd Pole or German too. My god, they'd need to have a bigger wall now – or several walls – because of the league of nations now represented at City. And they're *all* internationals these days.

I can, of course, look back at the era before 1992 when the domestic game was dominated by British talent. Today's transfers are the currency that excites supporters, and it was just the same decades ago. Let's have a look at a couple of the moves that tickled me!

One of the most astonishing transfers conducted by Manchester City – and I'm glad I was nowhere near the place at the time – was when chairman Peter Swales spent £1,437,500 of the club's money on Steve Daley, back in 1979. This happened when Malcolm Allison returned to Maine Road for his second spell as manager. It was a British record transfer at the time and no one, me included, could understand why it had happened.

Steve had earned an okay reputation as a goalscoring midfielder for Wolves, and I actually played against him in that 1974 League Cup Final. He'd got a few England B caps, but it was not a pedigree that labelled him worthy of that outlay. Swales and Malcolm both claimed the other had inflated the fee, but I know one thing: Malcolm told me he never wanted Daley in the first place!

Daley didn't last long. He stayed only 20 months before he was shipped out to Seattle Sounders in the North American Soccer League. City got just £300,000 for him, a pittance when contrasted with his original cost.

City were still reeling from the trauma of buying (and selling) Steve Daley when they bought Britain's first £1m player, Trevor Francis, in 1981. But Trevor, who'd been signed for that monster fee by Brian Clough in 1979, played even fewer games than Daley's 48 for City. Francis cost City even more than Cloughie had paid for him ... signing on for £1.2m. This was another odd one as everyone knew Trevor had struggled with injury niggles at Forest. By this time, John Bond was managing City and he had to go to the brink of resigning to get Swales to cough up another huge fee.

I knew early on there was something badly wrong with Trevor Francis. He'd only been at Maine Road a matter of months when I was speaking about him to my solicitor, Michael Horridge, who was then on the board at City. We were on the way to London – on paper mill business – and we were driving down because of some industrial disruption. Michael was telling me how well Trevor was doing following his arrival. I had to tell him: 'Michael, I don't know if it's true or not, but I've heard the only reason Cloughie sold him is because he has a very dodgy Achilles tendon, or problems with his calf. It's up to you to find out.'

Six weeks or so later, City sold him to Sampdoria. End result? Francis played just 26 games for Manchester City, scoring 12 goals. He was at City no time at all. The poor lad definitely had muscle problems. He was a good performer – not an aggressive forward, for sure – but if it was his day, he was a very fine player. Yet, just as with Daley, City made a massive loss. He cost Sampdoria just £700,000.

It's not just transfers that are worth highlighting, looking back. Sometimes I see real reflections of the era I played in when looking at the modern game. One of the big areas of concern for today's managers is having at least one top-quality 'holding midfielder', operating ahead of the back four; someone to break up the play so that others can play. A modern concept? Nonsense.

That's exactly what Nobby Stiles did for Manchester United and England more than five decades ago. Nothing changes, does it? In that 1966 team, England ended up with Bally on the right of midfield, Peters on the left, with Bobby Charlton in the middle – and with Nobby 'holding' or screening midfield, ahead of his four defenders.

In my first derby match with City, I played against Nobby. At one point, I played a one-two – knocked the ball and drove forward for the return – and he grabbed me by my shirt neck. I turned round and smashed him straight in the face. He didn't tackle me again in that match!

Nobby once said at a City function, when I was chairman, that wing-backs were becoming the vogue. He said he'd have dreaded modern wing-backs facing the likes of me and Mike Summerbee ... from a physical point of view, never mind anything else. It's true that I could look after myself, although I never went out to start anything. If it happened, I could react.

Mike, for sure, could be a nasty piece of work! He was first in – bomp! I once saw him and Chelsea's Scottish full-back Eddie McCreadie up against each other. Eddie had a bit of a reputation, and they spent half the game kicking lumps out of each other. They were both having a real good go! Yet as soon as a match ended, Mike was a completely different person, nice as pie.

I couldn't be like that. If someone was a tosser on the field to me, I just wouldn't speak to them, and leave it at that. But Summerbee, bless him, would go up for a chat – even if his opponent was on crutches! He'd say, 'Is it hurting? It'll be all right in a couple of weeks – it'll settle down.'

Mike left City pretty swiftly after me. He went to Burnley. I was surprised that Booky sold him – it must have been Swales's influence – because they were pals, they'd been room-mates when Tony was a player.

Let's move forward again and look at England's two best forward players in the Premier League era, before the emergence of Harry Kane. I'd say the best have been Paul Gascoigne and Wayne Rooney.

We've not had many in that period; Shearer, perhaps – but we've not had too many, have we? And, in my opinion, Rooney was a very good forward, especially earlier in his career when he was lean. But, in the final analysis, he was just a little too clumsy at times to be a real, world top-notcher. He was always going to get heavier and heavier as he aged, and that's what happened. He got a huge number of caps and a lot of goals, but he was just off being really world class.

In the 2012 Euros, I remember watching Wayne, and after five minutes of one game I said to the lads who were watching with me that Rooney, already red-faced, was 'blowing like a train'. He wasn't naturally athletic and fit, and struggled to be at peak-level fitness in his latter playing days.

Paul Gascoigne? He was a wonderful talent but had very different problems to Rooney, as we all know. Graham Taylor, when he was in charge of England, cloaked it nicely as a 'refuelling' problem. But Gazza could naturally go past people, brilliant ball control and upper-body strength, whereas Rooney very rarely did that. Gazza, before the demons devoured his talent, was the outstanding English talent of his generation.

So, arguably our best two forward talents, before the arrival of Harry Kane, were flawed. Don't get me wrong, I think Wayne was top, top drawer in the Premier League, but that's it. He wasn't at that top, top level on the international stage.

One of the greatest contrasts in the life of a player in, say, 1972 and 2022 is the way the modern footballer lives and trains. As I've said, I don't think any side trained harder than City in those years after I joined them in 1967. We were very fit. But this is many decades before the Arsène Wenger era in those Premier League days when the Arsenal manager led the way with a comprehensive rewriting of players' training, conditioning, diets and supplements.

I've always liked a drink and a smoke – and I did so when I played, as did many players. So, things that we thought were professional and acceptable in 1972 would be completely off-limits now. Everyone knows I was a stocky young lad when I played, and I was on a diet from being 19 or 20. I never ate chips. My mother was a good pastry cook and so was my first wife, but I cut down on high-calorie food. I didn't take sugar until the Thursday or Friday before a weekend game – honey before a match for energy. If I was training really hard, I may take sugar for the same reason. But if I had a day off, or wasn't training, I'd have no sugar and I wouldn't eat potatoes, pastry, ice cream or sweets after the main course. I never had a pudding, and even now, as I'm much older, it gets remarked on in the family if they see me with an ice cream. I didn't eat fattening foods. I did this because it was hard to keep yourself at your best, match-fit weight.

Other players, who would never put weight on, could eat anything. I had to be more careful. A lot of players wouldn't eat at all before a game, because they'd just throw it back up. Charlie George was one, Tony Coton another. I didn't eat much myself, a bowl of soup or a Dover sole – or omelette and a couple of rounds of toast with honey.

But I've always liked a few drinks and, if you do, you have to watch what you're eating on top of that. When I went to Derby, I'd have something light, soup or sole, a fillet steak, if I fancied it – which might not go down too well with today's club nutritionists! On Saturdays I liked to get up at about 8am and have cereal with maybe a boiled egg, plus toast and honey. At lunchtime, before a 3 o'clock kick-off, I'd have a Dover sole off the bone – no chips or anything like that! Again, with some toast and honey to follow.

It tickles me in today's game that the players, on good pitches and with excellent diet and advanced, modern training regimes, collapse with bloody cramp! What's that all about? I can't believe it – I've never had cramp in my life. And I played on bogs, when Maine Road could be a mud heap and fans still remember the awful pitch at the Baseball Ground. I played at the old Wembley in the late 1960s, too, when the pitch had never been in a poorer state.

When I did get injured, I healed quickly. My medial knee ligament injuries didn't keep me out long, no more than about three weeks. I was lucky, perhaps, to be resilient in the first place and then a swift healer if I did get a knock.

One of the other big differences between the modern English game and football in my playing era is how the competitions are perceived. Don't get me wrong, winning the league title was always the yardstick for deciding the most consistently successful side in the land – and it unlocked the route into what was then the European Cup.

But it wasn't the be-all and end-all it is today, with all the riches of the Champions League on offer.

That's because winning the FA Cup was the big thing. You know, the glamorous thing … the prize that united a massive TV audience once a year at a time when live football on TV was as rare as hens' teeth. For although we'd won the league title in 1968, the cup was regarded as the big one, because it was every schoolboy's dream – and a much bigger deal than it is today. It not only had the glamour of live TV and Wembley, but it also provided the pathway into what was then the second-biggest UEFA competition, the European Cup Winners' Cup, sadly no longer part of the football calendar. It was a big, big thing.

City's FA Cup Final win against Leicester, in 1969, though not one of my personal favourite performances, was a good game of football and it was won by a very good goal from Neil Young, made by my old pal Mike 'Buzzer' Summerbee. And it was, *ahem*, all started by an excellent throw-in down the right wing … what was *I* doing taking a throw from there? I have no idea. I was playing centre-forward but had been caught up in a couple of challenges and just threw it into space down the right for Mike to run on to. I never took throws. Everybody talks about Mike's excellent run and pull-back for Neil's superb strike past Peter Shilton. My long throw-in never gets a mention!

Chapter Nineteen

A Life Well Lived

SO, THAT'S my life. What a life I've enjoyed. I've loved it and still do. Football, business, racing, football again and a constant curiosity and search for a good deal. It's all been great fun. I've squeezed more into my threescore years and ten – and now beyond that – than most folk manage. And I was actually forced to confront my life and times, perhaps rather too early, when I was surprised by the *This Is Your Life* TV programme back in 1994, ironically just as I'd moved in as chairman of Manchester City. Neither the TV people nor I could know that the life they were spotlighting was about to get a whole lot more stressful!

In true *This Is Your Life* fashion, I was very much in the dark about this TV surprise. I knew that *something* was going on but Gill, on the other hand, did know all about it. The *TIYL* team were up in Granada's Lancashire area and they ended up recording three shows in three nights. Mine was on, Joe Longthorne, the singer and impressionist, was another to be surprised, and I'm not sure who the other target was.

I was kept out of the loop but the TV team wanted to know from Gill who I'd want to have there as guests of the show. My elder son and my daughter, Gary and Charlotte, had walk-on parts, and my younger boys, Jonny and Nik, got special permission to be off school. Oblivious to all this, I got to Maine Road and my friend and fellow director Colin Barlow told me we had to go to Granada Studios, in Manchester. He spun me a story that Granada were recording a show about football people in the Premier League. It was to feature Peter Johnson, then chairman of Everton, plus me and others in the game. We drove to the studios and Colin insisted I pull up at the front door, whereas I insisted on going around the back!

They sent a chap out to get me and I was shown into an anteroom. Then Paul Doherty, of the Granada sports team, popped in and he carried on with the same cover story about businessmen and the Premier League. I had some wine and a bite to eat and then they asked me to put make-up on. I still had no clue when they said we were going off for a light test.

I walked around this corner and suddenly that familiar music started! Michael Aspel, the host, stepped out of nowhere to surprise me with that famous Big Red Book. Everyone was there, all the old City team, Malcolm Allison, my mum, Millie, sister, aunties, uncles and people who worked for me. I thought *What the fuck is all this?* I'm glad I thought it and didn't say it!

I later had to apologise to everyone for being so ratty because I thought I was being messed about! Bobby Charlton very kindly did the interview with host Michael Aspel at the start – even comedian and City fan Bernard Manning came on! Bernard got a lot of stick for his old-school humour, but he was a great guy and raised millions for charity. The party afterwards went on until very late and the Granada staff said it had been one of their best after-show parties … no one wanted to go home!

That was my TV 'life', when I was just 50. So much still to do then, but was there anything missing, even then from my packed life? Some might say so … because the one part of the Francis Lee jigsaw that's incomplete is pretty obvious. I've had a great career as a footballer, a successful career in business and then went on to train horses and return as chairman of my club. What's missing? Well … I was never a football manager.

I think I could have been either a coach or a manager. Whether I'd have been any good, we'll never know. What I do know is that I was a good manager of the 300 people who worked for me in my paper business and we had very good working conditions. People seemed to enjoy working for me; they were pulling their weight, and we were all in it together. The most important thing to instil in your staff is that you're all pulling in the same direction – together – and you motivate each other. Oh, and you have to enjoy it.

My staff did enjoy it. One of the workforce who certainly helped with that – at times! – was a young lad who has gone on to have a brilliant career as a comedian and comic actor: Bolton's own Peter Kay. We were lucky to have Peter working for us for a time, long before his big break in comedy. He kept all his colleagues happy – although we eventually dissuaded him from coming in because he could disrupt the production on the nightshift with all his joking around!

Fun – and having fun at the right times – was a big part of my life, both in football and in business. When we were together at Hazlewoods, run by my pal Peter Barr, there was room for a bit of fun when the health and safety revolution started to bite. Peter's brother-in-law, a board meeting was told, would be coming by for an inspection and he'd be looking into our first-aid room. What he wouldn't have expected to see when he walked in was a coffin strategically placed, especially for the inspection. Did we laugh? You bet we did!

Or there was the time when one of our employees lost his balance on a shallow step and broke his ankle. An inspection followed and the scene had been taped off like a police crime scene – with the outline of a body chalked on the floor!

Does this sense of fun apply to management in football? Well, having fun, working hard, aiming for a common goal … sounds to me like the same approach would do well in a dressing room.

The football manager's job is tougher now than ever, because it's seven days a week for at least 48 weeks of the year. There's very little respite. If you get more than two weeks a year away from it, you've done pretty well. But, at the highest levels, it's a very, very well-rewarded job. A basic wage of £3 million isn't bad, is it? And that was a few years ago. It's even higher now. If managers stay employed at the top level for ten years, they'll be better off than me, so it's a very good job.

One of the problems is that today's manager has to try to motivate and extract the best out of players who may well be earning even more than they do. Not easy. You can't try to bully the modern player, not with today's terms and conditions, in the way the players in my Bolton dressing room were treated.

Looking back to my own playing days, though, I used to think I could suss a team-mate. What made him tick? A bollocking or an arm round the shoulder? A harsh word or quiet encouragement? That's what today's boss has to do. The 'hairdryer' alone will simply not cut it.

In today's Premier League, you can have all the right attributes to be a top manager, but you have to have the wherewithal to succeed. You need the resources, the cash to build a side. It would have been fun for me to find out, but it was not to be. I'd moved on. Instead, as chairman, I was appointing managers, and we know how that worked out!

But as my old racing pal Sir Alex Ferguson famously said: 'Football, eh? Bloody hell!' Where else in life can you get highly paid for something that comes relatively easy to you; for doing something that you enjoy and that also keeps you very, very fit? I can't think of any other sport outside the United States. It also gives you the buzz of winning something special, a league title, an FA Cup Final, other cups and European titles. That's some adrenalin rush.

For myself, if I take stock and look back, what would be my ultimate moment – the moment you have to cough up on something like *Desert Island Discs*? What's the memory that I'll take in a time capsule to my palm tree paradise? Well, it wouldn't be my running shoes! I'd have taken that salmon from the Tay if I could have kept it on the line – but it got away!

It's very, very difficult, but the moment I have to go for is the match that clinched the 1967/68 league title for Manchester City, at Newcastle's St James' Park. I got the goal that proved to be the winner in that 4-3 thriller, but it was a match that had everything, and we were roared on by 20,000 Blues fans who'd made the trip up to Tyneside. Wonderful. You can get great satisfaction with business success, certainly, but nothing like that soaring elation I felt at that moment, as I celebrated with our fans that day. A big deal in business might take two weeks to pull off. And if you do clinch something like that, the lawyers and accountants get involved – then it's on, it's off, on again, off again. The buzz in business is far less concentrated, much more strung out. It could be months before it's concluded, even if you've shaken hands on the deal. Football, in my view, isn't like that – not counting the Brian Kidd deal! The handshake didn't do the trick there. But if I shook hands with someone on a deal, there's no way I'd go back on my word.

I finished in 1976 as a player and went out at the top. I could have gone on for another two years, no doubt about that, but my fitness would undoubtedly have started to dip. I managed to finish without injuries … I was quite lucky that way. I was fortunate, too, to have made a success of my business, so much so that I was almost certainly the country's first millionaire footballer, thanks to my dual careers at such a young age. That's not the case today, when even average top-flight footballers will be millionaires if they manage to stay fit for just a few years.

So, do I think my own two-job model would be a good one in the current football era? Well, yes, I do! I think all players should work, even if they don't *have* to. That doesn't mean I want to see them cleaning windows, roping and sheeting a lorry or emptying coal wagons. But I do think they should train and work for another career. And they should learn how to handle the media, instead of just sloping off and wiping their nose on their sleeve. Although they're very wealthy, perhaps even millionaires, they're not yet prepared for life – not if the modern footballer wants to *maintain* the lifestyle and income that they've enjoyed as a player.

The day they stop playing football and their income turns off like a tap, they then have to think: *If I want to maintain these standards, I have to start working.* If you start living off your savings aged, say, 32, with £10 million in the bank and you live until you're 82, what money will you have left in 50 years' time?

When I finished my playing career at Derby, let's say I was on £800 a week and I was the highest-paid player in the country. Of course, £800 was very nice then, but that's no good to me now. I'd never have enjoyed the lifestyle I now have on £800 a week.

In 1996, when Alan Ball was City manager, he said there were players on our books who were millionaires – but most, if not all of them, will have run out of money by now. Around that time, our winger, Nick Summerbee, was on around £6,000-plus a week – roll on two decades and his money was gone.

Players have to do something with their money, and they have to have more ambition in life than simply what they do at the football ground. Many modern players sensibly invest their playing-days cash into property; others want to join the army of pundits on TV and radio. That's good, but they should have even more vision about possible post-football life than that. I used to say to my team-mates at Bolton: 'If, after training, I can go and do something, learn something and earn something, and not just play golf, drink or go shopping with the wife, then I'll be creating something useful for myself in later life.'

I say the same to my children: if they can be part of the ten per cent who want to go to work and *really* make a difference, be the very best they can be, then they'll do very well. Because 90 per cent of the people who do work simply turn up to earn a living without caring about what's involved beyond the pay packet.

Even when I was lorry driving, I was a bloody good lorry driver! I could sheet and rope 15 tons of baled paper just as well as any professional driver – because I took great pride in it. I have pride in anything I do, even the garden window boxes. If you do a job, do it well.

Even after I'd left the City boardroom and I'd sold my businesses, I never lost my restless desire to explore new opportunities, to strike a good deal. I had interests in property, and I never lost my entrepreneurial zeal. I looked at road-marking machines to help with safety in places such as Africa, and in the 2010s I patented a new recycling machine, the Enviromatique, which was designed to take household waste and compact it to a fraction of its original size. It could have been installed in all new-build houses and I was close to getting it fully launched. A good idea – and who knows, something similar may still take off.

The easy way in life is not the right way. Make it more difficult for yourself – and earn more money!

If Bill Riddings had been right all those years ago, and I hadn't made it – at least, not as a footballer – I'm convinced I'd still be comfortably off. Maybe not as well off as I am today, but I'd have done okay. I'd have gone on to work for myself, own my own house and car and had a good living. I'd have been successful. My dad, Colin, would have approved of how things turned out.

We're all only here once so we may as well have a good crack at what we're doing. Having said that, I drink as much as the next guy; I've enjoyed my fair share of cigars and I love my holidays … but I always strive to achieve.

And I don't like to waste a day. On to tomorrow!

Epilogue

Life in FrannyLand

Francis Lee died on 2 October 2023, aged 79, after living with – and fighting – cancer for more than two years. When his funeral was held in Manchester Cathedral, three weeks later, it was attended by many hundreds of mourners, drawn from his family, friends, business colleagues and a massive turnout from the world of football, including colleagues from Manchester City, old and young. It was truly a service celebrating Franny's life – and it was a life well worth celebrating!

What follows are the reflections of his family, those who knew him best, including his wife of 36 years, Gill, sons Jonny and Nik, and daughter Charlotte. They were the fellow travellers in what became known to them as FrannyLand – the world of Francis Lee.

Let's start with an excerpt from the moving and, at times, downright funny funeral eulogy delivered by son Jonny Lee, co-written with younger brother Nik, which Franny himself would have loved …

Funeral Eulogy

So, the tale of a working-class lad with a tough start, who defied the odds playing football for his country; had a number one hit single; ran multiple businesses; trained racehorses; owned a football club and was made a Commander of the British Empire, all washed down with good wine and champagne. Sounds like a good novel doesn't it, a dream if you like? Well, it was real and that's pretty cool – and it's something worth celebrating rather than being sad about.

You may have read lots of lovely things in the media, but I'm going to share the memories of Dad you may not know or have read about. Dad the *Dad*, if you like. I'm going to apologise now as most of what I'm about to tell you isn't serious, which is what he told me he wanted!

There's no doubt Dad was a great man, in my mind, who lived life to the full, but he was also one of the strangest and most eccentric men I've ever met. Living with him at times was near impossible as his banter was relentless, and he could be the world's most awkward man on his day. I'm going to share some of the highlights reel with you.

Waking up in the morning at our house was like an army barracks. Dad up first, making as much noise as he could in a rickety old 17th-century house. Greeting the dogs underneath my room by encouraging them to attack any small mammals that may have been in the garden before roll call. The next phase was to impersonate the major from *Fawlty Towers* by shouting 'Morning Fawlty!' as loud as he could when entering Nik's room. Nik followed back with a volley of abuse before Dad repeated the exercise with me. The dogs brought up the rear to ensure you were definitely out of bed. This was every day!

To the amusement of everyone, his breakfast lasted for hours and everything was left out. He had this strange trait of putting kitchen towel everywhere, on chopping boards, around the sink and underneath where he was prepping food. This process got longer and messier with age. Nik and I once staged the most monumental mess to add to Dad's – and when Mum got back from the shops she went nuclear with cries of 'I've been set up' falling on deaf ears.

There was further madness around food and meal times:

- He bit the tops off grapes to 'avoid pesticides', which I never understood.
- He hated takeaway coffee cups with a passion.
- He said he didn't like desserts, despite loving them, and considered eating burgers and pizzas as a sign of weakness.
- When ordering chips at a restaurant he always asked for 'six chips please'.

He constantly ordered things off menus that weren't on there. And when he did choose off the menu, there was a good chance he'd order badly, especially when it came to starters. It turned into such a minefield that he invented the 'Mystery Guest' who was ordered a full meal and often had a place setting to spread the risk of his poor choices.

On our last trip to Barbados he ordered steak at *every* meal we had out and described all of them as 'moderate', 'cold' or 'crap'. When it was suggested that he opt for something else we were told where to go, which brings us nicely on to one of his favourite pastimes … holidays.

Holidays always got off to a bumpy start, as Dad didn't like flying, so got very stressed. There was then the Manchester Airport security roulette. If it was a City fan on duty, his bag would get pulled for a search so they could get a picture or autograph with him, but if it was a United fan on duty, his bag would get pulled for a very long and thorough search. He always took things like this with good grace and whispered to us afterwards, 'I must have really annoyed them when I played!'

He often got his own back and liked winding up United fans, and, on one flight to Portugal, he sat next to an elderly lady who was a lifelong United fan. She was being picked up by her husband, who had been a season ticket holder in the Stretford End all his life. Dad asked her to show him a photo, tell her his name, where he sat at Old Trafford and informed her of his plan. He went through arrivals, walked up to the guy and said, 'Bloody hell, it's you! About ten rows up to the right of the goal in the Stretford End. I can still picture your face from 40 years ago shouting abuse and trying to put me off!' … and then Dad walked straight off. Years later they bumped into the same couple and the husband was still telling that story … his wife clearly hadn't spoiled Dad's plan!

He loved getting family and friends together in the same place before disappearing for much of the day to play golf. More latterly, when he couldn't play golf to the standard he wanted, he liked to spend time with the grandkids, by taking them to the driving range to watch him hit golf balls, before buying their silence with ice cream.

His peculiarities continued with a penchant for outdoor showers after an evening dip in an unlit (Barbados) swimming pool. That detail is important as he had an innate fear of swimming pool lights being on and electrocuting him! To our amusement, we always used to switch them on while he was in there and listen to the vast swathes of expletives, questioning the abilities of Bajan electricians.

As a former sportsman, Dad thrived in competition and gave no quarter. He preached practice and I think I was 16 when I finally beat him at snooker. I can remember the feeling like it was yesterday. Patio cricket on tour was like the Ashes, scorecards were prepared and, according to Dad, Sky Sports News were watching with a keen eye. He bowled unplayable spinners, creamed shots all over the park, dived for catches and appealed for everything, all in front of an applauding bunch of ten-year-olds. However, the loudest cheer of the day was when Dad got out as he approached another 50, or he dropped a catch, having said he had never dropped one since Garfield Sobers in 1963!

Tensions could be high on the golf course. On one occasion, Nik fired the first shot by trying to turn up to the first tee at Quinta (in Portugal) in pyjama shorts! And after a round of niggle, it boiled over when Nik stamped on Dad's putter 'Excalibur' while leaving the 17th green … needless to say we didn't finish that round.

When the sun set and the dinner table was cleared, the sporting coliseum really came to life with the evening card game. Anyone who has played trumps with us knows exactly what I'm talking about. Dad was primed and ready to sabotage any game he wasn't in with a chance of winning. Tactics included shouting nonsense like 'diamonds are forever' whenever diamonds were played, or referring to jacks as 'hairys' to annoy everyone. He wound Mum up by calling her Geoff Boycott for her defensive play – or he simply just cheated.

On a trip to the Swiss Alps to see sister Charlotte and the family, he went up the mountain to meet everyone for lunch after the morning ski. He was seen walking up to the restaurant at 2,000m wearing white golf shoes and a flat cap. Onlookers could only assume he'd lost a bet or was on a stag do!

Life was never dull with Dad, partly due to his ability to find fun blurring the lines between fact and fiction. This became fondly known as FrannyLand.

He wasn't shy when it came to giving himself titles. The self-proclaimed world's greatest BBQ chef; the best amateur putter and reader of greens in his generation; Lord Lee, which if anyone has received wine from Dad via Majestics, will note this is the name on the account, as well as being inscribed on his BBQ utensils in Portugal.

To be fair, he dished out as many titles as he gave himself, and here are some of my favourites: Sir Harold Cumberbirch & Lady Julie (even after 20 years Sandra in Portugal still thinks these are real titles and addresses them as such), The Brigadier Neal Briggsy Briggs, Commander Gordon Beech, John the Ageing Grocer, Domino Dave Lang, Dessie Duck, Little Red Rita and The Great Dane Maynard.

The co-founder of FrannyLand and partner in crime is Mike Summerbee. Fans, members of the public and even family were left amazed and confused when they were in full flight. Old football stories quickly took a turn when Mike and Dad switched into being Cold War spies during European away games. You'd then be whisked off to pre-season, where they found themselves behind enemy lines in the Burmese jungle or escaping Viet Cong POW camps, before being dropped into the race at the Monte Carlo Rally. Novelist Wilbur Smith has nothing on these two.

Some of you may know that Mike's nickname for dad was 'Malibu'. For those who don't, this came from a pre-season tour/mission to the US Pacific Coast. Dad was missing in action, but then Mike saw something on the horizon, which turned out to be a man on a piece of driftwood surfing a big wave with a gin and tonic in hand. Riding through the barrel of the wave, the man appeared to spill none of his drink. It turned out to be Dad, and a relieved Mike swam out to greet him. A remarkable tale made more remarkable by the fact neither of them could swim very well and were petrified of the sea!

Dad's 'spy training' never left him, and when we had a big family gathering in Portugal, a team photo was taken. Years later he saw the photo and outright denied it was him – as he'd put on a bit of timber for that trip. Despite fierce interrogation, pointing out the stooge was wearing his clothes, in his garden, with his family, he stood firm.

The sense of fun carried on even when he wasn't here. It was obvious reading some of the amazing obituaries of the last few weeks that a number of journalists and people quoted had taken the bait and become victims of FrannyLand. The recollection that he could play the piano to a concert-level standard got the loudest chuckle.

And that's the main thing I want to leave you all with. Laughter.

However, it wasn't all smiles. To smash moulds and operate like Dad it isn't always plain sailing and you can't please everyone. He was a complex man at times, and he would have periods of sadness and being low, but he'd always find that inner fight and dust himself off and go again, regardless.

One example I'm most proud of is after having his face disfigured (by surgery after his cancer diagnosis), a lesser man would have hidden away, but not Dad. He went to City's home game with Aston Villa (in 2022) and watched City win the league. That must have taken some courage.

He had a restless mind, unwavering self-belief and an incredible work ethic. He did crave being number one at everything and being the centre of attention but, wow, he was good at that and, unsurprisingly, he wasn't very good at getting old.

He was a tough man who didn't dish out praise easily, but when it came it meant something, and when you did get him in a serious moment, he provided wise advice to many problems.

He was an extremely generous man, as many can testify, and he always welcomed people into his home with a champagne reception and was a fabulous host. He helped countless people out over the years, even auctioning his own

England caps off to help former players. A special bond was forged with the Hay family (from Bolton) when Dad relentlessly helped their young daughter Debbie back from the brink during her battle with anorexia. He gave her a daily Man City-related reward for listening to the doctors, which often included players going with him to visit her in hospital.

He believed sport was the one of the great ways to give people hope and channel their energies. He was passionate about the Bolton Lads and Girls Club, where he was a vice-president, which does exactly this. It's now the blueprint for the new age of youth clubs popping up all over the country in some of the most deprived areas of the UK. He broke the law in apartheid South Africa to go and host football training sessions with the Cape Coloured community in Cape Town. He was warned not to do it, but went back regardless before being escorted out of the country. More latterly he was made honorary president of the International Club Almancil in Portugal and his fundraising led to the purchase of a new team bus.

On reflection, of all the amazing messages and memories I've seen over the last few weeks, the real magic of Dad was time and love. He gave the person in the street the same time as the biggest celebs, and time is the most precious commodity we can share as humans. He gave us all laughter and love and we'll miss him.

Love you, Dad.

Gill Lee

Gill married Francis in 1987 at Macclesfield Register Office. Married for 36 years, they had two sons, Jonny and Nik. She now lives less than a mile from Little Stanneylands, in Wilmslow.

When I first met Francis, the thing that attracted me to him was that we just laughed, we laughed so much. I didn't get that from my first marriage, and we had so much fun.

Yes, he could be very demanding because he had such high standards, especially when I discovered that he liked opening the house up to everyone. It came as a shock as I didn't even have my own children at that stage. Now, it was his mum, his kids and several dozen other people! And I was thinking, *Are they looking at me?*

Suddenly, I was inundated! Have I got this job now? I thought I was just getting Fran! But it was never that – and, to be fair, his family were great, especially Millie, his mum, who was a wonderful woman. She was very funny, a lovely lady, and Fran loved her to bits. He was a very caring, giving, but demanding man. He used to say, 'I'm so easy to live with!' – and everyone in the room would say, 'What? Really?' He'd tell people that he'd often catch me at the end of the bed, saying, 'Thank you, God, for delivering this man to me!' As if! That was Francis.

Our children, Jonny and Nik, would probably say he was never a 24/7 father, and he wasn't the arm-round-the-shoulder guy telling them they were wonderful at everything. I read these days about how the current generation of 20-somethings can't cope with life because they've constantly been praised too much for small things. That would never be true in our family – because Fran would never do that.

Yet if there was a problem, if the children needed something, or there was something he could sensibly talk through with them, such as a school matter or a job, then he was there. But his idea of going to school for a parents' night – which I'd drag him to occasionally – was to sit down with a teacher. If the teacher said, 'Your boy is doing well in this subject,' then Fran was up and off! I'd tell him to sit down because the teacher had more to say, but he'd insist he'd heard enough. The lad's doing well – it was all he needed to hear!

There were a lot of places Fran *didn't* want to be. And his idea of taking the grandchildren – Charlotte's children – out for a day was often a trip up to the golf driving range! I'm sure two little girls didn't want to go to the driving range. I'd say, 'Do something nice with them!' but often it was me taking them to get a lolly, a toy or a new frock. Fran wasn't that sort of man.

Our place in Portugal – a house that we bought in Quinta do Lago, where he loved to play his golf – was always his happy place, especially in the last few years, and he loved every day there. He loved his garden space and especially his pots – his pots were the talk of the Quinta! Everyone at the golf club wanted to know what he did with his pots!

He did so much at home for the youngsters of Westhoughton, his home patch, through the Bolton Lads and Girls Club, and when we had our bolthole in Portugal he did the same out there through our friend, Jose Fernandes. His family ran a restaurant, and he led International Club Almancil – a great place for kids of all age groups to learn their football. Fran first got involved by putting on a golf day and subsequently raised them a lot of money.

He'd already raised many thousands of pounds for the Bolton Lads and Girls Club and he was made their club vice-president. Then he did the same for Jose's club – so much so that Franny was made president in 2020!

Franny just loved opening up the house to all our family and friends and had lots of parties and fun. It made no difference if it was at home at Little Stanneylands or in Portugal – Fran loved entertaining. That has been reflected in all the letters I've had from many people, some very random people, who have told me how much they loved our hospitality. Franny loved doing that when we were away, whether it be in Quinta or at our rented place in Barbados, where we enjoyed spending time with racing friends after the end of the flat season. All those who wrote to me had been to some do or other that we'd put on.

He did love those Barbados trips, too. It was a special place for us. We'd go out in January, and we kept it largely for ourselves before Jonny and Nik were born. The children went everywhere else with us, to Portugal, for example, but our place in Barbados was initially for the two of us. We'd meet up with the racing fraternity such as the Sangsters and many others. It was a good life, if hard work at times.

Francis's home was his castle, so he wanted to be there and have others come to him. He never really wanted to visit other people's homes. And he was a good barbeque chef – as he liked to tell people!

He'd also tell people he was a very good dentist, that he could treat teeth better than a dentist! He thought he was good at all sorts of things. He'd tell Richard, his own dentist, how he should be doing things! He was a one-off, and that's just how he was. And I'm glad he was, because he provided for all of us, his family, and his mum, his brothers and his sister. He was the go-to man in his family, even though he was the second-youngest. If there was a crisis in anyone's life, it was a case of 'Fran will sort it out'... and he invariably did.

One of our very good friends from Fran's F.H. Lee company days, Kevin Carter, was left in a pickle once after arriving on holiday in Sorrento. His car from the airport had a tyre shot out and robbers stole his passport, money and cards. He was asking for help from the concierge at the hotel, only to be told, 'Don't worry, Mr Carter, a Mr Lee has sent us his credit card details and he will cover everything.' It's the way he was.

As for golf, especially in Portugal, he adored it. I bought him a set of clubs for his 40th birthday and that's when he took up the game, and he was off! He needed something to occupy himself at that point because he was less busy, and he quickly became a very good golfer. It proved untold misery for his brother, Arthur, who'd played the game for years and yet – in what seemed the blink of an eye – Franny was a better player with a better handicap!

So, Portugal was our retreat and we spent up to six months a year in Portugal, once our kids were old enough to be left. He loved the sun there and could indulge his love for golf. He played golf virtually every single day in Quinta. He adored it there and it was my goal to get Franny out there as recently as last September/October (2023) but that was not to be.

He was a very social person and a very generous man.

We enjoyed so many special days, and one of those was the presentation of his CBE in 2016 for services to football and charity … going to Buckingham Palace and then off to the Savoy hotel for lunch. Franny was very emotional that day. It was a big thing in his life for him, it really was. He was very proud. He never prompted you to say 'well done' or whatever – well, maybe he did over a barbeque! I said to him, 'What d'you want? A Blue Peter badge?' Of course, I congratulated him, and he was immensely proud.

Another thing that made him immensely proud was knowing that the statue of himself, Mike Summerbee and Colin Bell was to be erected at Manchester City's Etihad Stadium. He got the letter with the details from the club chairman, and the club delivered it personally. He was really emotional when he got that. The statue, crafted by the renowned sculptor David Williams-Ellis, helped bring all three families together – the Lees, Bells and Summerbees, as we got together to discuss it. Colin had only recently died and, of course, Francis and Colin had had their differences, but his widow, Marie, joined Franny and I, with Mike and Tina Summerbee, to look at the plans. That was good.

Francis would also have loved the recent news we got about the new Walk of Fame around the Etihad. He didn't live to see that, but I've given permission for the club to use Fran's signature along the walk – I know he'd have loved that.

He kept up his drive and enthusiasm for business and striking deals almost to the end. He patented a machine called the Enviromatique a few years ago. It was a unit that would go into your kitchen, and he was hoping that it would be fitted into all new homes the way you can fit a microwave. You could put in used cans that would be crushed into a fraction of their size. And it was all recyclable, for metal and plastic. It was patented and it should have flown, it should have taken off, but it didn't quite get the right backing. Francis never stopped thinking, never switched off. He had a machine – a lorry that he converted – that painted crash barriers along the road. It would spray white or black – any colour you wanted – and it was quick. The paint had reflective beads in it for extra safety. He did do quite a bit with that. Most entrepreneurs, I'm sure, are like Fran and don't switch off. They can be difficult and demanding!

If I had a problem, such as when I was being a mum but also doing the washing and drying of all the racing colours when he was into racing, I might go to him and say, 'I've too much to do, I can't cope with all this.' He'd just turn and tell me to hire some help – knowing full well I'd not want to do that, and that I'd knuckle down and show him. In other words, he was saying, 'Get on with it!'

When he became ill, he wasn't a good patient. He didn't want to be in the place he found himself. He prided himself on being fit and we tried as much as we could, but latterly it was difficult.

He wasn't happy and he was depressed because he didn't find it easy being ill. He found it difficult to delegate things he'd normally do himself and generally not being in charge. He didn't want to do certain things but didn't want to hand it over to me, either. The last two years, perhaps, were challenging, but that's life.

But what a life he had … and we were all privileged to share it with him.

Nik Lee

Nik, Francis Lee's third son, is 35. He works in real estate, UK residential property developments off-plan, based in Dubai, with his girlfriend, Lauren.

He was very entertaining and there was never a dull moment with Franny. There were obviously lots of ups and downs over the years but, from my point of view, my relationship with him only got better.

I think our personalities were very similar and that meant we clashed a fair bit in my mid-teens up until I was about 18. By the time I was 22 or 23 there was maybe a nod of appreciation between us. We then had a really strong relationship all the way through, and it improved as the years went on.

Yet he was one of the most difficult humans to deal with, in terms of him being just the way he was. He made no apologies for being difficult. In his own mind he thought he was the easiest person in the world to get along with. But deep down I think he knew, in reality, that he was single-minded and could be hard to deal with at times. That's what made him the bloke he was – and that also gave him a lot of his charm.

He could have come across as a bit selfish at times because of the way he ploughed through his days as number one. On the broader scheme of things, everything he has done for the family and the way he has provided for all of us over the years … it was all towards that goal.

On a day-to-day basis it may have seemed we were all running around after him. But when you look back at all the things he did and laid on for us, there's no doubt that we owed him more. Or that it was a great team effort, one of the two!

I moved abroad about five years ago and we got stronger from that point on, too. He was a dad I could always rely on and talk to, and I'd check in with him once or twice a week. That was probably the most difficult thing – when the dust had settled and you start the grieving process, you realise you no longer have that touchstone, the missing part of your life. And you know you're never going to have that conversation again but, thankfully, I'd had a lot of them.

He was very supportive of me. I'd had a blip in my life where I had a marriage break-up, which led to me moving abroad. That's when he stepped up. When the shit hit the fan, he was the most supportive person I could have imagined. He'd been through it all himself and so many different people were offering so many opinions. Even other members of the family were perhaps well intentioned but inadvertently caused me problems, whereas Dad took a step back and kind of looked after me. He guided me a little bit more and took the stress out of the situation.

He was able to juggle a lot of things in all the different aspects of his life: football, business, horse racing, and he was present for us. I'm sure his first family suffered more from him being a figure pulled in every direction when he was still playing football and building his businesses. If you put a full stop to the part of his life after he sold his business and wound down his horse racing … that came to an end largely before he returned to Manchester City as chairman. For Jonny and me, from about 1994, we saw his last day-to-day involvement in 'going to work' at that point.

We didn't really experience any great absence – he was very much a man of routine with us. He liked his lunch set out at a certain time and his dinner set out in a certain way. He was ever-present, really. And the really annoying thing for us, as kids, is that everything he tried his hand at, he was bloody good at!

He was a tough act to follow! Not only was he, obviously, a very, very good footballer, he was pretty damned good as a racehorse trainer, he played off seven at golf, he'd beat us at snooker when we were about 12, on the table at Stanneylands, so there was a bit of pressure … how could we follow him! But I think Jonny and I may have learned a bit from his first marriage and his first children, Gary and Charlotte. That breakdown was probably Dad's fault and they perhaps suffered from having a famous father, whereas, with less pressure in later years, Jonny and I were able to embrace it. There are obviously a few negatives to it, but having Francis Lee as your dad is a great door-opener in life, and the vast majority of people want to talk to you about it.

Jonny and I are both in business roles, Jonny in commercial property and me in residential property, and it's an amazing help in getting invitations to events or getting to talk to people. It can help in deals and, even if you don't get the deal, you know it helped you talk about a deal. We embraced being sons of Francis and, when we realised we wouldn't be professional sportsmen ourselves, we benefitted from the education he provided and the advice he had time to pass on. Perhaps he, too, was older and wiser, with more time to devote to us.

Much of that time was so entertaining – and downright funny. The photograph Jonny referred to in his funeral eulogy was a case in point. He'd often put people on the spot when greeting them, saying, 'You look well, you've put on weight! What have you been eating?' And it rebounded on him when I picked up that photo of him in the garden, looking portly.

That was so typical of him … he just wouldn't admit it was him! Hilarious. We could do that sort of mickey-taking with each other. It just shows what a unique and unusual character he was.

I was involved with the Enviromatique crusher, patented by Dad. I tried to help out and direct it in certain ways. But we didn't have the manpower and maybe Dad was at the wrong stage of his life, and I didn't have the experience. It showed just how much he still wanted to create, do deals and try something different. He continually had ideas and was always entrepreneurial.

Being made CBE in 2016 was special for Dad. We found out, as a family, about three months before it was announced in the New Year's Honours List. He was chuffed at the time … when it was announced he was his normal, guarded self and didn't want to show too much excitement. It was water off a duck's back. But when we actually went to the Palace with him, he got emotional that day. We were sat in the black cab going from the Palace to The Savoy hotel, which was a place where he'd had many a celebration in the past. It had a lot of memories for him. We were going down Pall Mall with the insignia around his neck and it all came rolling back to him … how far he'd come. He was going to the famous Savoy Grill where he'd dined and raised a glass to so many different things down the years … and now he was going back again as a CBE. It was another chapter and one that made him extremely proud. He hadn't shown much emotion beforehand, but he did on the day. I think, in typical style, he said: 'Well, I fucking deserve it!'

The last chapter of Dad's life was a roller coaster. It was a weird one, it was the summer of 2021 and a family holiday in Portugal was the plan. Mum and Dad were pretty much living in Portugal during Covid and I was set to fly down with my new girlfriend. We had to fly to Spain and drive to Portugal; it was all a bit of a battle because of the restrictions.

We arrived at the house, and I'd not seen Dad for perhaps six months. I saw him and called my brother upstairs because I was so panicked – I thought, *Jesus, he looks so different*, and I'd never seen him look like that. I could just tell that he was ill. It was like seeing someone you've not seen other than a photo for a while. He'd lost a lot of weight, he looked a bit confused and then, on that trip, he had a lump behind his ear and he went into hospital and had that lump removed. It seemed a routine operation. He ended up coming through that and the lump was gone, and the doctors didn't think it was cancerous – but it had been affecting his eyes and his ability to chew, things like that.

One of the wounds then haemorrhaged while he was in hospital. I'd been in to see him earlier in the day and he said, 'I want to get out,' but that same night the haemorrhage happened, and he was in a coma for two weeks. That was very stressful for the family. This was the first time my girlfriend had met the family. She and I ended up being in Portugal for about a month.

And then he came through that, but he was super-confused for about a month. We thought it could have been the end of the road then. But it wasn't. He was wheelchair-bound for a bit, and he wanted to fire all his nurses and escape from his captors on a golf buggy! It was quite funny, in a way; he didn't want anyone else in the house.

He was confined to sleeping downstairs for a while but then he started getting himself upstairs and, while he was still a bit confused, he got his determination back.

Later on that year, he found out it was cancerous. He was going to have another operation done at The Christie hospital, Manchester, but the day before he was due to go in, they rang up to say there was too much risk. It was a double-whammy, finding out it was cancerous but, also, no operation.

Afterwards, leading up to Christmas 2021, it was clear his treatment was for life extension, rather than cure. The family winter holiday to Barbados was cancelled and he started his radiotherapy. At that point they'd given him probably three months to live. He went through the radiotherapy and was out of that by about January. I was back in Dubai, and we got Mum and Dad out here in February 2022, just to give them a break, really. And guess what? We had virtually another two years with him, and he got back into some amazing form. Obviously, we were very upset, especially when he nearly died at the time of the coma. We thought we'd lost him mentally when he first came out of the coma, but to then have him back to something like his old self and have all that time with him was a real bonus.

He got his spark back and it was definitely one last hurrah: being able to go out for dinner, drink what he wanted to drink – whatever wine he wanted – all the things he wanted to do. Yes, he carried on having his favourite tipple … but no cigars now. He'd quietly given up on his Havanas some years ago, without ever admitting it! We were all really blessed that we had that time with him.

We knew Francis Lee couldn't live forever – and we had those chances to say what we wanted to say, all of the family did. We were so lucky. And – *and* – he got to see Manchester City win the treble! They say things are written in the stars … perhaps they are.

It's wrong to say his return to City in the 90s was a vanity project. Maybe he did want to exact a bit of revenge because of how he'd been forced out of the club as a player, but he really wanted to restore City to its former glory. It didn't happen for him, but not through lack of effort.

So, for him to see where the club is now and, especially, winning the treble in 2023 was a major connection for all of us. He didn't show an enormous amount of emotion throughout his life, but that was special for him, and for us.

Long before that, I'd been sat next to him in 2012 when the last-minute Sergio Agüero goal went in against QPR and we won the Premier League for the first time. There was the FA Cup win 12 months before that; we were all on that City journey together. Jonny was with him in Portugal as we clinched the treble.

After that, he'd lost the use of his legs, really, to get around the house. Something told me to get back home and see him, and I did that. Just to help him around the house, help out Mum and just to spend some time with him. We had a carer for four or five hours a day to relieve some of the pressure on Mum.

Getting around the house was getting to be a real effort for him and you don't want to see him having to make that effort. But he could still watch his football and we had a good weekend. When I left – and this was very out of character – he got hold of me and thanked me for looking after him that weekend. I'm so glad I did that as it was the last time I spoke to him in person and one of the last times we chatted. It was special.

Charlotte Barnes (nee Lee)

Charlotte, aged 54, is Francis Lee's oldest surviving child. She's married to Daryl and has daughters, Eve 24 and Holly 21. She lives in Zürich ('I went for six months and I've stayed 22 years!'). She's a furniture artist and is known as 'The Furniture Lady'.

I didn't really see a lot of Dad as a youngster because he was either busy with his football, at Manchester City, or with building up his paper business. I didn't really go to his City matches, because I was so young.

One of my funniest and earliest memories is being the 'world's best wheel cleaner'. He used to take me with him to the car wash on a Sunday and I remember he had a big car – a Jaguar, I think – with intricate spoked wire wheels. We'd go back home and he'd fill a bucket with water and tell me, 'Now, the world's best wheel cleaner is going to clean the wheels!'

I also recall, when I was about three or four, my brother Gary and I helping to clean out our concrete pond in the garden of our home, Higher Landedmans, in Westhoughton. I wanted to help but they wouldn't let me go in the pond because I was so young. So, I decided that I'd help with the fish, which had been put in a big black bin while the concrete was cleaned. I decided to clean the fish – so I put Fairy Liquid into the bin! I swilled it around and very proudly went over and told Dad, 'I've cleaned your fishes!' – then all hell broke loose. They took the bin upstairs to the bathroom, where we had a corner bath, and poured fresh water in to give the poor fish as much oxygen as possible. I was responsible for mass murder of fish! Not many survived … we had to restock the pond. Back to the fairground for more fish!

That house was beautiful, very old and thatched, with gardens on three sides, but quite small. We loved it there.

It was like a smaller Little Stanneylands, the house in Wilmslow that Dad moved to later.

He was extremely busy, having two jobs at the same time. Playing for City and building up his business. He did work incredibly hard. I don't remember him ever sitting down, he was always doing something – even on the rare occasions he wasn't obviously busy. He'd take me to the cricket pitch in Westhoughton to train and he'd get me to do some runs with him.

Nik and Jonny did get a more relaxed Dad, in that he wasn't still building up the business when they were young. He didn't have two full-time jobs then, but that's how it was for so many kids.

The difference, I suppose, is that my dad was famous. To a certain degree, I didn't even realise that I had a famous father, it was only as I got older that it became apparent. I actually noticed it most when my mum, Jean, and Dad split up, and that attracted a lot of media interest. That's the only time I really noticed that my dad was different to most other kids' dads who worked full-time.

We did, of course, have a lot of people around at our house at Higher Landedmans, and he used to have dinner parties. I'd be able to say hello to all the guests and then I'd be off to bed. It was just a normal way of growing up, the same as any kid whose father worked a lot. I didn't know any different.

Dad said this about when he was working: 'The Franny that scored all the goals and knew everyone was scared of him, when he was on the pitch – that Franny was so impatient and determined. That was the key.' And it was, even when he filled his car up with petrol, he was impatient and determined. He used to pull the trigger on the fuel pump so hard – because it wasn't quick enough for him! He wanted it badly – and he wanted it now.

So, he was so incredibly driven and focused. He was totally determined, and I think that came from his upbringing in Westhoughton. The fact that he was told he wouldn't amount to very much was the trigger. He decided when he was young: 'I'm going to show these buggers!'

Whatever he did, he gave it 100 per cent, it would be all-consuming for him. He wanted to succeed in everything he did. One thing he said to me, when I was younger, was: 'It's not the taking part that counts – it's winning!' – the exact opposite of the famous quote from Pierre de Coubertin, the father of the modern Olympics! That was Dad's philosophy.

He also said: 'You've always got to do things in life that you don't want to do, in order to succeed.' Another favourite line of his that he'd repeat was: 'If you want something doing, ask a busy person.' And he *was* a busy person!

After Mum and Dad divorced, my brother Gary was getting older, and when he left school he went to live in

Wilmslow. That left Mum and myself and I would then go to Dad's at the weekends. Maybe once every other weekend, I'd go off to the races with Dad or I'd be round at the house. When he moved to Little Stanneylands, I had a horse as well, so I used to ride a lot – and I loved that. There were times, growing up, where if your mother said, 'You have to go and see your Dad this weekend,' I'd sometimes want to be with my friends – just like any teenager. But Dad and I had good times and fantastic days out at the races, a lot of fun. He'd invite friends along too, and it was particularly exciting when we had a winner.

I loved that part of Dad's life when he became a trainer, and I loved watching him grow it. The first horse he ever bought was Clydebank; it got him hooked into racing. This was before he became a trainer. The horse was stabled up in Yorkshire and it won a couple of times. I think Dad saw it win and thought, *I've bought a horse, it's winning, it's easy – I'll have some of that!*

Dual family life, post-divorce, had its pros as well as cons. It gave me two different lives. At home with my mum, who was very creative, and we were always doing crazy things like knocking down walls; then at the weekend I'd be with Dad and we'd be off to the races! They were two very different aspects to my life and that was great. It was very positive in that respect. The negatives? I can't see anything particularly negative – obviously it would have been nicer to have my parents together but, the older I got, I realised that's the way it had to be.

Dad was the centre of the family, and his wider family. When he bought the paper mill, all the family went to work there! Brothers Trevor and Arthur, sister Irene, his mum – Millie – they all were there. Previously, they'd all have been in the cotton mills around Westhoughton. F.H. Lee was more modern, with better working conditions and better hours, and he looked after them. He always looked after his family, especially Grandma, his mum. She'd always come on holiday with us all, too, and she never wanted for anything. Dad bought a house for her but *none* of the family wanted for anything once he'd made his money.

I was working in Brussels at the time Dad was surprised by *This Is Your Life* on TV. Gill gave me a ring to say that it was happening, and it's just as well I was away from it all, as I'm hopeless at keeping a secret! It may have slipped out, had I been there! All I do remember is that I got to the studios and it was a really fantastic day. And it was a really, really good party afterwards. Dad was a great provider in general – but a great provider of parties, in particular!

It's true that he'd take my girls, Eve and Holly, to the driving range to watch him practise his swing as *their* treat. He wasn't a natural-born matriarch, he was a patriarch and maybe a little distant with grandchildren; he wasn't a great lover of little ones when he got older.

Portugal was so important to him. I think he'd have loved to live there permanently, if he'd been able to. He used to make me laugh about his plants out there. You'd think he was Alan Titchmarsh! What he'd actually do was go to the garden centre and choose some geraniums or pelargoniums and then he'd bring them back and his gardener would put them in the pots. My dad would then religiously water them, probably give them too much water, but he used to go on and on and on about his pots. In fairness, they were nice – but you'd think he'd done absolutely everything himself!

He was always so much more relaxed out in Portugal, and another memorable thing was the Lee barbeque. When we had people around and we had a BBQ, or even if it was just the family, he'd make this big production about cooking the meal, but, really, all he did was put the steaks on the grill! He used to get the kids to go and gather the pine cones from the golf course to light the barbeque. The cones are a good starter for charcoal. Quinta really was his happy place.

He was immensely proud of his CBE and his investiture, and he liked to write those letters after his name, if it was appropriate!

Towards the end, as such a determined achiever and always being in control, he did get frustrated with being ill. The frustration was in not being able to do those things that he'd always done. Anyone would be frustrated in those circumstances, but perhaps more so for Dad because he had that sense of wanting to achieve everything, be the best at everything – and he couldn't do that anymore.

He did, though, listen a lot more in those last 18 months or so – indeed, he listened more in his latter years, even before he became ill. He was never one for title-tattle or small talk. There usually had to be a purpose to a conversation for him. But then he got to listen more and come out with something quirky or a joke. Or he'd offer his advice – and nine times out of ten, of course, Dad would be right.

Even when he wasn't right, he was still right!

Jonny Lee

Jonny, Francis Lee's second son, is aged 37, and married to Suzi. They have children, Freddie and Darcey, and live in Barnes, South West London. He's a partner in a London commercial real estate company.

Looking back, the vast majority of our life with Dad was fun. He was very eccentric, mind-boggling at times. You could look and think all those sorts of disorders, such as OCD, were wrapped up in him. Life with him was so enjoyable, and an enormous amount of piss-taking went on. I think he recreated at home those things he missed from the football changing rooms and his business boardrooms. We gave a fair bit back, constantly doing impressions of him and mickey-taking.

He was a fantastic entertainer and host – he loved having people around to our home. He loved treating and sharing things with people, and he was very generous; generous with his time and also materially. Was he strict? Well, he could be hard when he needed to be, but Mum was the main disciplinarian in the house and he only got involved when really required. He'd usually be trying to tell us off while trying not to laugh, to be honest. We'd get the odd whack on the back of the legs back then – which many would frown on now.

We had a different upbringing to Gary and Charlotte, as Dad was older and possibly had a more stable platform when we came along. With Gary and Charlotte he was a travelling sportsman and he was often away, working hard both to play elite sport and to set up his business. It was very different.

He was very good to me and to others with his advice. He taught me very good principles, which I still live by, such as working hard to get on, and when I was starting in my career he'd tell me to treat the business I worked for as my own. When you're taking someone to a big lunch, he'd say, treat the money as your own. Having a work ethic was very important to him. He was keen to keep us grounded and I remember he took us to the first house he grew up in. It was a very small, terraced house and must have been crowded. I keep a picture of that house saved on my phone.

The power of outworking someone and outhustling someone was his way. He was well ahead of his time, in many ways. Anyone reading Matthew Syed's books about psychology and the power of practice would read about principles that Dad lived by decades ago. He spent hours with us in the garden practising various sports.

It's been fascinating reading Dad's book. He didn't divulge everything in his past to us and I found his account of his relationship with Peter James fascinating. I knew nothing about that. It obviously had a big impact on him.

And I think what helped make him the man he became was that he was a bit of a rebel. These days you're encouraged to positively challenge people at work. But in the days when Dad was a young man, it was so different. You just got told you were shit and had to get on with it, even if you knew there was a better way. Dad always challenged convention and always pushed his view if he thought it was the right thing to do.

A lot of people were telling him he wouldn't be a success, in that austere post-war period, when he was trying to get on. Many accepted that, but that wasn't washing with Dad. You'd think superiors would be pushing people up, not keeping them down, constantly telling a young lad from a working-class background, with far from the best start in life, that he wasn't good enough. I'm sure that built a considerable level of resilience and determination in him.

He was a rebel, not in a later-generation, fashionable punk way, but just in him being unbending and determined to prove others wrong. Later, he'd always encourage us to challenge authority and to question what people were doing – not necessarily accept that what we were being told was right.

Growing up with Dad was so much fun – at times we were like a travelling circus, going with him to race meetings during his years as a trainer. There would be the odd big one, such as Royal Ascot, but we'd mostly go to the tracks on the northern circuit. He had his own box at Haydock, so we'd go there quite a lot. And we liked going to meetings at Chester. We'd park up in the middle of the track and have a picnic. Just growing up around the stables at home was so brilliant. There would always be company and we'd have so many mates to play with. Gary, his eldest son, was around a lot then. He loved those racing trips, and City, of course, and we had some good times together.

Gary was a complex lad, and he later made some bad decisions. He was a bit of a scorched-earth character and, ultimately, I don't think he'd ever have found real happiness. Dad and Jean had him when they were very young, and he perhaps suffered when their relationship became unhappy.

For the rest of us, life at Little Stanneylands was fabulous. Here was a lovely 17th-century black-and-white thatched home, yet it was mostly only one room deep. And then there was the pool house at the back, where we spent hours having fun while Dad held court around the BBQ. We even had chickens behind the pool house for a while, and the fox sadly got in one evening and we were left with one ... who Dad named Lucky!

And Dad would always have us outside when he could, playing football, rugby and cricket, or just going down the fields rather than see us on our PlayStation. The kitchen was the hub of everything – whether it be having breakfast with the racing stable team or Sunday roast. It could be hard work for Mum, washing racing silks or sorting out food for another houseful. It was always buzzing and a real centre of things, and friends were always keen to stay. It was the essence of that home.

He was always keen to see us improve our sports skills (and his own!). He'd throw countless balls down at me, hours and hours of it, to improve my batting – but he didn't just toss them on the half-volley like a coach, he'd be trying to get me out, every ball! He was good at pretty much all sports – a very good cricketer and golfer. And snooker! He never, ever let you win – and he always beat us in our snooker room. Then, one day, when I was 15 or 16, I beat him for the first time. I was so excited that I celebrated like Sergio Agüero against QPR! I ran the length of the house to tell Mum that I'd beaten him. But then, of course, Dad said, 'I let him win!' Did he hell! We had a bust-up and I said, 'That's fucking bollocks!' But it just shows how ultra-competitive he was; he wanted to win at everything he did.

And yet he never pressurised Nik and me to follow him into pursuing sport. I was a decent rugby player and played football and cricket too. He never pushed us to follow his exact path because, I think, he knew from experience the pitfalls that could follow trying to get to the very top level. In an empathetic way, he didn't want that for us.

I remember injuring my shoulder, it popped out and I needed an operation. Dad came to the side of my bed and said, 'Look, you're not going to make a living out of this, you won't make any money. If you do that again, and they tell you there may be restrictive use of your arm, as much as you love that game it would be best to knock it on the head.' And he was right. He was a self-proclaimed injury expert, doctor and physio, and he'd always help us nurse sports knocks and injuries with long-winded ice routines and homeopathic remedies. We used to rip him massively for his love of Savlon!

I remember telling him at one point that I liked the idea of going to the Royal Military Academy at Sandhurst. He gave me quite a bollocking and told me to forget it. 'Absolutely not!' he said. 'I didn't work my bollocks off my whole life for you to get blown up in some foreign country! This family has given enough in that regard.' There was some family history in that because Dad's Uncle Harold died in the Far East fighting the Japanese, and an older uncle on his mum's side was very affected by his service. He became a right evil so and so. He once slapped Dad across the face with a fish. Francis had asked, 'What's that, Uncle?' and he said, 'It's a fish,' as he swiped it across his face! Dad saw the effects of war and was adamant that I'd not be doing that.

Little Stanneylands was like an island or a fortress for us, when you closed the gates. Yet Dad had an open-door policy and that could be surreal, seeing famous people rock up, or a Premier League footballer suddenly stroll in. We were always encouraged to come down and say hello and be polite to them. It was the same on holidays, which Dad loved, in Portugal and in Barbados. He'd always take us golfing with him, whether it was to play or tag along, and we'd be sitting next to cricket greats Sir Garfield Sobers or Brian Lara, just chatting away.

He certainly loved Portugal but, equally, he loved Barbados, the Bajan people, their banter and the Caribbean way of life. We made so many friends, and unfortunately his friends there couldn't get to his funeral, but we saw them at Christmas a couple of months later, and so many were upset. We had so many loving messages of support.

Holidays were a great thing with him, and we *all* went. It was like the royal court moving to Sandringham, except, with Franny and the Lees, plus friends, it was the season for our family moving court to Portugal or Barbados! Before the days when you could get decent meat in Barbados, Dad would take a whole suitcase of vacuum-packed meats.

It was a toss-up as to which was his happiest place.

At home, Manchester City were just a huge part of all our lives, not just Dad's. He passed on his love for the club to all of us, despite what had happened when he was chairman. It was not always easy following City; 20 years of my life as a fan were utter shit before things got better! All your mates at school supported the other lot, United, during one of the golden eras of English football. But it was a life lesson; you stick with your team and it turned for the better – and how.

Dad didn't do anything by halves. He lived and breathed everything City. I think when he returned to the club as chairman in the 1990s he underestimated the level of corruption and the level of challenges he'd have to face, the resistance to change and all that kind of stuff. I think initially he thought he could walk in, as he did when he was a player, and the glory days would follow. But it was so multifaceted and multidimensional and the rot had set in. He had to deal with that.

I think he did well to accomplish what he was able to, in the end. He got the merchandise back under control, got the club on a level playing field financially, and eventually started rubbing shoulders with the right people, such as Sir

Howard Bernstein, just as that legacy 2002 Commonwealth Games was in the planning. What Dad did then was key to City's future.

That return to City took a lot out of Dad. I could see it myself, though I was young at the time. He'd had a lot of success in life, and everything usually turned to gold, but that was a challenging time … the only time in his life when it seemed it was all falling in on him. He'd gone in with good intentions and it didn't quite happen for him. I felt sorry for him.

He threw a lot of money at it, as well, and probably lost a lot of it. It all took its toll. It has to affect your health, that level of stress. He probably hid a lot of the strain and worry, not that he was diagnosed with any illness, but he was under strain. I'm sure he internalised a lot of it, yet he dusted himself down and got on with things.

He could be up and down, certainly, and, as Churchill would say about his spell of depression, the Black Dog would come over him at times. He had so many constant highs but then naturally there would be a dip. Being him was quite exhausting. He'd have a week when he was down and morose and he'd decided he'd need to go away and have a holiday or do something fun.

But following City as fans was something for all of us. Dad, who stayed away in the immediate period after his chairmanship, went back to watching games and he loved it. The move to the new stadium helped because he felt, rightly, that he was part of that rebuild. But following City always seemed to be one step away from disaster.

Then, in 2008, we signed Robinho! I couldn't believe it. The Brazilian came in with our new owners. There were still a lot of false starts but gradually, with Roberto Mancini, the good football really started to happen. I was there with Dad for that QPR game when Agüero scored and we won the Premier League. It was a different level, and Dad absolutely loved that.

Last year I watched the FA Cup Final with him as City beat United 2-1 – and then we watched the Champions League Final on 10 June as we beat Inter Milan 1-0 to secure a fantastic treble. That was really special and we opened a nice bottle of champagne.

He was never jealous, unlike some ex-professionals, about the success of City's new generation. In recent times he celebrated those in City's blue who followed his own example. Some don't want their achievements to be eclipsed. He was happy to see the team playing a style of football under Pep Guardiola that was not far removed from the way Malcolm Allison coached Dad's great City side. He just wanted to see beautiful football, played in the right way.

I think he'd stopped watching football, to a large extent, in the 80s and early 90s because he hated the way it had gone. He couldn't watch it and really hated it. This City side was so different to all of that.

Exactly a year before he died, he saw both Erling Haaland and Phil Foden score a hat-trick in the Manchester derby against United at the Etihad. City won 6-3. No City player had scored a hat-trick against United since Dad did it, back in 1970. In one game, Haaland and Foden did just that! Dad loved that City players had scored hat-tricks against United again. I said to him that we'd battered them and the two lads had beaten his record. He couldn't help but quickly correct me: 'They haven't beaten my record, just equalled it,' he told me. 'But these lads did it at home against a shit United team, while I got my hat-trick against a great United side when they were European champions – and I did it at Old Trafford!' You couldn't argue with that.

The City-United rivalry could be funny for Dad. Growing up, I'd see United fans giving Dad abuse, and City fans would too, sometimes, when things were bad. If there was a City fan on security at Manchester Airport, Dad would get stopped for an autograph, but if it was a United fan on security, he'd be stopped for a bag search! There were downsides as people sometimes took it too far, but Dad was quick to highlight how long ago he'd played and what an impact he must have made if they still hate him!

We got to spend much longer with Dad than we thought we would – and my work were very good to me in the latter couple of years, letting me spend extra time away with him. They were precious moments and he got to spend more time with Freddie, who really loved his 'Dodo'. He still talks about him a lot. The extra time meant he got to see my second child, Darcey, born. She reminds me of him. She's cheeky, can be stubborn and has a real mischievous glint in her eye. It was really special for Suzi and me that our kids got to meet him.

I get sad that he's not around and we can't chat or have banter anymore, but that sadness dissipates quickly because I feel very lucky to have spent so much time with him, had so much fun, navigated his quirks and been given a great start in life. I've made peace with his death as he wasn't designed to sit in a chair and do nothing. He was a hard patient to help and got very frustrated, so I'm thankful there wasn't too much of that for him and us.

We were so overwhelmed and humbled by the levels of media coverage upon his death and around the funeral. It helped so much. The Manchester City family were also incredible and supported us. It was sad he didn't get to see the statue's unveiling but I think he'd have found it a bit awkward on the day, as much as he was impressed by the plans.

He was an incredible man who had one hell of a life, and I hope people enjoy his story.